ADOBE® PHOTOSHOP® CS5
RESTORATION AND RETOUCHING FOR
DIGITAL PHOTOGRAPHERS ONLY

Adobe® Photoshop® CS5
Restoration and Retouching FOR
Digital Photographers ONLY

Mark Fitzgerald

WILEY
Wiley Publishing, Inc.

Adobe® Photoshop® CS5 Restoration and Retouching for Digital Photographers Only

Published by
Wiley Publishing, Inc.
10475 Crosspoint Boulevard
Indianapolis, IN 46256
www.wiley.com

Copyright © 2010 by Wiley Publishing, Inc., Indianapolis, Indiana

Published simultaneously in Canada

ISBN: 978-0-470-61816-5

Manufactured in the United States of America

10 9 8 7 6 5 4 3 2 1

For general information on our other products and services or to obtain technical support, please contact our Customer Care Department within the U.S. at (877) 762-2974, outside the U.S. at (317) 572-3993 or fax (317) 572-4002.

Wiley also publishes its books in a variety of electronic formats. Some content that appears in print may not be available in electronic books.

Library of Congress Control Number: 2010926853

about the author

Mark Fitzgerald has spent the majority of his life helping photographers to get the most from their photos. He cut his "photographic teeth" in the professional photolab business when digital photography was only a dream. In 1999, as the possibilities of digital began to emerge, Mark left the lab business and devoted two years to exploring everything digital. After that, he was ready to begin using his new skill-set to help photographers solve their digital retouching and workflow problems.

Today, Mark is an Adobe Certified Photoshop expert who specializes in helping photographers, ranging from established professionals to people who are just finding their passion for photography. Mark has taught countless photographers how to smooth out their workflows through private training, classes, and workshops. He and his wife Julia (with their three dogs, Ruby, Hazel, and Sam) live in Portland, Oregon, where Mark owns a consulting business, The Digital Darkroom. To learn more about Mark, visit www.ddroom.com.

Other Wiley titles by Mark Fitzgerald are *Adobe Photoshop CS3 Restoration and Retouching Bible*, *Adobe Photoshop Lightroom and Photoshop Workflow Bible*, *Adobe Photoshop CS4 After the Shoot*, and *Adobe Photoshop Elements 8 After the Shoot.*

credits

Acquisitions Editor
Courtney Allen

Project Editor
Chris Wolfgang

Technical Editor
Mike Vraneza

Copy Editor
Kim Heusel

Editorial Director
Robyn Siesky

Business Manager
Amy Knies

Sr. Marketing Manager
Sandy Smith

Vice President and Executive Group Publisher
Richard Swadley

Vice President and Executive Publisher
Barry Pruett

Project Coordinator
Kristie Rees

Graphics and Production Specialists
Elizabeth Brooks
Jennifer Mayberry
Ronald G. Terry

Quality Control Technician
Melanie Hoffman

Proofreading
Lisa Young Stiers

Indexing
Estalita Slivoskey

To my wife, Julia, whose unconditional support enabled me to become the person I am today.

acknowledgments

I want to thank the following photographers for letting me use their images. The sample images they so generously provided made it much easier to write this book. Please visit their Web sites to see more of their work.

> Emily Andrews, Emily Andrews Portrait Design: www.emilyandrews.net

> Jerry Auker, Jerry Auker Photography

> Dan Christopher, Dan Christopher Photography: www.danchristopherphotography.com

> David Hitchcock, Hitchcock Creative Photography

> Dave Hutt, Dave Hutt Photography: www.davehuttphotography.com

> Ted Miller Jr.: mrmontana.blogspot.com

> Brannon McBroom, Brannon McBroom Photography: www.bmcbphotography.com

> Carl Murray, Seattle Photography, Inc.: www.seattlephotography.com

> Denyce Weiler, Something Blue Photography: www.somethingbluephotography.com

> Mark Wilson, Hakuna Matata Photography: www.hakunamatataphotography.com

> Doreen Wynja, Eye of the Lady Photography

All other photos were shot by me, or in the case of older, restored photos, are part of my collection of family photos or photos I restored for clients.

Thank you to Springhill Suites by Marriott in downtown Seattle for allowing me to use a photo of the hotel, which is one of my favorite places to stay when I'm in Seattle.

Thanks also to the editing team at Wiley: copy editor Kim Heusel, who noticed so many small details that made big differences; technical editor Mike Vraneza, who used his expertise to check the technical points of this book; and project editor Chris Wolfgang, who managed this project from start to finish.

Finally, a thank you to Courtney Allen, Acquisitions Editor for Wiley Publishing, who so kindly invited me to join the Wiley team. Without her, this book would not be a reality.

contents at a glance

contents

chapter **2 Adjusting Brightness and Contrast   29**

chapter **3 Managing and Correcting Color   49**

chapter **4 Understanding the Advantages of Layers   73**

Part II Photoshop Tools and Techniques   **91**

chapter **5 Using Selections to Isolate Content   93**

chapter 6 Taking Control with Layer Masks   117

chapter **7 Using Photoshop's Main Retouching Tools 143**

Part III Restoration: Rescuing Damaged Photos 165

chapter **8 Starting with the Scan 167**

chapter 9 Solving Typical Repair Problems   185

chapter **10 Finishing the Image 207**

chapter **11 Hands-on Restoration Project: The Complete Workflow 233**

Part IV Retouching: Taking Your Images to the Next Level   257

chapter 12 Using Strategies for Success   259

chapter **13 Solving Special Portrait Retouching Problems 269**

chapter **14 Hands-on Portrait Retouching Project: The Complete Workflow 289**

chapter 15 Hands-on Architectural Retouching Project: The Complete Workflow   311

introduction

You may be asking why the topics of photo restoration and retouching are being covered together in the same book. That's a reasonable question, considering that on the surface the goals of these two processes seem quite different. The goal of restoration with just about anything — old cars, antique furniture, and so on — is to repair and refurbish something until it resembles mint condition. In the case of old photos, the goal is to erase the years and return the photos to what they looked like when they were new.

The goal of retouching, on the other hand, is to take the original image to a higher level by enhancing its positive aspects and reducing or removing the distracting elements. The finished product becomes something more valuable than the original image because of those enhancements.

Though these two goals seem at odds, the truth is many of the same Photoshop tools and techniques are used to achieve both goals. Because of that, it doesn't make sense to discuss one of these subjects without the other. It also doesn't make sense for you, as a student of Photoshop, to learn to use these tools and techniques for only restoration or retouching. You never know when you may want to try something new. If you take the time to learn everything in this book now, you'll be ready to handle just about any image-editing challenge you're likely to encounter.

WHAT'S IN THIS BOOK?

This book is divided into four main parts. Part I deals with the fundamentals as they apply to restoration and retouching. This is where I show you how to create a solid foundation that supports all of the subsequent work that's done with an image file.

Part II concentrates on the Photoshop tools and techniques that are used in the restoration and retouching processes. Here you focus on what are called Photoshop's *retouching tools*, comparing and contrasting them. As I describe these tools and techniques, I offer conceptual insight into why one way of doing things is often better than another.

In Part III, you learn to apply everything you learned in Parts I and II to the subject of photo restoration. You learn how to repair typical problems and add finishing touches to an image, and you also learn about scanners and scanning. Finally, you get to work on a hands-on restoration project from beginning to end so that you can experience the entire workflow. By the end of this section, you'll know everything you need to know to begin restoring your own old photos.

Part IV is all about retouching. I discuss some of the conceptual issues surrounding retouching, including workflow. Then I show you how to solve some special retouching problems, such as glass-glares and skin smoothing. You finish off this part with two complete hands-on retouching projects. The first one is a typical portrait-retouching project. The second is an architectural-retouching project. By the end of Part IV, you'll have all the tools you need to do just about anything to fine-tune an image.

Throughout this book there are several step-by-step projects with practice files. These files can be downloaded at your convenience at www.wiley.com/go/phoprestorationandretouching.

WHO SHOULD READ THIS BOOK?

Adobe Photoshop CS5 Restoration and Retouching for Digital Photographers Only is intended for anyone who wants to know how to restore old photos and/or retouch new ones. You don't have to be an accomplished Photoshop user, but it is helpful if you have some experience with the software and its interface. With that said, even a beginner benefits from reading this book. It just may take a little longer to get up to speed with the basics.

This book is not intended as a comprehensive guide to all things Photoshop. My intention is to give you the things you need to accomplish these processes, without distracting you with what you don't need. There are times when I'd like to go into deeper detail, but can't because those details are outside the scope of the book. If I don't cover some topic in detail and you want to know more about it, find a resource to help you explore it. One of the best places to begin your search is Photoshop's online help files (www.adobe.com/support/photoshop).

HOW TO USE THIS BOOK

To get the most from this book, start at the beginning and go through it sequentially. This allows you to experience the learning process in the way I envision it. In many cases, ideas in one chapter build on information introduced in previous chapters. This amplification process won't make as much sense if you experience it out of order. Also, take the time to read each chapter, even if you think you already understand its subject. You never know when you'll turn up a nugget that will completely change the way you work with your images.

Download all the sample files from the Web site. Most of them are fairly small files. After you work through a project, take the time to explore those new processes with some of your own photos. I know from my own experience that working with personal files makes a big difference in the learning process. This is where you'll find the time to go as deep as you need to go while exploring the content of this book.

After you've been through the book from front to back, you can use it as a reference guide to help you solve your own restoration and retouching problems. When a specific issue pops up, find the relevant references in the book and review them as needed.

Conventions Used in This Book

I'm big on using keyboard shortcuts in my own workflow, but I won't be stressing them much here because there are potentially hundreds of shortcuts in Photoshop and I don't want to confuse you with them. I also think it's more important that you know where to find a command in the menus, rather than the fastest way to execute it.

With that said, I do think you should begin getting used to the idea of keyboard shortcuts. So I'll share some of the more useful shortcuts. When I first introduce the most common tools and commands, I give you their keyboard shortcuts in parentheses like this: the Lasso tool (L).

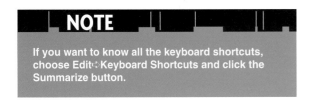

NOTE

If you want to know all the keyboard shortcuts, choose Edit⇨Keyboard Shortcuts and click the Summarize button.

Because this book was written on a Mac, all the screenshots are from the Mac version of Photoshop CS5. That shouldn't make much difference, because almost everything is the same in the Mac and Windows versions of the software. If you're using a Windows machine, the only real differences are the keyboard modifier keys.

Macs use the Option (Alt) key and the Command (Apple) key as modifiers, and Windows machines use the Alt key and the Ctrl key for the same functions. (This is all the more confusing because a standard Mac keyboard has a Control key on it that has a completely different function!)

> Mac Option (Alt) key = Windows Alt key
> Mac Command (Apple) key = Windows Ctrl key

Because every modern Mac keyboard I've seen has an Alt label on the Option key, I refer to this key as Alt, which should be straightforward. When I need to mention the two other set of modifier keys, I say ⌘/Ctrl. The only reason I'm putting the Mac command first is to be consistent with the screenshots.

Products Mentioned in this Book

On several occasions I recommend products I use or like. I want you to know that I do not have relationships with any of the companies that sell these products. In other words, these companies do not sponsor me. The only reason I endorse these products is because I think knowing about them will make your Photoshop experience more efficient and enjoyable.

DIGITAL EDITING FUNDAMENTALS

Chapter 1

GETTING ORGANIZED

Photo by Mark Fitzgerald

Photoshop has forever changed the way the photographic postproduction process is carried out. Image modifications that were unthinkable only a few years ago are easily accomplished in only a few minutes. Now a skilled Photoshop user is limited only by her imagination.

However, this digital dream can quickly turn into a nightmare when important files are hard to locate or when they completely disappear. Because of that, it's important to build an organized system that ensures every file is stored in an appropriate place, and that each is backed up in the event of a hard-drive crash.

UNDERSTANDING FILE FORMATS

Adobe Photoshop CS5 works with a variety of file formats. Most are created when edited files are saved with the Save As command. Figure 1-1 shows the options available in the Format pop-up menu. Choices here determine the kind of file that is created during saving. Be aware that this set of options is available only when saving an 8-bit file because 16-bit files can only be saved in a few formats.

X-REF

Bit depth is discussed in Chapter 8.

People who deal with digital photography don't generally use all of these file formats. I work with lots of professional photographers and typically, they use four file formats 99 percent of the time: RAW, PSD, TIFF, or JPEG.

RAW

RAW is a special type of file format that's used to capture images with dSLR cameras and some point-and-shoot cameras. The reason RAW is special is it contains a vast amount of information — almost as much as the camera's sensor can record. Most serious photographers are shooting in the RAW format because they want the largest amount of information available to them when they open a file for editing.

Because this book is concerned with repairing and perfecting photos during the editing process, I don't go into the RAW file format in detail. However, I do want to make a couple of important points. The first thing to be aware of is that each camera manufacturer has its own proprietary RAW file format. For example, Canon cameras use CR2 and Nikon cameras use NEF.

The second thing to be aware of is that the RAW format is strictly a *capture format*. This means that it's only used to capture images in-camera. When a RAW file is opened for editing, it must go through a conversion process in order to get it into Photoshop. This conversion process is handled by special software such as Adobe Camera Raw, which comes with Photoshop CS5.

Take a close look at Figure 1-1, and you'll notice that there is no CR2 option for saving. After a RAW file is open in Photoshop, it must be saved as a different file format — usually PSD, TIFF, or JPEG. One of the effects of this is that it prevents you from inadvertently overwriting an original RAW file. Cool, huh? You may notice an option in the Format section of the Save As dialog box called Photoshop Raw. This isn't a standard RAW file format. Photoshop Raw is used as a flexible file format for transferring files from one computer platform to another (Mac, PC, Unix, and so on) or between more exotic image editing applications, such as those used for high-end animation.

X-REF

To learn more about the RAW file format see *Adobe Camera Raw For Digital Photographers Only* by Rob Sheppard.

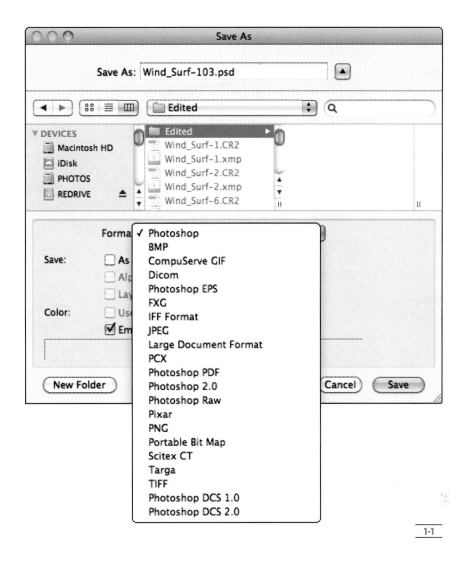

1-1

PSD

PSD is Photoshop's proprietary default file format. It supports more Photoshop features than JPEG or TIFF. In fact, the only other file format that supports as many features is the Large Document Format (PSB), but that's a file format I've never needed. One of the big advantages of working with PSD is that other Adobe products like Illustrator can open PSD files and access all the saved features. This makes life easier for people who move back and forth between Adobe software applications.

A special option can be set in Photoshop's preferences that maximizes PSD file compatibility when saving. With this option turned on, a composite version of all the individual image layers in the image is embedded in the file so that other non-Adobe applications, as well as earlier versions of Photoshop, can display a composite preview of the image. This option is especially important if you use Lightroom as part of your workflow because Lightroom can't catalog a PSD file unless it contains one of these composite previews. The only minor downside to embedding a preview is that the PSD file is a bit larger because of the embedded composite.

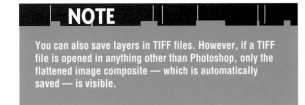

X-REF

Layers are covered in detail in Chapter 4.

Here's how to set this preference so that a composite preview is always embedded in your PSD files:

1. Go to Photoshop's Preferences. Choose

   Edit/⇨Preferences⇨General⇨File Handling.

2. Under Maximize PSD and PSB File Compatibility, click the pop-up as shown in Figure 1-2. Select Always, and click OK. If you want to make the compatibility choice on a case-by-case basis, choose Ask. Then Photoshop asks you if you want to save a composite before saving a new PSD file.

One of the big advantages to using PSD is that all layer information is preserved and stored. When the image is opened, it goes to the state that it was in when it was last saved. All the layers are there, and the last

active layer is still active. When you work extensively with layers, as you do in much of this book, saving them becomes important.

NOTE

You can also save layers in TIFF files. However, if a TIFF file is opened in anything other than Photoshop, only the flattened image composite — which is automatically saved — is visible.

TIFF

TIFF stands for Tagged Image File Format. TIFF is a flexible format that's supported by virtually all image-editing and graphics software. Layers can be saved in TIFF, and the format supports a number of color models like CMYK, RGB, and LAB.

Normally, a TIFF file is larger than a PSD file that's saved from the same image. That's because PSD files

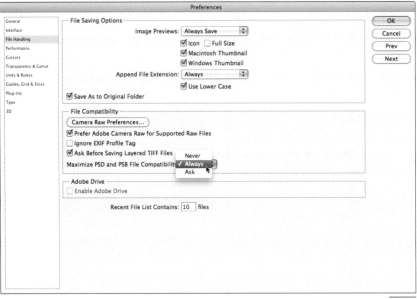

1-2

are *compressed* a bit to make them smaller when they're saved. Compression can substantially reduce file size when images contain lots of the same tones, such as solid backgrounds. Images with lots of details and colors won't compress as much.

Many file formats support file compression. With PSD, it's a transparent part of the process that happens automatically when a PSD file is saved. With a TIFF file, compression is an option. It must be selected in the TIFF Options dialog box when the file is first saved, as shown in Figure 1-3. Photoshop offers three types of TIFF file compression: LZW, ZIP, and JPEG. The main difference among these three compression methods is that LZW and ZIP are lossless compression methods and JPEG is a lossy method of compression.

When an image is compressed, the data is generally handled in one of two ways:

> **Lossless compression:** All information is retained during the compression. This means that an image can be resaved and recompressed without compromising image quality.

> **Lossy compression:** During compression, data is permanently removed. Higher levels of compression result in greater data loss. Every time a file is resaved with lossy compression, more data is lost. This cumulative data loss can greatly affect the quality of an image.

When compressing a TIFF file, stick with lossless compression by selecting LZW or ZIP. They're fairly equal in performance, and Photoshop opens either of them. However, be aware that ZIP is not supported in older software.

Another option with TIFF files in Photoshop is the ability to save layers. This seems pretty cool, except that few image-editing applications can open a layered TIFF file. I don't use layered TIFF files often. If I'm saving a layered file and planning to use Photoshop to edit it,

1-3

then I save it into Photoshop's native file format: PSD. If you're worried about hard drive space, go ahead and save your files in the compressed TIFF format.

NOTE

A layered TIFF file contains individual layers and a composite of the flattened file. If the file is opened in software that can't see the individual layers, the composite data is all that can be seen.

Because I don't use layered TIFF files, I have Photoshop warn me if I forget to flatten a file before saving it as a TIFF. To do this, I select the Ask Before

Saving Layered TIFF Files option in the Photoshop File Handling preferences, as shown in Figure 1-2. When this box is checked, a warning pops up to remind you that you're about to save a layered TIFF file, as shown in Figure 1-4.

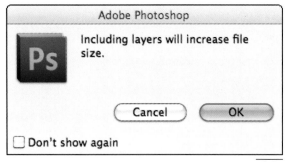

1-4

JPEG

JPEG (sometimes abbreviated as JPEG) files are always compressed because JPEG was designed to be a space-saving file format. JPEG is one of the most widely used file formats for digital imaging. Virtually any software that can open an image file can open a JPEG. What's more, nearly all the photographs you see on the Internet are JPEG files — at least the ones that look good. JPEGs can be compressed to very small sizes, which is perfect for online delivery or e-mail.

Like RAW, JPEG can be used as a capture format. In fact RAW and JPEG are the two primary capture formats. Because many cameras and photographers don't shoot RAW files, JPEG is by far the most widespread capture format. This came about because of JPEG's ability to be compressed. In the early days of digital cameras, memory cards were small and expensive, so the files had to be small so that more would fit onto the card. With the large capacity of memory cards, you can save thousands of JPEG photos on a single card.

Though it's useful, JPEG compression is a double-edge sword. Very small files can be created with high compression, but JPEG compression is lossy, so image quality can be affected. Additionally, whenever a file is resaved, more data is lost. The amount of loss depends on the level of compression.

You select the amount of JPEG compression in Photoshop when a JPEG file is saved. Figure 1-5 shows the JPEG Options dialog box.

In this case, an image that is 24.8MB as an uncompressed TIFF file becomes a 4MB JPEG with a compression quality of 12. If the Quality value, which controls the amount of compression, were lowered to 10 instead of 12, the file size is reduced 1.4MB without adversely affecting the image quality. The key is to try to compress a JPEG file only once when possible by not resaving (and further compressing) the file.

NOTE

JPEG is an acronym for Joint Photographic Experts Group, a committee that created the format in 1992. The committee's goal was to establish a portable standard for compressing photographic files that would be universal.

NOTE

Some photo labs are beginning to require that all JPEGs submitted be saved at a level of 10 instead of 12. This saves space on their servers, which, as you can see from the previous example, can add up quickly.

As you can see, the higher the Quality number in the JPEG Options dialog box, the lower the amount of compression will be. (Lower amounts of compression equal higher quality files.) When saving at a quality of 12, you can make a few multiple resaves to JPEG files without noticeable image degradation (it's happening, you just can't see it yet). If you think you'll be reopening a JPEG and resaving it, choose the highest quality when saving.

With that in mind, JPEG files can be quite useful. As I mentioned, they're perfect for the Web and e-mail. PSDs and TIFFs are mostly useless for those two purposes because of their relative sizes. Also, most photo labs want only JPEG files because they move through the lab's workflow faster. Many labs won't accept TIFFs, and I've never heard of one that will accept PSDs, though I'm sure you could find one. The real trick to working with JPEG is picking the right time in your workflow to save a file as a JPEG, which is usually at the end of the process when you're ready to create a file for output.

CREATING AN ORGANIZED SYSTEM

Organization has always been important for photographers. Now with digital photography, organization is more complicated for a couple of reasons. For one thing, if you aren't careful, the place where image files are stored isn't quite so intuitive. Sometimes, files end up in cryptic places requiring three software engineers to find them. For another, working with digital images tends to create lots and lots of derivative files from some original files. When so many similar yet different files are created, organization takes on a whole new meaning. If all of these files are stored in the same folder it becomes difficult and time consuming to locate a particular version of the image.

CONSIDERING THE NONDESTRUCTIVE WORKFLOW

Photoshop, by its very nature, is destructive to the pixels in an image. That's because editing the image

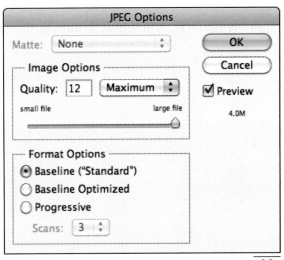

1-5

changes the pixels in it. Sometimes pixels are even removed. If precautionary measures aren't taken, ordinary things, such as tonal and color adjustment, change the pixels permanently and can't be undone at a later date. The idea behind a *nondestructive* workflow is to keep your options open at all times so that it's easy to change individual elements of the editing process. For example, one way to limit the destructiveness of image editing is to avoid cropping and resizing in Photoshop whenever possible. That's because if you make these changes and close the file, they become permanent.

The problem with this is that you need to crop and resize files at some point. You usually do this when you're giving someone else a copy of the file, taking it to a lab to be printed, or uploading it to a Web site. To solve this problem in a nondestructive way, you save two separate files: an editing file (TIFF or PSD) that retains all the flexibility possible, and an output file (JPEG or TIFF) that has been sized, cropped, and prepared for output. Often, you'll prepare multiple output files from the same original image for different uses. These versions begin to add up, creating a level of complexity that was never a problem when shooting film.

THREE KINDS OF WORKFLOW FILES

When creating a nondestructive workflow it becomes necessary to organize three different kinds of files: original files from the camera, edited master files that contain as much information as possible (usually in layers), and final files for printing or display. Both a master file and any related final files are derivatives of the same original file. Look more closely at these three kinds of workflow files:

> **Original files.** These are the capture files from your camera that should never be overwritten. Original files need to remain pristine so you can go back to them when necessary — for example, when you learn a new technique.

> **Master files.** These editing files contain all the flexibility and options that are built in to the file as it's edited in Photoshop. These files are usually saved as PSD files, though they can be saved as layered TIFF files.

> **Output files.** These final files have been prepared for some final usage, such as for print, Web, or e-mail. They have been cropped and sized to a final size and sharpened for output.

When all these files from the same image are stored in the same place, they become difficult to manage. They all look similar so you spend time sorting through them. To minimize confusion, these three file types need to be organized in two ways: They have to be in special folders, and they need to have unique names based on the original file's name.

CREATING A VIRTUAL FILING CABINET

Think of your hard drive as a big filing cabinet. It's divided into separate drawers that are used to organize documents. Folders are stored in these drawers, often with other (sub) folders stored inside of them. This system insures that everything is in its place and can be found when needed.

Figure 1-6 shows a typical hard drive filing strategy with the following file path: Photos⇨2010⇨Smith. The folder named Photos (in the first column) is my filing cabinet. It has three drawers (folders) named 2008, 2009, and 2010. Each of those drawers has a bunch of folders in it. The third column shows the Smith folder and the photos in it. The last column shows two sub-folders that are inside of the Smith folder.

The previous example uses three levels of organization:

> **One main folder (Photos) contains all images in subfolders.** This is incredibly useful when it comes to backing up photos because only one folder — with its subfolders — needs to be backed up.

> **Subfolders are created for each individual year.** This level of organization prevents you from having to sort through folders from previous years unless you want to.

> **Shoot/job folders are used to store the files from an individual photo shoot.** This folder contains the original images and subfolders containing different kinds of derivative files.

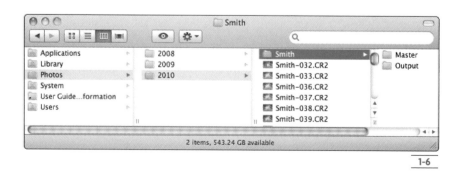

1-6

Creating a filing system like this is the first step to becoming organized. The next step is to begin using a folder and file naming system that complements the kind of photography you do.

FOLDER AND FILE NAMING STRATEGIES

When it comes to naming folders — and the files stored inside them — there are two predominant schools of thought. One is to name folders with pertinent dates and the other is to use descriptive names that describe the photos in the folder. Take a look at both of these strategies to determine which is best for you.

Naming folders with dates

Some photographers prefer to name all shoot/job folders with the date they were shot, or in some cases uploaded. That way every folder is listed in chronological order. The key to using this naming strategy is to use the correct date format so that folders are sorted in the correct order. The preferred method is Year_Month_Day.

This way, every file is sorted in the correct order, beginning with the year, then the month, then the day. Some people like to make life easier by adding a descriptive name to the end of the date. For example, if I shoot some scenic photos at the Oregon coast, I name my folder 2008_08_21_Oregon_Coast.

One of the main drawbacks to using this Year_Month_Day system is that it tends to spread out similar images too much. In its purest form, all photos are placed into dated folders that represent the day they were created.

If I take a trip to Europe for two weeks and then download all my photos using the date naming system, I end up with a folder for every day. If I took pictures every day, then my vacation photos would be spread out into 14 folders. I prefer to see them all together. A better organizational system in this case is to create a main folder with a general date — such as the date the files were uploaded — and then add all files to this one folder instead of placing them into individual daily folders.

Naming folders with descriptive names

Another strategy is to use a descriptive name to identify a shoot. With this strategy, the folder from my European trip is named Europe_2010. If I took more than one trip to Europe, I would add the month after the year. An advantage to this strategy is that folder names are more descriptive. Another advantage is that all photos from the shoot are automatically located in one main folder.

The main disadvantage with this strategy is that folders are sorted alphabetically, instead of chronologically. If chronology is important to you, then this system may not be the best choice. Another disadvantage is that a single descriptive name doesn't always describe everything in the folder. This happens when you allow lots of images to collect on your camera's media card before uploading them.

One way to solve this is to do multiple uploads from the camera's card — placing groups of images into individual folders with descriptive names. A better way to solve this is to regularly upload your photos so they don't accumulate on the card.

Choosing your naming strategy

I know photographers who use both the date and descriptive systems to file images. The people who tend to use the date system are photographers who shoot lots of images, such as commercial and stock shooters. They also tend to be photographers who are highly organized because they often have to locate stored files over long periods of time. The photographers who tend to use the descriptive name method are mostly portrait and wedding photographers who are more oriented to locating jobs by the client's name.

Some photographers don't fall squarely into either of these camps. They tend to use a blend of the two naming systems. If the images in the folder can be categorized with a descriptive name — such as Hawaii 2010, or Jones Wedding — then they use a name. When the images don't have a predominant theme, they use a general date for the name and then use keywords to identify the individual images.

No matter which system you choose, make sure that you're consistent in the way you use it.

Naming original files

Digital cameras automatically create filenames for every photo you shoot. Sometimes those names, such as the filenames shown in Figure 1-7, are quite cryptic and don't tell you much about the photos they represent. That's why I always like to change these names to descriptive names — often the same name I use for the main folder.

For example the Smith job's folder is named Smith, and the individual files are named Smith-001.CR2, Smith-002.CR2, and so on. Renaming is often done as the original files are transferred from the camera's media card to the computer, but it can also be done after the files are in the system using Bridge, as you see later in this chapter.

1-7

_MG_0886.CR2	8.1 MB	Canon Camera Raw file
_MG_0885.CR2	8.1 MB	Canon Camera Raw file
_MG_0884.CR2	8.1 MB	Canon Camera Raw file
_MG_0883.CR2	7.9 MB	Canon Camera Raw file
_MG_0882.CR2	8 MB	Canon Camera Raw file
_MG_0881.CR2	8.1 MB	Canon Camera Raw file
_MG_0880.CR2	8 MB	Canon Camera Raw file
_MG_0879.CR2	7.6 MB	Canon Camera Raw file
_MG_0878.CR2	7.4 MB	Canon Camera Raw file
_MG_0877.CR2	7.1 MB	Canon Camera Raw file
_MG_0876.CR2	7.3 MB	Canon Camera Raw file
_MG_0875.CR2	7.4 MB	Canon Camera Raw file
_MG_0874.CR2	7.6 MB	Canon Camera Raw file

When I rename files, I generally use a naming strategy like Jane_Doe-123. A name like this makes more sense on a couple of levels. First, if I ever need to find Jane's photos using the photos' names, I can do a system search with my computer's operating system for Jane_Doe. Without a descriptive name, this becomes impossible.

The second reason a descriptive filename makes sense is that eventually derivative files for editing and output will be created from some of the originals. It's easier to keep those files organized when you begin with a meaningful name.

For example, suppose the original file is named MG_6337.cr2 because that's what the camera automatically named it, the master file is named Sarah_Jones123.psd, and the final file for 8×10 printing is named Girl_in_Boat.JPEG.

This causes problems in two ways. First, if the files are all placed into in the same folder and they're being sorted alphabetically, they're scattered all over the place among the other files. Second, if you learn some new tricks next year and decide to redo the Girl_in_Boat.JPEG image, you may have trouble remembering from which original file it's derived.

If I rename the original file as soon as it's copied from the media card to the computer, any new derivative file can use that name as a base.

In the previous example, the original file becomes Sarah_Jones123.cr2, the master file becomes Sarah_Jones123_edited.psd, and the final file becomes Sarah_Jones123_8x10.JPEG. This way, I know exactly what kind of file I'm looking at just by looking at the name. In the case of Sarah_Jones123_8x10.JPEG I even know that it's been prepared for an 8×10 print.

Filing Photos in Your Virtual Filing Cabinet

After you establish a naming methodology, you must address the second level of file organization: filing different kinds of workflow files into the appropriate folders. Figure 1-8 shows how I organize my file folders.

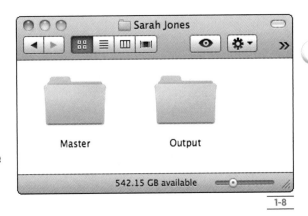

1-8

When I begin a new project, I create a folder for it. In this case, the parent folder is titled Sarah Jones. This folder contains all of the original photos as well as two subfolders named Master and Output.

PRO TIP

Sometimes it's hard to find the Master and Output folders in a job folder because they get buried with all of the original files. I solve this by placing an underscore in front of the folder names, such as _Master. Doing this places these files at the top of the sorting order when files and folders are sorted alphanumerically by your system.

My goal with this organizational system is to make it so intuitive that I know where everything is without looking. Even though I never do it, I want to be able to call my assistant back at my office and ask her to send a particular file to me if I need it. I can do that because I know exactly where the file should be, and so does she.

Your system doesn't necessarily have to look like mine. Create something that makes sense to you because you're the one who needs to understand it. The thing that's most important here is to get a system in place and begin using it now.

MANAGING YOUR ORGANIZATIONAL SYSTEM WITH ADOBE BRIDGE CS5

Early versions of Photoshop had no file browser. If users wanted the ability to visually browse through files to find a particular image, they had to purchase a separate file browser. When Adobe released Photoshop 7, it finally included a very useful file browser that came as part of Photoshop. When Photoshop CS2 was released, the file browser was retooled and separated from Photoshop.

This new file browser was named Adobe Bridge, a stand-alone software that could be used even if Photoshop wasn't running.

> **NOTE**
>
> Bridge is named Bridge because it's more than a Photoshop file browser. It's a central file browser for a number of Adobe titles, such as InDesign and Illustrator. It acts as a bridge between these applications.

Compared to most file browser programs, Bridge is like a browser on steroids. With Bridge, you can view and organize images in a very flexible and intuitive environment. You can rate images and sort them with colored labels and stars, and you can attach a variety of metadata so they can be quickly located later. Because Bridge is such a comprehensive program, it would be easy to dedicate a couple of chapters to it.

My goal here is to introduce you to it and point out some of the highlights so that you can begin using it to manage your files now. If you're already working with Bridge and feel comfortable using it, you still might want to review this section to insure that you're getting the most from this useful piece of software.

> **NOTE**
>
> Bridge comes with Photoshop CS5. When you install Photoshop, Bridge also is installed. You can launch it independently of Photoshop by clicking its icon in your Applications folder (Mac) or from the All Programs button in the Start menu (Windows).

GETTING A BIRD'S-EYE VIEW OF BRIDGE

I talk to lots of professional photographers, and I'm continually amazed at how many use Photoshop on a regular basis but don't use Bridge. In fact, many of these people don't even know how to launch it from Photoshop. It isn't because they don't like Bridge; they just don't understand it. After they learn to use Bridge, they seldom go back to their old system.

To open Bridge from Photoshop, choose File⇨Browse in Bridge. You also can launch Bridge by clicking the Launch Bridge button with a Br icon at the top left of the Photoshop CS5 workspace. When Bridge is already running, this button provides a quick way to jump to it from Photoshop.

When Bridge opens your screen will look something like Figure 1-9.

If your screen looks different than the one shown in Figure 1-9, it's because your *workspace* is different. You can use different layouts of the Bridge workspace for different tasks, which is a great asset. This is covered in a moment. First, set Bridge back to its default view by choosing Window⇨Workspace⇨Essentials (⌘/Ctrl+F1), as shown in Figure 1-10.

The Bridge CS5 Default workspace consists of a series of panels. Here's what some of them are used for:

> **Folders panel.** This displays the folder tree of the folders on the hard drive. Notice the folder structure in Figure 1-9. The folder currently being viewed is the main job folder.

1-9

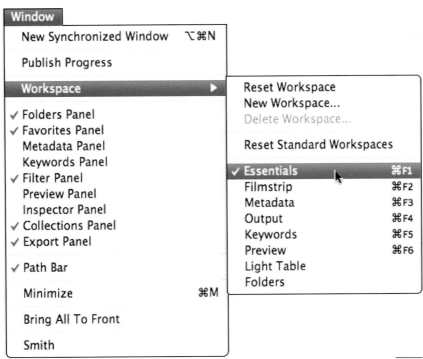

1-10

> **Favorites panel:** This panel allows you to have easy access to some of the areas you use most. It comes with a few common locations, such as Desktop, loaded into it. Click and drag a folder from the Content area to the Favorites panel to add it to the list.

> **Filter panel:** Whenever the content of a folder is displayed in the Content area, the Filter panel looks at the content and dynamically displays all the different ways that the particular folder can be filtered. If you are viewing a new folder where few changes have been made in Bridge, then the options are limited.

In Figure 1-9, you can see that the Filter panel opened headings for Labels (colored labels), Ratings (rating stars), and File Type. Sorting for one of these criteria is easy. You just click it in the Filter panel. For example, if I want to see only the six files that have a green label, I click on the green (Approved) label under the labels heading. You can even sort for more than one criterion by selecting multiple criteria. To turn filtering off, deselect the filter criteria by clicking them.

The other, collapsed headings allow you to sort for other criteria. For example, to see only the vertical images, open the Orientation heading by clicking on the sideways-pointing triangle and choose Portrait.

> **Content panel:** This is the main viewing window. Thumbnails of the selected folder in the Folders panel are displayed here. Use the thumbnail size slider at the bottom right of the workspace to change the size of these thumbnails. Double-click on a file to open it in Photoshop.

Another important part of the Bridge user interface is the Application bar at the top of the interface. This bar provides a number of useful buttons that give you quick access to features, such as access to recent folders and the Bridge photo downloader.

Just below this bar is the Path bar, which displays the path to the currently displayed folder for easy reference, as well as other buttons that are used to sort, rotate, and filter photos in the Content panel.

An important button on the Path bar is the Thumbnail Quality button that's just to the left of the star in Figure 1-9. Clicking this button opens a drop-down list, as shown in Figure 1-11, that controls the quality of the thumbnail images as they're rendered in the Content panel.

Shortly after Photoshop CS5 was released, a longtime client called to tell me that all of her thumbnails in Bridge looked horrible. The cause was due to Prefer Embedded (Faster) being selected. This helps to render the thumbnails quickly, but quality can suffer. When she switched the menu to Always High Quality, the thumbnails were rerendered and the low quality issue disappeared.

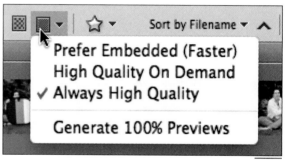

1-11

CREATING CUSTOM WORKSPACES

As I mentioned earlier, predefined workspaces are used to set up the working environment to suit the way you like to work. One of my favorites is the Light Table workspace (Window⇨Workspace⇨Light Table). When you activate it, all side panels are instantly hidden and the Content area is maximized, allowing you to focus on only the thumbnails.

What makes these workspaces even cooler is that you can create your own custom workspaces. Though Bridge comes with a Preview workspace for viewing a large preview of the selected file(s), I like to create my own custom workspace that gives me large preview workspace that suits my needs. I show you how to do that in just a moment. First, I want to show you how to modify the default layout so you can save your own custom workspace:

1. I don't use the Export panel, which can be used to upload photos to online storage sites such as Photoshop.com or Flickr.com, so I just turn it off. To turn yours off, go to the Window menu and click Export Panel to uncheck it. If you don't want to see other panels, now is the time to uncheck them.

2. I also like to change the accent color in the Bridge preferences. Here's how: For Windows, choose Edit⇨Preferences; for Mac choose Adobe Bridge CS5⇨Preferences.

3. Make sure that the General preferences are highlighted in the menu on the left. Click on the Accent Color to open it and choose a different color, as shown in Figure 1-12. I like to use Amber because it's easy to see. If you want to remove some of the default items from the Favorites panel, deselect them from the Favorite Items area at the bottom of the dialog box.

4. Click OK.

5. Click and drag the vertical and horizontal bars that separate panels to make any adjustments to panel positions until you have a workspace that you like and can use every day. When you're ready to save it, choose Window⇨Workspace⇨New Workspace and name the workspace, as shown in Figure 1-13.

If you select Save Window Location as Part of Workspace, the Bridge window always opens in the same location. Choosing Save Sort Order as Part of Workspace uses the current file sorting order every time you use the workspace. I recommend you don't select this one because it can be annoying to have a special sort order change when you switch workspaces.

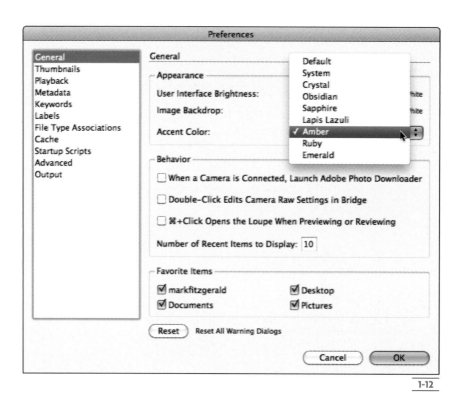

1-12

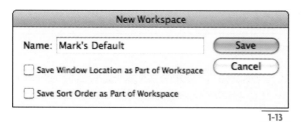

1-13

Okay, now that you have a default workspace saved, here's how you can create another one that's designed for focusing on a large preview of the selected file(s).

1. Go to the Window menu and deselect all the panels except Preview. You'll have to uncheck them one at a time. This removes them from the interface. When you finish, you should see only two panels: Content (which can't be removed) and Preview.

2. Move your cursor over the line that divides the Preview panel and the Content area. When you see the cursor change to a double-sided arrow, shown circled in Figure 1-14, click and drag to the left until a single column of thumbnails is visible on the left.

3. The only thing left to do is to save the workspace. Choose Window⇨Workspace⇨New Workspace. I named mine Large Previews.

Now you can instantly jump back and forth between these two workspaces by choosing them from the Workspace menu. When I work in Bridge, I use these two custom workspaces, along with the Light Table workspace, exclusively.

1-14

Now that you have the Bridge workspace laid out the way you like it, it's time to put it to work.

USING BRIDGE TO BATCH RENAME PHOTOS

I mentioned earlier that naming should happen to an original file early on so that any derivative images use the original name as the root of their own name. For this to be truly effective, you must apply meaningful names to the original images as early as possible.

To rename a file in Bridge, simply click its name below the thumbnail in the Content panel. Sometimes, it takes a moment for the name to highlight. Be patient. If you're in a hurry and click twice too quickly, Bridge interprets it as a double-click and opens the file in Photoshop.

Being able to rename a file is useful, but for this to really work you need to be able to rename all files at once. This is called *batch renaming*. Batch renaming is extremely useful for dealing with digital camera files

19

because there are usually quite a few of them. Fortunately, batch renaming is quite simple and straightforward in Bridge.

Here's how it works:

1. Select the files that need to be renamed. If renaming happens early enough in the process, you usually rename all files. If that's the case, select all files by choosing Edit⇨Select All (Ctrl/⌘+A).

2. Choose Tools⇨Batch Rename (Shift+⌘/Ctrl+R) to open the Batch Rename dialog box, as shown in Figure 1-15. The look of this dialog box varies depending on whether the Batch Rename function has been used before. These settings are *sticky*, meaning they stay where you last left them.

3. The first thing to check is that the Rename in same folder option is selected in the Destination Folder section; otherwise, the photos could be copied to another folder, or even moved.

One of my clients inadvertently selected the Move to other folder option when renaming a wedding she photographed. When she did, all the files disappeared from her folder and she thought they had been deleted. If this happens to you, do a search for the new name to find the folder to which your images were moved.

4. Go to the first menu box in the New Filenames section. If it says anything other than Text, click on it and choose Text from the drop-down list. Then type the new filename as you want it to appear. In my case, in Figure 1-15 I typed Smith-. The reason I added a hyphen after the name is to add a bit of separation between the name and the sequence number that is added in the next step. This is especially useful if you use a date naming strategy.

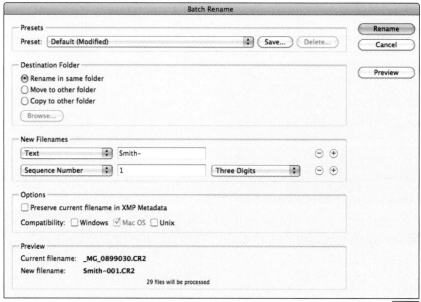

1-15

5. Now you need to add a sequence number to the filename so that all files are named sequentially. If no other boxes are below the Text boxes, click the plus button (+) to the right to add an additional naming element. Then use the drop-down list for that element to select Sequence Number. Use the pop-up on the right box to set the number of digits to what you want. I selected Three Digits. In the middle box, type the starting number of your sequence.

6. Click Rename to complete the process and rename your files.

PRO TIP

At the bottom left of the Batch Rename dialog box is a section called Preview. It allows you to preview what the new filename will look like before completing the process. Checking this can be very useful, especially if you're using dates for filenames and you forget to add a hyphen to separate the filename and the sequence number.

WORKING WITH LABELS AND RATING STARS

After the files are renamed, it's time to sort through them and identify the winners and losers. The best way to do that is to use colored labels and/or rating stars. When these are in place, you can quickly find images that have them applied by using the Filter panel. However, before you begin adding labels there's an interesting preference you should look at.

For some reason, the engineers at Adobe decided a couple of versions ago to rename the colored labels to names other than the name of the color. For example, green is named Approved and red is named Select. This causes confusion in two ways. First, when you go to the Label menu, it's difficult to know which label is a specific color. The other, and more serious, problem concerns people who use Lightroom. When colored labels are added in Lightroom and then viewed in Bridge, they all appear white instead of colored.

To switch your label names to the old defaults, follow these steps:

1. Open the Bridge preferences and choose labels from the menu on the left. This opens the Labels Preferences dialog box shown in Figure 1-16.

2. Click in each text box and rename the label to its color using an initial cap. For example, Select becomes Red. Then click OK to make the change. Now your label names make more sense.

PRO TIP

Deselect the Require the Command Key to Apply Labels and Ratings option to shorten the keyboard shortcuts for colored labels and rating stars to a single numerical keystroke.

Colored labels can be added to an individual image or to a group of selected images by choosing the Label menu and selecting the color you want. For example, if I want to add a green label to a photo, I choose Label⇨Green. This adds a green label beneath the selected thumbnail(s). If you don't like digging through menus, learn the shortcut keys for the labels you use most often and use them instead. These shortcuts are listed next to the labels and stars in the Label menu. Purple is the only one that doesn't have a shortcut because the engineers ran out of numbers. To remove a label, choose it again from the menu or use its shortcut key.

Preferences
Labels

☑ Require the Command Key to Apply Labels and Ratings

Select	⌘ + 6
Second	⌘ + 7
Approved	⌘ + 8
Review	⌘ + 9
To Do	

1-16

Rating stars work pretty much the same way. Go to the Labels menu and select the number of stars that you want to place on the thumbnail, or use the shortcut key. To remove a rating star, choose Label⇨No Rating.

Another way to quickly add stars to a file is to use the shortcut that's built in to the thumbnail. Just below the image on each selected thumbnail are five little dots that represent the five rating stars. Just click the dot number that represents the number of stars that you want; in other words, click the second dot from the left to add two stars. To remove stars, click the Cancel icon that appears just to the left of the first star when you move your cursor there.

> ### NOTE
>
> If the thumbnails are scaled too small, the dots (and labels for that matter) may not be visible. Use the Thumbnail size slider at the bottom right of the Bridge interface to increase their size until you can see the labels.

You can use labels and stars to identify and sort image files in a variety of ways. I use a fairly simple system: Green labels mark images I like, and red labels mark images I want to delete. I do this very quickly, usually in the large preview workspace so I get a good look at each image.

1. When I see an image I like, I add a green label to it. When I see one I want to delete, I add a red label to it.

2. After all images are labeled, I go to the Filter panel and click the Red label to display only the red labels.

3. I select all the red-labeled images (⌘/Ctrl+A), and press Delete. This opens the dialog box shown in Figure 1-17. It gives me two options for removing the files. Clicking Reject hides the file without deleting it, which can lead to endless confusion.

Clicking Delete sends the files to the Trash on a Mac or the Recycling Bin on a PC. Notice in Figure 1-16 that you can press ⌘/Ctrl+Delete to delete an item, eliminating the need to go through this dialog box.

4. Then I click the red label in the Filter panel to turn the filter off so I can see all the remaining images.

5. Now I can click the green label in the Filter panel so I can focus on my favorites. As I go through these, I look for the best of my favorites and use stars to make them stand out even more. One star = mild interest; two stars = more interest; three stars = very interested.

6. After that's finished, I go to the Filter panel and select three stars under Ratings. Now the only images I'm viewing are the most important images in the folder.

> ### PRO TIP
>
> Stars also are a great way to let clients rate their images after you've done a rough sort with colored labels. Show them the green ones, and let them use stars to indicate their favorites.

You don't have to use colored labels and rating stars exactly the same way I do here. Just develop a system with them that means something to you. After you have that system, try to use it all the time. When you see a particular colored label or a certain number of stars on an image, you'll instantly know how important it is.

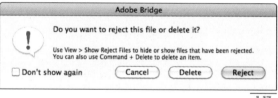

1-17

INTRODUCING MINI BRIDGE

As I stated earlier, Bridge is an incredibly powerful application. What you've seen in this chapter is only the tip of the iceberg when it comes to Bridge's feature set. Sometimes, though, you don't need all of that power — you simply need to quickly find and open a file. Because Adobe realized this, it introduced a slimmed-down version of Bridge, named Mini Bridge, with the release of Photoshop CS5.

Mini Bridge is not a separate application like the full version of Bridge. It's a panel that can be opened within Photoshop, even when Bridge isn't running. This allows a great deal of flexibility because the panel can be left open for use without consuming the system resources required by a fully functioning program like Bridge.

To open Mini Bridge in Photoshop, choose File⇨Browse in Mini Bridge. You can also open it by clicking the Launch Mini Bridge button, which is just to the right of the Launch Bridge button on Photoshop's Application bar.

Figure 1-18 shows the Mini Bridge panel. This elegant design incorporates all of the most important features of Bridge in a very small space.

Using Mini Bridge is fairly straightforward. When you click on an option in the Navigation pod, its content is displayed in the pod to the right.

In Figure 1-18, I clicked Favorites to display the list of my favorites on the right. When I click one of these headings, such as Pictures, the Content pod below is populated with its contents. Just like the full version of Bridge, double-clicking on a folder in the Content pod reveals the contents of that folder in the Content pod. Double-clicking on a file opens it into Photoshop. If you decide that you need to open the full version of Bridge, click the Go to Adobe Bridge button on the top row. It's the button with a Br icon on it.

Even if you're a longtime user of Bridge, I guarantee you'll find that the new Mini Bridge improves your workflow because it gives you quick access to your files without ever leaving Photoshop.

BACKING UP AND ARCHIVING

Why organize all your photos if you don't take the time to back them up? Digital photography offers all kinds of creative opportunities that have changed the way photographers work with images. Unlike film, though, digital files can disappear in an instant when a hard drive crashes.

If proper archiving measures aren't used, a hard drive crash can be catastrophic. The following sections explore some archiving options and strategies.

1-18

One of the easiest ways to create a backup is with a separate hard drive that backs up all image files. In its more sophisticated form, this is often an array of multiple hard drives that are set up to act as one. This kind of array is called a *RAID* (Redundant Array of Independent Disks). Several different schemes are used to protect file integrity on a RAID. Here are the two main methods:

> **Mirroring:** (Sometimes referred to as RAID1) Identical data is written to more than one disk. If a disk in this array crashes, identical data is recovered from the mirrored disk.

> **Striping:** (Sometimes referred to as RAID0) Information is spread out across multiple disks. This greatly enhances performance because several disks are doing the job of one disk when reading and writing. However, unless some form of redundancy is built into the system, there is no data protection as in mirroring. Setting up some form of redundancy allows for striped data to be recovered after a crash. One method of doing this is to have software that can reconstruct missing data from a crashed hard drive by analyzing data that wasn't lost on the other hard drives.

All the workings inside a RAID, mirroring and striping, happen in the background. The best part is that it happens automatically. The RAID just looks like a big hard drive to the computer's operating system. After a RAID is set up, it does its job whether you think about it or not. With the low cost of hard drives today, a RAID is a great option if you're dealing with lots of files.

PRO TIP

I know many photographers who are using a RAID system called Drobo from a company named Data Robotics, Inc. (www.drobo.com). Drobos come in a few different configurations as to the number of hard drives that are used. These systems are easy to set up and configure. Once that's done, your data is backed up automatically.

A less sophisticated, yet equally effective hard drive solution is to have a secondary hard drive that's used for storing backup copies. These backups can be created automatically with specially designed software, or they can be created manually by dragging and dropping files. Of these two schemes, the automatic solution is by far the best because you don't need to remember to do it. With backup software like ChronoSync by Econ Technologies (for Mac) and Microsoft Sync Toy (for Windows), multiple auto-backup scenarios are easy to set up so that you never have to think about them again. Mac users with the Leopard operating system can also use Time Machine to back up their system, though it isn't as flexible as a program like ChronoSync.

Hard drive storage is a great solution for storing backup files, but this also can lead to a false sense of security. A few years ago, shortly after relocating my office, I had three hard drives crash within months of each other. They were all from different manufactures, and they weren't in a RAID. One of those drives was my main drive that had lots of data files on it. One of the other drives was a backup drive of that same data. Unfortunately, I hadn't taken the time to restore all the backed-up data, so when the second drive crashed everything was gone.

PRO TIP

I solved my crashing hard drive problem by purchasing an uninterruptable power supply (UPS). A UPS is little more than a big battery that you plug your computer into. If the power goes out unexpectedly, the UPS kicks in, giving you time to close important files and shut down your computer. Most UPS units also do something else: they clean up the incoming power so it's more stable. That's what solved my crashing problem.

More extreme nightmare scenarios that can make your life miserable are fire and theft. Either of these events can wipe out years of work. You have to think about all these possibilities when you consider the storage of image files. I know several photographers who locate a backup drive or RAID in a hidden portion of their home or office in case of theft. With some of the wireless hard drive solutions available today, this is an even more viable option.

In the case of fire, the best protection is to have a backup of important data that's stored off-site. To do this, add a second hard drive to your backup regimen and store it in a fireproof safe or at a friend's house. Then every week or so swap this drive with your main backup drive so that the drive with the most recent data is placed in a safe place.

CD/DVD

Another system for backing up and archiving images is using CDs and DVDs. CDs and DVDs are cheap, and almost any computer can read them. If handled properly, they faithfully preserve data for many years.

CDs and DVDs are not as easy and seamless as using a hard drive, and they don't offer quick access to data. In my mind, they're best used as an adjunct to a hard drive backup — more of an archive that can be pulled out anytime a file needs to be resurrected. In a well-designed workflow, they should be used at two different times:

> **As soon as you finish transferring, sorting, and renaming a new job or project burn a CD (or DVD if necessary) of all original files and store it in a safe place.** In the case of a professional photographer, that would be in the job folder or client's folder.

> **After all work for the job or project is done, burn a DVD(s) of all related folders — originals, masters, and finals folders.** File this DVD with the first CD/DVD backup you created. If the job or project is important, burn a second copy and store it off-site. Now everything is completely covered. You will probably never need these discs, but it's comforting to know that they are there in case you do. If the job or project is a big one that takes lots of time, then intermediate DVD backups are a good idea. You can use rerecordable media for this.

When working with optical discs, you need to observe some basic ground rules regarding handling. They scratch easily when dragged across rough surfaces, so they should be stored in some sort of acid-free sleeve at all times. It's important to use acid-free sleeves because acids in other types of plastic or paper sleeves can deteriorate the plastic that the discs are composed of. Also, keep these additional things in mind when working with CDs and DVDs:

> **Try to avoid writing on the top surface.** These discs are read by a laser beam that shines up from the bottom through the lower layers of plastic. It reflects off the shiny layer on top and bounces back down to read the data. If anything is done to degrade the reflective nature of the surface on the top of the disc, the laser won't be able to read it. Sometimes the acid in a pen's ink can destroy the shiny layer on top.

If you need to write on a disc, try to do it on the inner circle where the plastic is clear. Another option is to purchase printable CDs and DVDs. These are designed to be printed on with an inkjet printer, so they have a more durable surface that you can write on.

> **Only use labels that are approved for CDs and DVDs.** These use adhesives that are acid-free. You really don't know what kind of adhesive is used on a standard mailing label. Besides the adhesive issue, mailing labels can cause a different problem.

A couple of years ago, a client dropped off a CD with files he wanted me to work on. He labeled the CD with three small, rectangular mailing labels.

Each label had a different set of information. I was unable to read this disc on any of my systems because when it was spinning at 10,000 RPM in the disc drive, the labels threw it out of balance.

> **Store disks in proper, acid-free sleeves or envelopes.** Keep them out of the sun, preferably in the dark. Store them lying flat if possible, rather than upright.

When it comes to backing up, you don't need a sophisticated system, but you do need a system. Working without one is like a trapeze artist working without a net. When things come crashing down, it can be a real showstopper.

Q & A

I want to implement an organizational system similar to the one you described in this chapter. However, I already have thousands of files that aren't very well organized. The thought of going back and organizing them now seems overwhelming. How do you suggest I proceed?

The best thing to do is start organizing all new work now. Any new files, whether they're originals or derivatives, need to be named and filed in organized folders. As you do this, your new system begins to materialize. When you have time, you can go back and roughly organize older work. Begin with files that are the most important to you. Group them into a hierarchal folder system whenever possible. Don't worry about renaming the individual files unless the process seems straightforward to you. Naturally, the level you go into with older files will depend on the type of photography you do. If you're a wedding photographer, you may never really need to go back to older files so it might not be worth the effort of reorganizing them. If you're a stock photographer who makes a living from selling photos, organization should be one of your highest priorities. One big sale will make any invested time worth the effort.

You mentioned Lightroom a couple of times earlier in this chapter. What exactly is Lightroom?

As you work your way through this book, you'll find that Photoshop is a powerful piece of editing software. It enables you to completely transform an image. Sometimes, though, a photographer doesn't need all of Photoshop's power. This is especially true on the front end of the workflow when large quantities of images need to be organized and processed. Lightroom, which is the newest imaging product from Adobe, solves this problem by making it easier for photographers to efficiently organize and process photos.

Lightroom isn't a replacement for Photoshop; it's designed to work with it. In fact, its official name is Adobe Photoshop Lightroom. Lightroom is more like a combination of Adobe Bridge and Adobe Camera Raw, merging most of the features of these products in a single intuitive workspace. When more advanced tools or techniques are needed for a photo, it is moved into Photoshop for the heavy lifting Photoshop is famous for.

If you're not currently using Lightroom, it's not necessary to run out and get it now. But do put it onto your radar. If you decide to add it to your digital editing toolbox later on, many of the things you learn in this book can be applied to learning and using Lightroom at that time.

Chapter 2

ADJUSTING BRIGHTNESS AND CONTRAST

Photo by Mark Fitzgerald

UNDERSTANDING HISTOGRAMS

The primary tool used to evaluate the tones in a digital image is the *histogram*. A histogram is a graphical representation of the distribution of the tones in an image. It consists of a graph that ranges from pure black on the left to pure white on the right.

To understand how the graph is created, imagine 256 side-by-side columns, one for each of the individual tonal values. The columns start with pure black (0) on the left and end with pure white (255) on the right. In between, there are 254 other columns representing all the shades of gray between black and white. Together these 256 tonal levels equal the sum total of the tones in an image. The height of each column is governed by the number of pixels in the image having that particular tone. Because these columns are standing right next to each other, they form a graph when viewed as a group. This graph is called a histogram.

Figure 2-1 shows a photo of photographer David Hitchcock. The histogram next to it shows a graph of the tones in this image. In this example, it's easy to see how the histogram is mapping the data. The darker tones in the image are represented by the taller regions on the left side. The lighter regions, which are mostly in the wall behind David, are represented by the tall region on the right. Because the photo doesn't have many middle tones, the middle region of the histogram is relatively flat.

HOW EXPOSURE AFFECTS ITS HISTOGRAM

The histogram in Figure 2-2 covers a broad range from almost black to almost white. This tells you that most of the midtones are represented. There's a tall area on the left, representing the darkest areas in the stems and greenery on the lower left. However, the darkest and the brightest tones fall short of pure black and pure white so you know that the image is holding detail in the shadows and the highlights — which is usually the goal in photography.

When a photo is underexposed, the entire histogram shifts to the left. The emphasis is on the darker tones and fewer highlights are represented. Figure 2-3 shows an underexposed version of the daffodils. Notice that everything is darker and that it's difficult to discern detail in the deepest shadows of the greenery. This tonal shift is confirmed by looking at the histogram.

The darkest tones on the left, which were fully represented in the histogram of Figure 2-2, are now being pushed off the end of the graph. When this happens, all those tones that used to describe the darkest shadows are forced to black (0). This tonal loss is called *clipping* because the tones are essentially clipped off the end of the tonal scale.

Figure 2-4 shows what happens when highlights are clipped by overexposure. The histogram is pushed to the right and the tones that used to describe bright highlights that still held detail in them are forced to pure white (255).

This highlight data loss is easy to see in the photo where the lightest parts of the sky are clearly being blown out. There's still a tall section on the left of the histogram representing the darker areas in the stems of the flowers, but it's moved to the right indicating that the darkest areas are much lighter now.

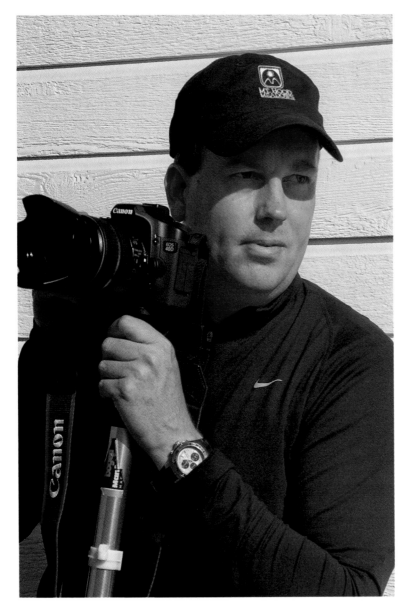

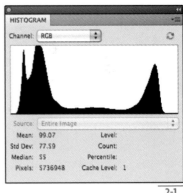

2-1

How subject matter affects a histogram

Something else to consider when evaluating a histogram is the tonal key of the image. When an image is a bright scene (high-key) or a dark scene (low-key), the histogram can fool you. Figures 2-5 and 2-6 show photos and their accompanying histograms.

At first glance, the histogram in Figure 2-5 appears normal and the histogram for Figure 2-6, which is the darker image, appears to indicate underexposure. However, notice that the dark tones are not being clipped on the left side of the histogram in Figure 2-6.

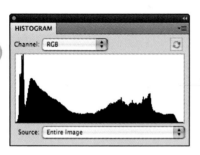

2-2

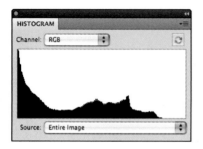

2-3

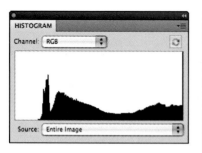

2-4

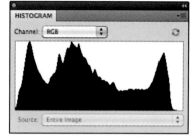

2-5
Photo by Denyce Weiler

In fact, both of these images were made with exactly the same exposure and lighting. The differences in the histograms come from the differences in subject matter. Figure 2-5 contains more medium tones and bright tones while Figure 2-6 contains more dark tones.

I can prove both photos were exposed the same by drawing a selection around similar areas of both faces. When I do that, the histogram displays information only about the tones inside the selections.

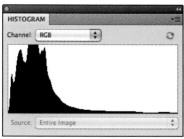

2-6
Photo by Denyce Weiler

Figures 2-7 and 2-8 show close-ups of the selections and their resulting histograms. Now you can be sure that these two images have the same exposure.

The histograms are different because of the tonal values of the subjects in the photo.

X-REF

Selections are covered in detail in Chapter 5.

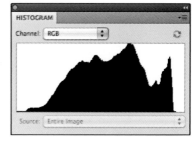

2-7

Always remember to factor in the tonal range of the subject matter when evaluating a histogram. Allow low-key images to have a histogram that's weighted to the darker regions (the left side) and allow higher-key images to have histograms that lean toward the lighter end of the scale (the right side). The main thing to watch for is shadow and/or highlight clipping.

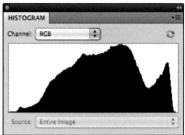

WORKING WITH THE HISTOGRAM PANEL

To see the Histogram panel, choose Window⇨Histogram. To remove the panel from its panel group so you can see it better, click and drag it by its header to make it free floating. There are several ways to display tonal data in a histogram.

Figure 2-9 shows the default view, which displays data for each of the three color channels in their specific colors: Red, Green, and Blue. (This histogram is for the photo shown in Figure 2-5.) Overlapping colors are displayed as the combination of those colors.

For example, where the Red and Green channels overlap, the overlapping area is shown in yellow. When the Red, Green, and Blue channels overlap, they're displayed in gray.

X-REF

Color channels and color theory are discussed in Chapter 3.

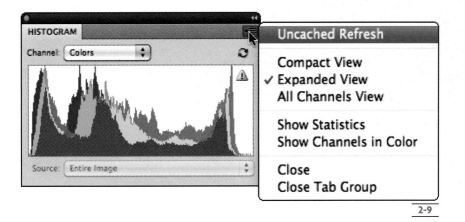

Click the panel menu button to open the Histogram panel's menu. This menu allows you to change some of the ways tonal data is displayed. Select from the options to change the display:

> **Expanded View:** Increases the overall size of the panel.

> **All Channels View:** Adds three additional histograms that display data for each channel.

> **Show Channels in Color:** Shows each channel in the All Channels view in its color (Red, Green, and Blue).

> **Show Statistics:** Adds a second window with interesting, though mostly useless, information for our purposes. (This information is shown in the histogram in Figure 2-1.)

PRO TIP

Almost every panel has a panel menu. These menus allow you to modify the way the panel is viewed. Many panel menus also provide quick access to commands used with the panel.

You can also display individual channels one at a time in the main histogram window by choosing them from the Channel pop-up menu, which is only visible when the panel is in the Expanded View. The default setting is Colors, as shown in Figure 2-9. I used the RGB preset for the other histograms I showed earlier in this chapter because I wanted to keep things simple by showing a black histogram.

You may have noticed a small, triangle-shaped exclamation icon in the Histogram panel. It indicates that the currently displayed histogram is being created with cached information — not the very latest info. This happens when you make an edit to an image. The histogram changes, but it isn't a precise representation of the changes. To update the histogram so it's using the most current information, click the exclamation icon or the circular Refresh button directly above it. (You can also select the Uncached Refresh option in the panel menu to update the cache.)

One of the cool things about the Histogram panel is that it updates in real time as you edit a photo, allowing you to monitor how your changes are affecting it. I recommend that you leave it visible in your workspace so that you can use it to help you get a feel for how tonal and color adjustments affect the histogram.

Even with the best exposure, the scene may not contain the darkest and brightest tones you want to see. In these cases, it becomes necessary to adjust the tonality of the image, which in turn affects the histogram. You can do this in a couple of ways: using the Levels command and using the Curves command, which are discussed in the following sections.

ADJUSTING CONTRAST AND BRIGHTNESS WITH LEVELS

The Levels command is one of the primary tools for tonal adjustment in Photoshop. It allows you to control the overall brightness and contrast of an image. More importantly, the Levels command enables you to pinpoint the darkest and lightest tones in an image. That way, you not only know whether you're clipping highlights or shadows, but you also know exactly where clipping is occurring in the image.

When you open Levels (choose Image⇨Adjustments⇨Levels), the first thing you notice is that it uses the histogram to display information about the image, as shown in Figure 2-10. The small triangles below the histogram at each end allow you to control where the ends of the histogram stop. These triangles are called *input sliders*. When you click and drag them inward, you modify the histogram by moving the endpoint. The numbers below the sliders tell you exactly which tones are being affected.

Black Input slider — White Input slider

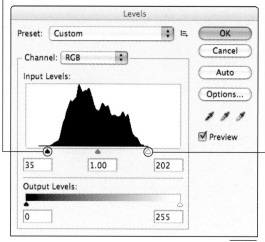

2-10

When the black and the white Input sliders are moved, they have a similar effect on their respective endpoints. The black slider controls what the darkest tone in the image is — a value of 0, or pure black. The white slider controls what the lightest tone in the image is — a value of 255, or pure white. This means that whatever values these sliders are set on become the new blackest black (the black-point) and the whitest white (the white-point).

In Figure 2-10, the black and the white Input sliders have both been moved inward. The black slider is set at 35, and the white slider is set at 202. If OK is clicked at this point, the current tone of 35 becomes 0 and the current tone of 202 becomes 255. Tones outside of these settings are clipped. This can be verified by looking at the display in the Histogram panel, as shown in Figure 2-11. It shows a preview of the modified histogram, which is overlaid on top of a lighter graph of the starting histogram.

Take the Levels command for a spin so you can get a feel for the three main sliders:

1. Open the practice file titled Snow_Dog.tif from the downloadable practice files on the Web site. (www.wiley.com/go/phoprestorationandretouching)

2. If the Histogram panel isn't showing on your desktop, choose Window⇨Histogram.

3. Choose Image⇨Adjustments⇨Levels (⌘/Ctrl+L) to open the Levels panel. The histogram for this photo of Ruby luxuriating in the snow shows that the image doesn't have deep shadows or bright highlights because the histogram data doesn't extend all the way to either end of the graph. This can be seen in the image in Figure 2-12 where the contrast is a bit flat.

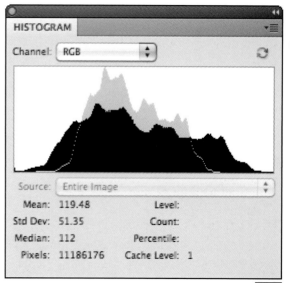

2-11

2-12

4. Click and drag the black Input slider until the value is 23.

5. Click and drag the white Input slider until the value is 226. Notice how much richer the image looks. The blacks have been punched up, and the whites look much cleaner.

6. Now click and drag the black slider to 45 and the white slider to 200. Now notice how the image's contrast has gone too far. The darkest tones and the lightest tones are losing detail because highlight and shadow information is being clipped.

7. Click Cancel.

When you use Levels, you need to be careful about clipping shadows and highlights when moving the endpoints. It's not only important to know when clipping is happening, but it's also important to know where it's happening in the image.

1. Open Snow_Dog again. If it's already open, be sure that no previous Levels adjustments have been applied by selecting the file's open state in the History panel. You can do this by clicking on the first history state labeled Open, or by clicking the small image thumbnail at the top of the Histogram panel.

2. This time hold down the Alt key while clicking and sliding the black slider inward. The first thing to notice is that the image goes completely white. Keep dragging the slider until you see detail appear in the image, as shown in the first frame of Figure 2-13. This is called a *clipping preview*. The dark areas that appear as you drag the slider are the shadow tones that will be clipped and forced to black with the current Black Point slider setting. These tones first appear as colors, indicating the color channel that's being clipped. As you continue to move the slider the tones are displayed as black, indicating that all color channels are clipping in those areas.

2-13

3. Move the black slider back to the left until the preview just becomes completely white, and release the mouse button. Now you know that detail in the shadows is preserved because none of them are clipping.

4. Do the same thing with the whites. Hold the Alt key, and drag the white slider inward toward the left. Notice that the screen goes black. Keep dragging until some detail appears in the image, and then back off until the preview is black again. Now you know that all highlight detail is preserved, which is important in a photo like this one because of the snow. If these tones are clipped, some of the snow becomes white blobs without any definition.

5. Look at the Histogram panel and note that the updated graph now covers almost the entire range from black to white. The adjustments you made to the black and white points increased the contrast of the image by making use of the entire tonal range without clipping shadows or highlights.

6. Deselect the Preview check box on the Levels window to see the image without the adjustment. Be sure to select the check box before clicking OK later.

7. Click the middle Input slider to adjust the overall brightness of the image. It's between the white Input slider and the black Input slider. This slider is called the gray Input slider. Just below it is a readout displaying 1.00, which is its default setting. Slide it to the left to lighten the image, and slide it to the right to darken. (Holding down the Option/Alt key here has no effect. Just move the slider until you like what you see.)

8. When you're happy with your adjustments, click OK.

Now the image has had its contrast and brightness fine-tuned. We know where the darkest and lightest parts of the image are, and we know that we're holding detail in them. This valuable information is provided by the clipping preview function in the Levels command.

Sometimes, I let the shadows of an image clip if I think it makes the image look better by providing deeper blacks. I just make sure that those shadows are not in my main subject. In this example, any detail loss in the shadows is in the dog's fur — which would be unacceptable to me. If shadow clipping is occurring in a dark background, I might let some of it clip if I thought the increased contrast gave the image a little more snap. However, I almost never allow a highlight to blow out if I can prevent it, now matter where it is in the image. When a highlight is blown out and it gets printed, it becomes the color of the paper it's printed on because there's no detail in it.

So here's the lowdown on Levels: When adjusting an image with Levels, always start with either the black Input slider or the white Input slider. Adjust both the black point and the white point before adjusting the image's brightness with the gray Input slider in the middle. If you begin with the gray slider before working with the end points, you'll most likely have to revisit it later to readjust it.

USING CURVES FOR ADVANCED TONAL ADJUSTMENT

Curves works along the same lines as Levels. You set the black point and the white point and then adjust midtone values. The main difference with Curves is that you have much greater control when adjusting midtone values.

The Curves dialog box is shown in Figure 2-14. This interface may seem intimidating at first, but after you understand what the various adjustments do, it begins to make sense. The main thing to understand is that the diagonal line that runs from left to right inside the graph represents the image's tonal range with black on the left and white on the right.

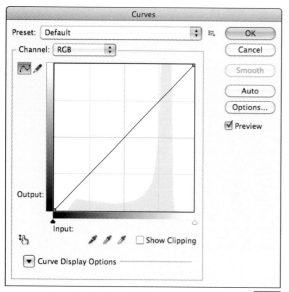

2-14

Follow these steps to use curves to modify the tonality of the photo of Ruby:

1. Open the Snow_Dog sample file again.

2. Open the Curves command by choosing Image⇨Adjustments⇨Curves (⌘/Ctrl+M).

3. Click and drag the black Input slider, below the graph on the left, and move it horizontally toward the middle. Notice that the blacks get blacker just like the black Input slider in Levels. Also notice that the Input box indicates the number you stopped dragging at and the Output box indicates the new value for that number.

4. Click and drag the white Input slider on the right, and slide it horizontally toward the middle. The whites get whiter just like the white Input slider in Levels.

5. Return the sliders to their starting points and then select Show Clipping. Notice that the photo turns white, much like it did when you held down the Alt key while adjusting the black point slider in Levels. When you adjust the white input slider, the preview switches to black, just like the white point clipping preview in Levels.

6. Slide the black and white sliders inward until you almost see clipping in the preview. After both sliders are set where you want them, deselect the Show Clipping check box to return the image to its normal appearance. Notice how much steeper the diagonal line in the Curves dialog box is now that the endpoints are moved inward. Something to be aware of with the Curves command is that the steeper this diagonal line is, the more contrast the image has. Keep that in mind as you modify the midtones in the next step.

7. To lighten the image, click the middle of the diagonal line to place a point. Then drag that point straight up. To darken, drag the point downward. This point is like the gray slider in the Levels command. It represents the midtones in the image.

The big difference, however, is in the effect that adjustments have on this point as compared to the Levels command. When you adjust the gray slider in the Levels, the effect on the tones around it is linear. With the Curves command, the effect of the adjustment is stronger on tones that are close to the point and weaker on tones that are farther away. That's why the command is called Curves because the adjustment slopes away.

Another difference is that the Levels command's gray Input slider is situated in the center of the midtones and can't be placed in a different tonal area before adjusting it. However, with the Curves command adjustment points can be placed anywhere on the diagonal line.

PRO TIP

If you want to nudge the settings of a point, you can use the up and down arrows on the keyboard to move them one increment at a time after you make the point active by clicking it. This works with almost any slider in Photoshop, including Levels.

Whereas the Levels command has only two endpoint sliders and one grayscale slider in the middle, the Curves command allows up to 14 adjustment points to be placed onto the curve line — although you rarely need more than a few.

To add adjustment points to the diagonal line, simply click the line. The higher up on the line you place the point, the lighter the tones that will be adjusted. Because these points represent tonal regions in the image, it's best to be informed about the tones they represent before placing them. The best way to see how the tones of your image correspond to the points on the curve is to click the image while the Curves dialog box is open. When you do so, a small circle temporarily appears on the Curves line to indicate where the tones you're clicking are located on the line. To place one of these preview points on the curve, ⌘+click/Ctrl+click the tone in the image.

PRO TIP

To remove a point from the Curves line, click it and drag it out of the Curves dialog box.

Typically, these additional points are used to modify midtone contrast. You can do this by placing a point in the highlight section of the curve and dragging it upward or downward, and then placing another point in the shadow region and dragging it upward or downward. To increase midtone contrast, drag the highlight point upward and drag the shadow point downward. Doing so increases the slope of the middle of the curve line where most of the midtone detail is located.

A side effect of this is that this flattens the curve on the toe (shadows) and the shoulder (highlights), and slightly reduces contrast in those areas. The result of this type of adjustment is called an *S-curve*, as shown in Figure 2-15. If you want to decrease midtone contrast, drag the highlight point downward and drag the shadow point upward. This flattens the midsection of the diagonal line, creating what's called an *inverted S-curve*.

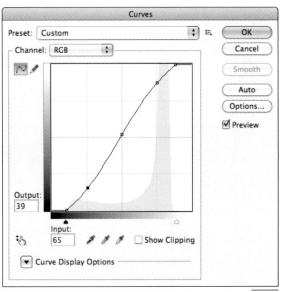

2-15

Follow these steps to adjust the midtone contrast of the image using the Curves dialog box:

1. Open the Snow_Dog photo one more time. If it's already open, use the History panel to undo any tonal adjustments that were applied in previous steps.

2. Complete steps 3 to 7 from the previous exercise and leave the Curves dialog box open.

3. Start clicking in the darker regions of the fur on the dog's hip. When you get an Input value near 55, ⌘+click/Ctrl+click to place a point on the line. This point represents the lower end of the darker regions in the photo.

4. Now click the side of the dog's face until you find an input value close to 150. When you do, ⌘+click/Ctrl+click to set a point representing highlights on the Curves line. Be careful that you don't go much higher than 150 because you don't want to have too great of an effect on the snow, which is mostly in the range of 200 and above.

5. Carefully drag the upper point that represents 150 straight up until the value for the output is about 160. Drag the lower point that represents 55 down until its output value is around 40. Now the midtone contrast has increased slightly, just enough to add some snap to the midtones while the snow and the dark fur retain most of their details. Try dragging the two points even farther. Notice how easy it is to go too far.

NOTE

The Output value in the Curves dialog box is what the Input becomes when OK is clicked. In this case, the dark region around 55 becomes 40 (darker), and the light region around 150 becomes 160 (lighter). If you make the darker regions of the midtones darker and the lighter regions lighter, then it makes sense that you're increasing midtone contrast because you're pulling the tones between 55 and 150 apart so that they now cover the area between 40 and 160.

You may have noticed a small button on the Curves dialog box that looks like a hand making the "we're number one" sign. This button is used to activate the On-Image adjustment tool.

This is a cool feature that enables you to click on the image and make tonal adjustments by sampling the underlying tone without touching the Curves dialog box. For example, in the previous exercise you ⌘+clicked/Ctrl+clicked on the image to add points to the curve line and then dragged those points up or down to affect them. When you use the On-Image tool and click on the image, a point is automatically added to the line. Then click and hold on the image while dragging the mouse up or down, increasing or decreasing the Output value for the range of tones you clicked on.

Naturally, this adjustment affects all tones in the image, but it is a more intuitive way of working with the Curves dialog box.

BALANCING DYNAMIC RANGE WITH THE SHADOWS/HIGHLIGHTS COMMAND

In the previous exercises, you used the black Input sliders and the white Input sliders to increase the contrast of the practice file. Sometimes, though, the *dynamic range* of the scene being photographed is too wide for you to get an exposure that maintains acceptable detail in both the shadows and highlights. Dynamic range refers to the distance between the brightest tones and the lightest tones. This scenario is common when you photograph a scene with bright backlighting where the main subject is in a shadow. When editing a file that suffers from this problem, making the image look its best with Levels or Curves can be difficult. Fortunately, there's a command named Shadows/Highlights that's designed to help solve this problem.

The Shadows/Highlights dialog box, shown in Figure 2-16, is opened by choosing Image⇨Adjustments⇨ Shadows/Highlights. This dialog box allows you to modify the shadows and highlights independently of one another by adjusting a set of sliders. If you don't see all of the sliders shown in Figure 2-16, select the Show More Options check box at the bottom left of the dialog box.

> **Amount:** This slider controls the amount of adjustment. Higher values in Shadows lighten the shadows more. Higher values in Highlights darken the highlights more.

> **Tonal Width:** This slider controls the range of tones that are affected by changes in amount. Higher settings in Shadows affect a larger range of shadow tones. Lower settings affect a narrower range. When working with the Highlights area, higher values affect larger ranges of highlight tones, and lower values affect smaller ranges of highlight tones.

> **Radius:** This slider works like this: When the Shadows/Highlights command looks at an image, it decides whether a pixel is a shadow or a highlight by evaluating its surrounding pixels. The Radius slider enables you to fine-tune this decision making by determining which surrounding pixels are affected by adjustment. Lower values restrict the area that's affected, and higher settings expand that range. Too large of a setting darkens or lightens the entire image rather than localized areas.

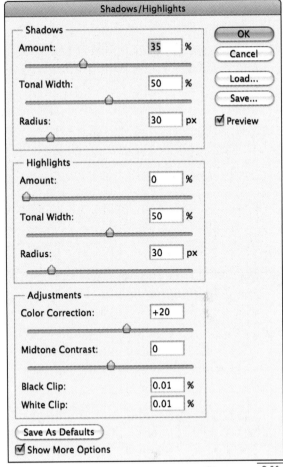

2-16

> **PRO TIP**
>
> If you start seeing halos around dark or light edges, you need to lower the Tonal Width setting for the respective tones — Shadows for dark tone halos and Highlights for light tone halos.

In addition to the Shadows and Highlights areas on the Shadows/Highlights command, there is an area labeled Adjustments. These sliders are used to help to undo any unwanted shifts that might occur when the shadows and highlights are adjusted. Here's what they're used for:

> **Color Correction:** When tonal values are changed, colors can shift. For example, when shadows are lightened, a color that was dark before becomes lighter. The Color Correction slider allows you to control color *saturation* — the intensity of the color. Increasing the value of the Color Correction slider tends to increase saturation, and lowering it tends to decrease saturation. This command is available only when working on color images.

Keep in mind that the Color Correction slider affects only portions of the image affected by the Shadows and Highlights sliders. When those adjustments are more extreme, the range of adjustment to Color Correction is greater.

> **Brightness:** This command is available only when working on grayscale images. It works something like the Color Correction slider. Moving the slider to the right lightens the entire image, and moving it to the left darkens the image.

> **Midtone Contrast:** Slider movement to the right increases midtone contrast, and movements to the left reduce it.

> **Black Clip/White Clip:** These adjustments are used to clip shadow and highlight tones. Increasing these values increases the contrast of the image. It's usually better to use the Levels or Curves commands to better control clipping.

In most cases, I'd rather modify image brightness, contrast, and clipping using Levels or Curves adjustments because of the greater degree of control these commands offer. However, if you're working quickly on an image, it may be faster to take care of these issues here.

Be sure to look for two side effects when using the Shadows/Highlights command. The first is that your image can become flat in contrast if you overdo it. If this happens, try making a Levels or Curves adjustment to compensate for it. In fact, if you think you'll need to make a tonal adjustment with the Levels or Contrast commands, try to do it after using the Shadows/Highlights command.

The second side effect is that when you open up shadows with any tonal adjustment tool, you reveal noise because most noise tends to be in the shadows. If you watch for this as you adjust the Shadows sliders, you know when to take it easy on areas of extreme noise.

Q & A

I've heard that most advanced Photoshop users use the Curves command to adjust an image's tonality. If that's the case, what's the point of using the Levels command?

The Levels command is like a chisel because it allows you to sculpt an image's tonal range. You have control over shadow and highlight clipping and you can make accurate adjustments to the midtones of an image.

On the other hand, the Curves command is like a scalpel because you can target small ranges of an image's midtones with much more control than the Levels command. However, a scalpel in the hands of someone who doesn't know how to use it can make a real mess. The same is true for Curves. If you aren't careful, you can do more harm than good with the Curves command. If you use Curves, take it easy and begin by making small adjustments until you become more comfortable and confident with this powerful tonal adjustment tool.

If you're new to Photoshop, you may find that you can do most of your tonal adjustments quite accurately with the Levels command. Quite often, you may not even need Curves. Because of that, when you first start out with Photoshop, you should master the Levels command before going too deep into the Curves command.

You mentioned that an inverted S-curve in the Curves command tends to reduce an image's contrast. Is this the same as using the Shadows/Highlights command?

Yes. You can reduce contrast using an inverted S-curve. However, the variety of adjustment sliders in the Shadows/Highlights command provides you with a great deal of control over the specific tonal ranges that are affected. If you simply need to lower contrast, an inverted S-curve will do the trick. If you're working with a difficult image with an extreme dynamic range, you may be better off using the Shadows/Highlights command, especially if you aren't comfortable using the Curves dialog just yet.

Chapter 3

MANAGING AND CORRECTING C

Calibrating Your Monitor

Digital files are viewed on a wide range of equipment. If appropriate measures aren't taken, predicting what an image looks like when someone else sees it in her particular viewing environment can be difficult, if not impossible. That's why monitor calibration is the first step to managing color in Photoshop.

The idea behind monitor calibration is to establish a set of standards and get everyone to use them. These standards refer to the color temperature, brightness, and contrast of a monitor. A hardware calibration device is used to measure these display qualities and then allow you to adjust your monitor to bring them into alignment with the standards. This is called *monitor calibration*.

After you calibrate your monitor, the calibration device allows you to create a custom *color profile* that describes the way the monitor displays color. A color profile enables all the devices in a digital workflow to interpret and understand color so that they all speak the same language. Cameras, monitors, and printers all have color profiles.

A number of monitor calibration devices are available. Two of the most popular devices are the ColorVision Spyder3 Pro (shown in Figure 3-1) and the X-Rite Eye-One Display 2.

These devices range in price from about $150 - $250. Both do a great job of helping you bring your system into alignment.

These calibration devices work a little differently from one another, but for the most part you use them in the following manner:

1. Install the software that comes with the calibration device.

2. Plug the device into a USB port on your system — preferably a port on your machine, not a USB hub.

3. Launch the software, and follow the steps to calibrate and profile your system. If the software has an advanced option, be sure to use it the first time you use the device so that you have access to all of the calibration and profiling options.

The software then takes you through some preliminaries and asks a couple of questions about your system. Pay special attention to the questions about color space and gamma. Choose 6500K for color temperature and 2.2 for gamma as your starting points to be consistent with most of the rest of the world.

The Difference Between CRT and LCD Displays

There are some differences in CRT (Cathode Ray Tube) and LCD (Liquid Crystal Display) monitors that affect the way they're calibrated. CRT monitors create color by using three electron guns that project color for each color channel (red, green, and blue). When calibrating a CRT the settings on these guns are adjusted to change their individual intensities. An LCD monitor doesn't use electron guns so color can't be adjusted in the same way. Even if the LCD monitor has buttons for changing color, they do not work on the monitor itself. Because of that, it's best to leave them at their default settings and allow your calibration device to calibrate the monitor by making changes to the video card.

4. When the calibration software is finished, it prompts you to save the newly created profile and automatically make it your default.

5. The profiling software reminds you to recalibrate at certain intervals so that your viewing environment stays consistent. This is a good idea because monitors tend to drift, especially CRTs. I recommend that you recalibrate at least once a month. When you do, it isn't necessary to run the advanced setup again. You can go with the easy/simple option to speed up the process.

Keep in mind that you can reach a point of diminishing returns when striving for perfect color — especially when you're dealing with outside printing sources. Make an effort to get calibrated, but don't worry if you aren't getting an exact match to your prints.

X-REF

Several things that can affect color matching when printing are discussed in Chapter 11.

UNDERSTANDING COLOR THEORY

The first thing to understand about color is that it's personal. Everyone has his or her own preferences. When I worked in a professional photo lab, we had a lab standard for skin-tone colors. However, there were certain customers who wanted the skin tones in their prints to have a particular tint. Even though we didn't like the color the customer liked, we did everything in our power to make him happy.

Some of this bias relates to personal taste, and some of it has more to do with individual color perception. Not everyone sees color the same. In fact, your own color perception can shift as blood sugar levels go up and down. Additionally, some people are deficient in seeing color on a red-green axis; others are deficient on a blue-yellow axis. However, few people are completely colorblind.

NOTE

Here's an interesting fact. More men are affected by color blindness than women.

Even though your experience of color can be highly subjective, the physics behind color theory is rock solid. The main distinction to make about color is whether it's *subtractive color* or *additive color*.

3-1
Photo courtesy of datacolor

SUBTRACTIVE COLOR

Subtractive color describes the way pigments, such as paints, dyes, inks, and natural colorants, reflect light. When white light strikes a pigment, the pigment absorbs some wavelengths of light and reflects the unabsorbed wavelengths. The wavelengths that are reflected are the colors you see and what give the pigment its color. That means that a subtractive color system begins with white light made up of colored wavelengths. The color you see is the reflected light with some wavelengths subtracted from it — or absorbed by the pigment.

Here's an easy way to remember how subtractive color works: If equal amounts of red, green, and blue paint are mixed together, the result is a muddy gray. It's impossible to mix any of these three colors together in a way that they create white. In order to get white, all paint needs to be subtracted from the white canvas.

ADDITIVE COLOR

Additive color describes the way light waves combine to create color. This is the way humans see things, and it's the system used for most color management and adjustment in Photoshop. This system is called additive because it begins with black (no light). A light source adds wavelengths of light that have a specific color.

With additive color, white is created by adding together equal amounts of red, green, and blue. This can seem counterintuitive to people who are used to working with pigments and subtractive color. Technically, six colors are used when working with additive color. The primary colors are red, green, and blue, and their opposites (or *complementary colors*) cyan, magenta, and yellow. Figure 3-2 shows the primary colors and their complements.

When you have equal amounts of two complementary colors, you end up with neutral gray — in other words, the colors cancel each other out.

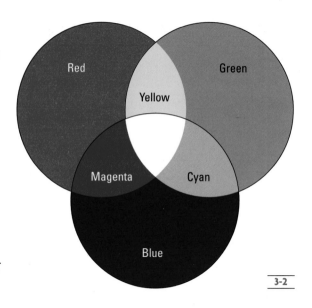

3-2

The relationship among these six colors gets even more interesting because each is composed of two *component colors* — and those component colors are always going to be two of the six colors. Here's how the colors break down into components:

> Red is composed of magenta and yellow.

> Green is composed of cyan and yellow.

> Blue is composed of cyan and magenta.

> Cyan is composed of green and blue.

> Magenta is composed of red and blue.

> Yellow is composed of red and green.

This may seem confusing at first, like an endless shell game, especially if you're used to thinking about the way pigments such as paint combine.

Figure 3-3 shows an easy way to remember these relationships: The primary colors red, green, and blue are directly above their complementary colors (the ones that cancel them out) cyan, magenta, and yellow.

Here's the trick to understanding this: The two component colors of any color are the two colors that are not directly across from it. For example, red is composed of magenta and yellow. Cyan can't be a component of red because it's the opposite of red (its complementary color).

When I learned this system many years ago, it completely changed the way I thought about colors and their components. All I have to do now is visualize this simple chart, and I know how all six colors relate to one another — which colors are complements and which are components.

MANAGING COLOR IN PHOTOSHOP

Photoshop CS5 gives you a great deal of control over color. This control begins as soon as you open a file. To understand the process, you first need to understand the method Photoshop uses for describing color.

COMPARING COLOR SPACES

The primary colors discussed here (red, green, and blue) are the colors of a *color model* called RGB. A color model is an abstract way of mathematically describing colors and their relationships to one another. This common vocabulary is important when discussing specific colors within that RGB model. Otherwise, when I say "red," how do I know you're picturing the same color that I'm picturing?

Colors are further classified into *color spaces*. A color space, among other things, defines the *gamut*, or range of colors, that a device is capable of capturing or reproducing. For example, my monitor is capable of displaying only a certain gamut of colors. Many of the colors I can see in nature can't be displayed on my monitor.

However, my monitor can display colors that can't be printed on my inkjet printer. The monitor's gamut isn't as large as the spectrum that a human eye can see, but in some cases it's larger than the gamut of the printer. These kinds of color spaces — monitor and printer — are called *device-dependent* color spaces. A device-dependent color space describes the range of colors that a particular device can see and/or reproduce.

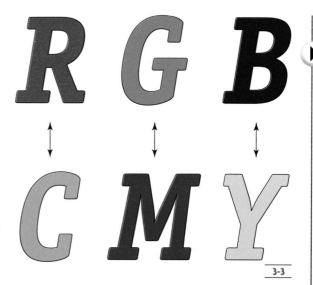

3-3

Digital Editing Fundamentals

> **NOTE**
>
> Devices can be subcategorized into input and output devices. A digital camera is an input device, and a printer is an output device.

The second type of color space is a *device-independent* color space. A device-independent color space is not limited by the gamut of any particular device. These color spaces are used to describe the range of colors in color *editing spaces*. An editing space describes the total palette, or gamut, of colors available when editing a photo in Photoshop. The two most common editing spaces in Photoshop are Adobe RGB (1998) and sRGB:

> **Adobe RGB (1998):** This is a large color space that is more applicable to high-end printing and reproduction.

> **sRGB:** This is a limited color space that is intended to be common to a wide range of devices.

The main difference between these two editing spaces is that the gamut of Adobe RGB (1998) is larger than sRGB, meaning it has a much wider range of colors than sRGB. Think about it this way: Imagine that you have two boxes of crayons. One box has 24 colors, and the other box has 120 colors. Suppose you and I both want to do a drawing of the same scene outside. If I give you the 120-count box and keep the 24-count box, the results of our drawings would be quite different. The greens and browns in my trees would be more limited than yours because I don't have the same range of greens and browns to work with as you do.

This is sort of the way it works in Photoshop. When you edit digital files, you need to standardize the way color is managed in your Photoshop workflow so that you're working with a predictable gamut. You can choose to work in a smaller color space like sRGB, or you can work in a larger color space like Adobe RGB (1998).

The graph in Figure 3-4, created with ColorThink software, a product of Chromix in Seattle, Washington (www.chromix.com), compares the color gamuts of Adobe RGB (1998) (the wireframed shape) and sRGB (the solid shape). Notice that the Adobe RGB (1998) gamut is much larger in some areas, especially the yellows and greens.

CHOOSING A COLOR SPACE

At first it seems like a no-brainer to choose to work in a larger color space so that you're working with more colors, but that's not always true. When you consider working spaces, you also must think about device color spaces — devices such as printers. Even though a working space may be device independent, the color of a print is limited to the printing device's gamut.

In many cases a printer's limited gamut is much smaller than the Photoshop working space. This means that some of the colors in the file are not printable because they are out of gamut. These colors are clipped to the nearest in-gamut colors, which can lead to disappointments at printing time.

sRGB

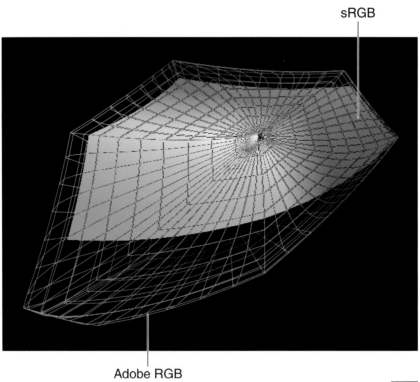

Adobe RGB

3-4

The real key to deciding which color space to use as your main Photoshop working space is how you plan to output your files. If you're using a commercial photo lab, ask what color space the lab prefers. Most will tell you that their equipment works in the sRGB color space. If you plan to do most of your printing at this lab, use sRGB as your working space. Some labs do work in the Adobe RGB (1998) color space. If your lab is one of them, take advantage of the larger color space.

Understanding color space is also important when preparing photos for the Web. The sRGB color space is ideal for the Web. In fact, it was created in the mid-1990s with the Internet in mind. If a file is prepared with a larger color space and then uploaded to a Web site, its color may look completely different.

Many people use inkjet printers for outputting prints. Most inkjet printers work with a limited gamut of color. However, this can be misleading because the gamut isn't limited in every color of the spectrum. Figure 3-5 shows the color profile of an inkjet printer, (the solid shape), compared to the sRGB and Adobe RGB (1998) color spaces (the wireframe shapes). In the left image of Figure 3-5, you can see that the printer is capable of printing greens that are well outside the limits of sRGB. In the right image, you can see that Adobe RGB (1998) contains all of the greens the printer can output. If I were photographing a green Corvette and planning to print it on this printer, I would edit it in the larger Adobe RGB (1998) space.

You must think about these sorts of things as you consider which working space to use in Photoshop because your working space choice really does depend on how you plan to output the files. With that in mind, here's the bottom line:

> Use sRGB when you know that all your workflow is oriented to producing images for the Web or for photo labs with printing equipment that is using sRGB. Doing this helps you to better predict what your color looks like when it's time to view images online or in print.

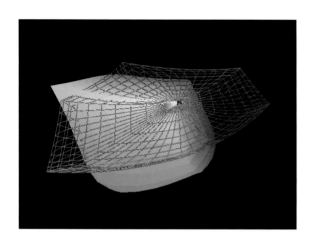

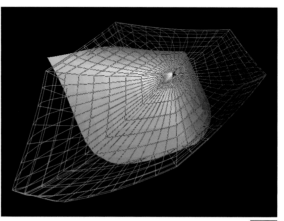

3-5

> Use Adobe RGB (1998) when you're dealing with a lab that uses the larger color space, when outputting to an inkjet printer, or when you just aren't sure what you're going to do and you want to keep your options open.

NOTE

A third editing space is gaining popularity in the photography world. It's called ProPhoto RGB. Its color gamut is even larger than Adobe RGB (1998). Currently, few output devices support such a large gamut, but that will change as technology moves forward. In the meantime, it's better to stay away from ProPhoto as a working space because converting images for output on some devices results in unpredictable color shifts.

SETTING UP PHOTOSHOP'S WORKING SPACE

Now that you know about color spaces, you need to tell Photoshop how you want color handled when you open a file — which color space to use as a working space and what to do when the color profile of the photo doesn't match the working color space. Do that by following these steps:

1. Choose Edit➪Color Settings to open the Color Settings dialog box.

2. Click the drop-down list in the Settings box, and select North America Prepress 2. This configures the color settings with the best starting points, as shown in Figure 3-6.

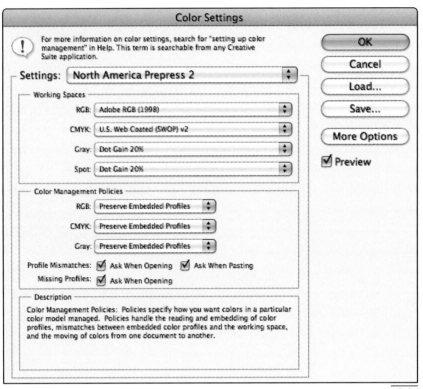

3-6

3. Click OK if you plan to use Adobe RGB (1998) as your working space as you're finished. If you plan to use sRGB, then click the RGB drop-down list under Working Spaces. Select sRGB IEC61966-2.1, and click OK.

For the purposes of this book, you're not concerned with the other working spaces in this dialog box (CMYK, Gray, and Spot), so leave them as they are.

The reason I encourage people to configure the Color Settings dialog box by initially selecting North American Prepress 2 is because this setting selects all the check boxes under Profile Mismatches and Missing Profiles. When these check boxes are selected and Photoshop finds a discrepancy between the color space you're using and the file's color profile, which is called a *profile mismatch*, it refers to the Color Management Policies boxes to resolve the conflict.

When these warnings are enabled and you open a file with a profile that doesn't match your working space, Photoshop prompts you to make a decision about how you'd like to handle the profile mismatch by opening the Embedded Profile Mismatch dialog box (see Figure 3-7). These are your choices:

> **Use the embedded profile.** Selecting this option opens the photo in its own color space using the photo's embedded profile.

> **Convert document's colors to the working space.** Selecting this option moves the file into your working space by mapping its colors to the appropriate equivalents in your color space.

> **Discard the embedded profile.** Selecting this option strips the image of any color information by deleting its profile. This usually isn't a good idea — though I have used it when experimenting.

Choosing one of these settings allows you to manage your color space choices on the fly when opening a file. In general, you don't gain anything by converting a file that's in the smaller sRGB color space into the larger working space of Adobe RGB (1998). When you begin with a small gamut, you pretty much have to live with it. The range of the original colors doesn't expand and change when the image is converted to a larger color space.

However, if you're opening a file with Adobe RGB (1998) into a working space of sRGB and you know

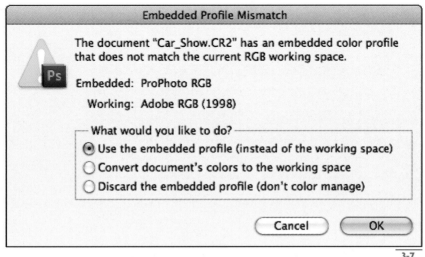

3-7

that you need a smaller color space for output, converting an Adobe RGB (1998) file to sRGB before editing it is a good plan; that way, you'll see only colors that are reproducible.

After you get a handle on what's happening with profile mismatches and you get tired of being asked the same question every time you open a file, you can deselect the question check box in the Color Settings dialog box. I generally recommend against this, but you may have reasons to make this choice.

CHANGING COLOR PROFILES AFTER A FILE IS OPEN

Sometimes it's necessary to change a file's profile after you open it in Photoshop. For example, you have a photo that will be printed on your inkjet printer and it will be uploaded on your Web site. Because you want to use Adobe RGB (1998) for the inkjet print and sRGB for the Web image, you need to open the file into Adobe RGB (1998), prepare it for printing, and then save the file. Then convert the profile of the image to sRGB and prepare it for Web usage and save it using a different name.

To convert a file's profile after it's open in Photoshop, choose Edit⇨Convert to Profile. When you do, the Convert to Profile dialog box shown in Figure 3-8 opens. Select the profile you want to convert to by using the drop-down list in the Destination Space section and click OK. The file is converted and tagged with the new profile so that it's permanently attached when the file is saved. This is also the method you use to convert files to your lab's color profile, if you received one from it.

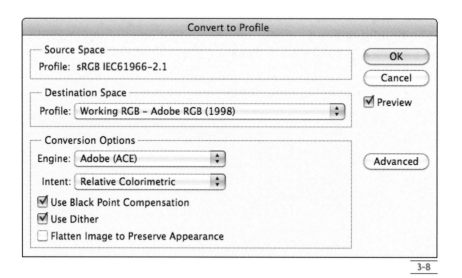

3-8

Understanding Color Channels

Because you're working with an RGB color model, your images are composed of three separate color channels. One channel represents the red/cyan content of the image, another channel represents the green/magenta content of the image, and yet another channel represents the blue/yellow content of the image.

Here's the weird part: Each of these channels is composed of *grayscale* data — all the tones are gray.

The best way to understand what's going on here is to look at the channels in a specific image. Follow these steps:

1. Open the Spring_Flowers.tif practice file from the downloadable practice files on the Web site (www.wiley.com/go/phoprestorationandretouching).

2. Find the Channels panel on your desktop; it's usually grouped with the Layers and Paths panels. If you don't see the Channels panel, choose Window⇨Channels to open it.

3. Click the Red channel icon. This hides the other two channels so that you see only the red data in your image preview, as shown in Figure 3-9. Notice that everything that is red in the photo is a light tone of gray.

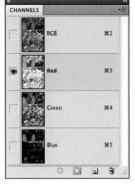

3-9

4. Click the Green channel icon. This hides the Red channel and shows the Green channel. Now the greens are lighter, and the deep reds at the top are quite dark.

5. Click the Blue channel icon to see only the Blue channel. Now just about all the flowers are dark except for a few pinkish flowers at the top. Notice that in all three channels the tonality of the fence stays about the same. That's because its color is mostly *neutral* — a shade of gray where red, green, and blue values are about the same.

6. To get back to full color, click the composite channel, labeled RGB, at the top of the stack. Notice that all three channels become visible again because the little eye icons next to them are turned on.

7. Even though each of these channels is a grayscale image, when combined, they create color. To see how it happens, start with only one channel visible. Then turn on the visibility of another channel by clicking the eyeball next to it. Notice how these two grayscales combine to create a limited amount of color. When the third channel is added, all the colors appear.

The main thing to get from this experiment is that when you're working in an RGB color model, every digital image is composed of three individual channels, one for each primary color: Red, Green, and Blue.

EVALUATING COLOR WITH THE INFO PANEL AND THE COLOR SAMPLER TOOL

Photoshop provides two useful tools for evaluating color in your digital photos: One is the Info panel, and the other is the Color Sampler tool. In combination, these two items allow you to monitor and measure each color channel as you make adjustments to your image. Follow these steps to explore the Info panel:

1. Open the Spring_Flowers.tif practice file. If you still have it open from the preceding exercise, return it to its opening state by clicking the image icon at the top of the History panel.

2. Click the Info panel; it's usually nested with the Navigator and Histogram panels. If you don't see the Info panel, choose Window⇨Info.

3. Move your cursor over the white horizontal fence section between the two vertical slats on the left. Look at the RGB readout on the Info panel while doing this. The three channels are very close in value — in the 220 to 230 range, as shown in Figure 3-10. That means the color of the fence in that spot is a very light shade of gray because the RGB colors are all high in number and almost the same values.

4. Now move the cursor over some of the flowers. Notice that the red flowers at the top have high values in the Red channel and low values in the Green and Blue channels. The yellow flowers in the foreground have readings that are high in the Red and Green channels and low in the Blue channel.

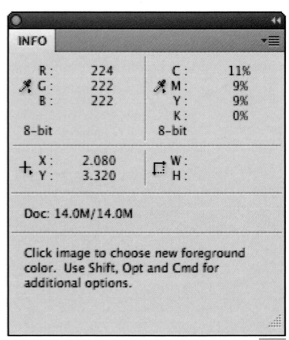

3-10

5. Move the cursor over the middle vertical slat. Notice that it has a high red value and a low blue value. That's because it's reflecting the red and yellow flowers in the foreground.

Having the ability to measure color is cool, but you can make this feature even cooler by adding the Color Sampler tool to the mix. The Color Sampler tool is stacked with the Eyedropper tool and some other measurement tools, as shown in Figure 3-11. (The Count tool is only available in Photoshop CS5 Extended.)

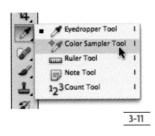

3-11

With the Color Sampler tool, you can place up to four sample points anywhere in an image. Each is labeled with a number ranging from 1 to 4. An RGB (Red, Green, and Blue) readout for each of these points is added to the bottom of the Info panel.

When you make changes to tone or color a second readout is added to the right of the original sample readout on the Info panel. This new readout displays the updated RGB values for the sample points, reflecting the changes your edits are having on the RGB values for those points.

1. Select the Color Sampler tool from the Tools panel.

2. Go to the Options bar at the top of the screen, which is used to set up the selected tool, and change the setting from point sample to at least 5 by 5 Average, as shown in Figure 3-12. Now the tool samples a grid of pixels that is 5 by 5 and averages them instead of sampling a single point. This assures that some renegade pixel isn't accidentally sampled alone. This setting also affects the Eyedropper tool, which is used to sample and copy colors.

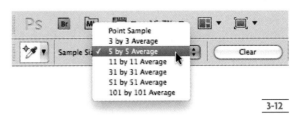

3-12

3. Return to the Spring_Flowers.tif practice file.

4. Find a spot that looks white, but where the three channels are not quite the same by monitoring the Info panel readout. Click in the area to add a sample point with the number 1 beside it. Notice that color values are added to the bottom of the Info panel with #1 beside them.

5. Add another sample point to the same area you measured on the middle slat in Step 5 from the preceding exercise. Its values also are added to the Info panel with #2 beside them.

6. Choose Image➪Adjustments➪Levels (⌘/Ctrl+L) to open the Levels command.

7. Move the middle gray Input slider to the left to lighten the photo while watching the Info panel. Notice that a second row of numbers appears next to the sample values. These new numbers change as you move the gray Input slider, indicating what the modified values are.

8. Click OK. The second set of numbers disappears, but their values become the new sample point values.

9. You use this image again in just a moment so press ⌘/Ctrl+Z to undo the Levels adjustment you just did.

The ability to sample a particular area of the image and measure any changes can be very useful. This is especially the case when you're adjusting the color of an image with something in it that should have a neutral color balance.

ADJUSTING COLOR

There are a number of ways to adjust color in Photoshop. In this section, you learn about the main color correction tools in Photoshop and some methodologies for using them. I begin with the least likely — the Levels command.

REMOVING A COLORCAST WITH LEVELS

When using the Levels command in Chapter 2, you may have noticed that its dialog box has its own set of three eyedroppers. They are, from left to right in Figure 3-13:

3-13

> **Black Point Eyedropper:** This eyedropper is used to assign a black point to the darkest part of the image. If you know where the darkest area of the image is, click it with this tool to set the black point and convert that spot to 0 red, 0 green, and 0 blue. Any tones that are darker than the tone you click on are clipped.

> **Gray Point Eyedropper:** This eyedropper is used for creating a neutral gray; the RGB values become the same anywhere you click.

> **White Point Eyedropper:** This eyedropper works just like the Black Point Eyedropper except that it's used to set the white point in the image. When you click the lightest part of the image, this tool sets it as the white point and converts that tone to 255 red, 255 green, and 255 blue. Any tones that are lighter than the tone you click on are clipped.

The tonal values that the Black Point Eyedropper and the White Point Eyedropper use for clipping points can be modified so that they don't clip to pure black (0) and pure white (255). For example, you can set them to clip at 15 and 240, meaning that the black point is 15 instead of 0, and the white point is 240 instead of 255. This allows you to leave some room for printing processes that don't handle extreme shadows and highlights very well, such as a newspaper. You can modify them by double-clicking the eyedroppers and setting the RGB values to the value you want to call pure white or black.

Although this sounds useful, I have never found much use for the Black Point Eyedropper and White Point Eyedropper tools. The biggest problem with them is that you need to know where the lightest and darkest areas in an image are. You also need to feel confident that these dark and light areas should be neutral in color. I would rather handle clipping manually with clipping preview in Levels or Curves where I have more control.

The Gray Point Eyedropper is designed to neutralize the color and remove all colorcasts wherever you click with it. It does this by setting the values to the Red, Green, and Blue channels to the same value. This new value is an average of the three original values unless a huge correction is being applied. You can use it anytime you know that a certain area of an image should be neutral in color.

Follow these steps to get a feel for how this tool works:

1. Go back to the Spring_Flowers.tif photo you were using in the preceding exercise. If that image is not open, open it and repeat Steps 1 through 4 from the previous exercise.

2. Choose Image➪Adjustments➪Levels (Ctrl+L/ ⌘+L) to open the Levels command. When you use the Gray Point Eyedropper, it affects any other Levels adjustments from that Levels session. Because of this, you should start a Levels adjustment with the Gray Point Eyedropper if you plan to use it. Then do other Levels adjustments to finish fine-tuning the tones in the image.

3. Click the Gray Point Eyedropper to activate it. Now, anywhere you click in the image becomes neutral.

4. Click sample point number 1 in the image. Notice that the readout in the Info panel shows that the numbers have been nudged into alignment. If they aren't exactly the same, it's probably because you didn't click in exactly the same spot as where the sample is located. Not a problem — they don't have to be absolutely perfect. Remember, however, that every time you click the image, the gray point is reset.

5. Click sample point 2. Notice that the whole image gets cooler. This is because that part of the white fence was reflecting all the red flowers. When you force the color to white, it removes the color being cast by the reflection, but adjusts the rest of the colors correspondingly, which is unacceptable. The lesson to be learned here is that not all apparent neutrals are created the same. When you use this tool, you must be sure that the color you're clicking is actually supposed to have neutral color values.

6. Click sample point 1 to get the color back into alignment.

7. Now the image is ready for Levels adjustments using the Input sliders, as covered in Chapter 2.

8. Click OK when you finish.

Sometimes, the image may not have anything that is supposed to be a neutral gray. Or maybe you use the Gray Point Eyedropper, but you still want to do some further adjustment to get the colors to look the way you like them. When that's the case, you're ready to move on to Photoshop's main color adjustment tools.

LEARNING COLOR ADJUSTMENT WITH THE VARIATIONS COMMAND

Correcting color is a skill that takes time to develop. The real trick to color correction is this: Identify the color that you don't like, and add its opposite until you don't see the offending color anymore. In order to pull this off, you must be able to see and identify the colors in an image. With that in mind, I want to show you one of the best color-correction learning tools: the Variations command.

Follow these steps to do some color correcting with the Variations command:

1. Open the Garden_Gnome.tif practice file from the downloadable practice files on the Web site (www. wiley.com/go/phoprestorationandretouching). This photo looks a little cool in color, though it's hard to know exactly what the color of a gnome's skin tone should be.

2. Choose Image⇨Adjustments⇨Variations to open the Variations dialog box. When the dialog box opens, you're presented with what's called a color ring-around. The uncorrected image is in the center, and it's ringed by equal amounts of the individual six colors, as shown in Figure 3-14. Notice that complementary colors are across from one another in the ring-around.

3. To warm up this image, you need to add some red and possibly some yellow. Click the thumbnail labeled More Red. Notice that the current pick at the top of the screen changes to reflect the addition of red. Also notice that the whole ring-around is updated based on the color of the Current Pick. The addition of red warmed up the photo, but it may have been too much. For accurate color adjustment, it's often necessary to have better control over this tool.

4. Click the Original thumbnail at the top left to reset the Current Pick thumbnail to its original setting.

5. Go to the Fine/Coarse slider and move it to the left so that it lines up with the first vertical mark on the left of the scale. Notice that the color value difference in the ring-around is much lower now.

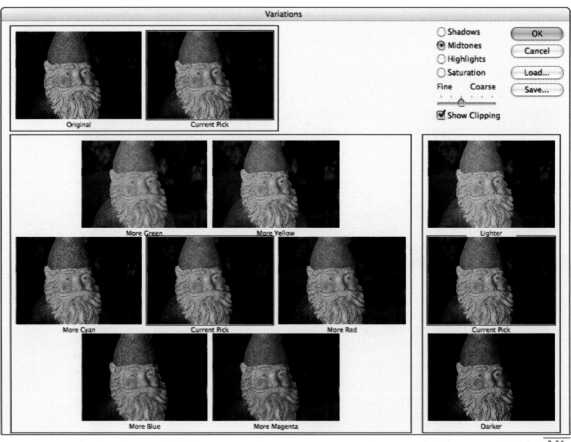

3-14

This gives you more control over the tool. Now you can make minor adjustments and build them up until you have added the appropriate amount of color.

6. Click the More Red thumbnail again. A small amount of red is added to the Current Pick preview. Continue to click the red thumbnail until you feel that you've added enough red. To back up and remove some red, click the More Cyan thumbnail — the opposite of red. If you want to add another color, such as some yellow, do it now by clicking on its thumbnail.

7. When you're happy with the new color, click OK. This is the moment of truth. It can be hard to see your adjustments in the Variations window because everything is small. After you click OK, you really get a look at it. If you're not satisfied with what you see, press ⌘/Ctrl+Z to undo the color adjustment. Go back to Variations and try again with a slightly different adjustment.

I encourage people who are new to color adjustment to begin with the Variations command because it can be a great tool for learning the differences among the six colors used. After you're able to identify these colors in a photo without the Variations ring-around, you'll find it much easier to use Photoshop's more powerful color-correction tools.

ADJUSTING COLOR WITH THE COLOR BALANCE COMMAND

The Color Balance command has most of the adjustments the Variations command has, but it has some differences, too. One of the main differences in the dialog box, shown in Figure 3.15, is that you don't get thumbnails in a ring-around for visual comparison, though you do get a better preview because you see real-time adjustments in the image itself as you move the sliders.

Another big difference is that you can make color adjustments one color unit at a time by moving these sliders. With Variations, you don't really know how many units of color you're adding when you adjust the Fine/Coarse slider.

After you become comfortable with color correction, you'll realize that Color Balance is the perfect tool for making global color adjustments to an image. I use the Color Balance command on just about every file that needs an overall color adjustment.

Try adjusting a file with the Color Balance command:

1. Open the Garden_Gnome.tif practice file again. If it's already open, use the History panel to reset it to its opening state.

2. Choose Image➪Adjustments➪Color Balance (⌘/Ctrl+B) to open the Color Balance dialog box.

3. Make sure the Preserve Luminosity check box is selected. This prevents any color adjustment from shifting the tonal values in the image, causing the image to get lighter or darker.

4. Move the Red/Cyan slider to the Red side and stop short of making a full correction to the Cyan tone of the image. As you do, notice that your image responds by getting redder.

Color Balance

Color Balance

Color Levels: `0` `0` `0`

Cyan ———————————— Red
Magenta ———————————— Green
Yellow ———————————— Blue

OK

Cancel

☑ Preview

Tone Balance

○ Shadows   ◉ Midtones   ○ Highlights

☑ Preserve Luminosity

3-15

3

Managing and Correcting Color

5. Select the Highlights option to switch to highlight correction, and add more red to finish off your correction. I use this technique of splitting my correction between midtones and highlights often, especially in portraits. I add some of the color I want to the midtones and some of it to the highlights.

6. Add some yellow to the midtones and highlights.

7. When you like the color, deselect the Preview option in the Color Balance dialog box to turn off the preview function. This shows you what the image looks like without the correction. Turn Preview on and off a few times to evaluate your correction.

8. When you like what you have, click OK. I used +39 Red and −8 Blue in the midtones and +14 Red and −2 Blue in the highlights. Figure 3-16 shows the image before and after color correcting with the Color Balance command. The left side is uncorrected and the right is adjusted with the Color Balance command.

3-16

FINE-TUNING COLOR WITH THE HUE/SATURATION COMMAND

Even though the Color Balance command is my faithful companion, my favorite color adjustment tool is the Hue/Saturation command. With this amazing tool, you can work with color in a variety of ways that aren't possible with the Color Balance command.

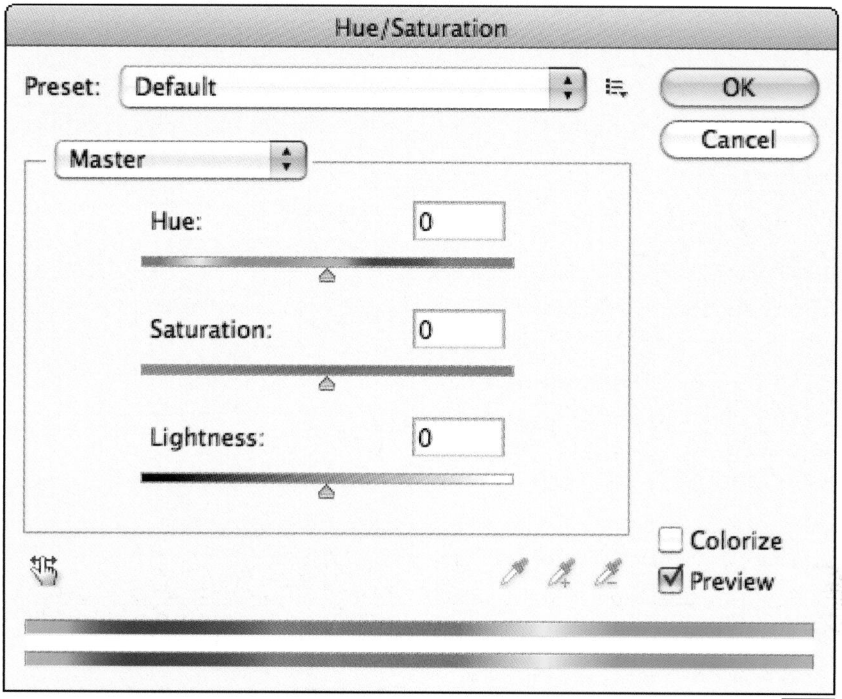

3-17

NOTE

You may have noticed earlier that the Variations command has a saturation control. There's a reason I didn't point it out during that discussion. It's because the control is quite crude when compared to the real thing.

To open the Hue/Saturation dialog box, shown in Figure 3-17, choose Image➪Adjustments➪Hue/Saturation. The sliders in this dialog box allow you to modify three different aspects of a color:

> **Hue:** This is the color of a color — the difference in the red of an apple and the yellow of a banana is the hue. Use this slider to change the base color of a color.

> **Saturation:** This is the purity of a color — the difference between a black-and-white print and a color print. Use this slider to increase the saturation of a color with positive values or lower it with negative values.

> **Lightness:** This is just what it sounds like — it's the lightness of a color. Positive values add white to the color, and negative values add black to the color.

These three sliders give you amazing control over the colors in an image. Explore some of the uses of the Hue/Saturation tool with these steps:

NOTE

The Colorize option is used to tone an image with an overall colorcast.

1. Open the Hot_Air.tif practice file from the downloadable practice files on the Web site (www.wiley.com/go/phoprestorationandretouching).
2. Choose Image➪Adjustments➪Hue/Saturation (⌘/Ctrl+U) to open the Hue/Saturation dialog box.

3. Move the Hue slider to right. Stop when you get to a value of +120. This changes the sky to red and shifts the other colors as well. Notice that as you drag the slider, the color bar on the bottom of the dialog box shifts to the left. This color bar, shown in Figure 3-18, gives you a preview of how the relationships in the color spectrum are changing as you adjust. For example, find the blue color on the upper color bar and look directly below it. Notice that the color below it is red, which is the same color as the sky. The color below yellow is cyan, which is the color of the yellow panels in the hot air balloon.

3-18

4. Reset the Hue slider to 0.

5. Drag the Saturation slider all the way to the left. When you do this, all color is removed from the image and it takes on a black-and-white appearance. This change is reflected in the color bars. Adjust the slider all the way to the right, and notice how all the colors become too saturated — almost fluorescent.

6. Take a moment to experiment with the Hue and Saturation sliders to see the different kinds of effects they have when used in combination.

Being able to make global adjustments to color with Hue/Saturation is powerful. However, the reason this command is my favorite color-correction tool is that it can be used on specifically targeted colors. This is where this amazing tool really shines.

Follow these steps to learn how to adjust specific color ranges within the image:

1. Open the Hot_Air.tif file again. If it's still open from the last exercise and you didn't click OK, hold down the Alt key and click Reset to reset the dialog box values to their defaults.

2. Click where you see "Master" to open the Channel menu. Choose Reds from the six colors shown in the Channel pop-up menu (see Figure 3-19).

3. Click and drag the Hue slider to the right and left. Notice that only colors that have red in them are affected. The same thing happens when you move the Saturation and Lightness sliders. That's because this adjustment is only taking place on the Red channel.

4. Reset all values to 0 and return the Channel menu to Master.

3-19

5. Choose any color from the Channel menu to activate the Eyedropper tools in the Hue/Saturation dialog box. These eyedroppers are different from the eyedroppers in the Levels and Curves dialog boxes. They enable you to take targeted adjustment to a much higher level. When the Hue/Saturation dialog box first opens, they're grayed out because you need to select a specific color from the pop-up menu to make them active.

6. Click on the first Eyedropper tool on the left, and then click on the darker green color in the photo, near the top of the balloon, to sample it. Click in a few different spots in the green region of the balloon and notice that the preview color bar at the bottom of the dialog box shifts to reflect the exact color range of the green you click. Also notice that the color in the Channel menu shows Greens when you click the colors on the right side and Cyans when you click those on the left. Clearly, all greens in this photo were not created equal.

7. Click on one of the darker green panels near the center of the green panels on the balloon. Adjust the Hue slider to -120. Notice that some of the greens are affected, but not all of them. That's because of the variety of the color green in the green panels.

> **NOTE**
>
> Be aware that when you target specific colors with the eyedropper tools, all similar tones anywhere in the image are affected.

8. Click on the eyedropper with a plus sign (+) next to it. This is called the Add to Sample Eyedropper tool because it's used to add other similar colors to the originally selected color, expanding the range that's affected. Click one of the green panels on the left that wasn't affected by the last step. When you click, the color is added to the colors being affected by the Hue adjustment and the image colors are modified. Continue clicking the green panels until all of them are affected. Select and deselect the Preview option to compare before and after.

9. If you notice that any of the yellow panels on the balloon are being unintentionally affected, use the eyedropper with the minus sign (–) beside it, the Subtract From Sample Eyedropper tool, to click on the colors you don't want to affect and remove them from the selected colors. Keep working with the Add to and Subtract From eyedroppers until only the two rows of green panels are being affected by the Hue adjustment.

10. Drag the Lightness slider all the way to the left to -100. This adds black to the selected color range, changing the panels to gray and black. Positive values with the Lightness slider add white to the color, which lightens it. Figure 3-20 shows a before and after of these adjustments.

> **NOTE**
>
> The Hue/Saturation dialog box has an On-image adjustment tool, much like the one discussed in the Curves section of Chapter 2. This tool enables you to directly select and adjust the saturation of a color by clicking and dragging on the image instead of choosing adjustments from the pop-up menu. After the color is selected, you can use the other sliders to make additional modifications.

In this exercise the goal was to experiment with the techniques for adjusting specific color ranges with the Hue/Saturation command. This kind of color-correction control allows you to do things like change the hue and saturation of the blues in a sky, change the color of the greens in the grass or foliage, or change the color of someone's shirt. Just be aware that when using Hue/Saturation to target a specific color range that all similar colors within that range are affected. For example, if you change the blues in the sky, it will most likely affect the color of the blue jeans someone in the image is wearing.

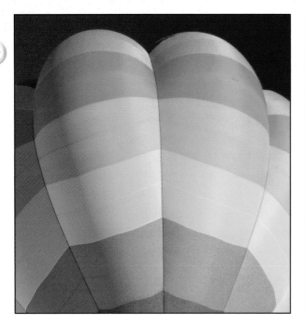

3-20

USING THE VIBRANCE COMMAND

The latest addition to the color-correction lineup in Photoshop is the Vibrance command. Its dialog box has two sliders: Vibrance and Saturation (see Figure 3-21). These two sliders combine to refine, and ultimately replace, the Saturation slider in the Hue/Saturation dialog box when adjusting overall saturation.

3-21

> **Vibrance:** This slider affects the image in a similar way to the Saturation slider in the Hue/Saturation dialog box, but there are some significant differences. One of the problems with using the Saturation slider in the Hue/Saturation command is that some colors that are already saturated become oversaturated as overall saturation is adjusted. The Vibrance slider minimizes oversaturation as full saturation of a color is approached. It does so by affecting colors with lower saturation more than colors that have higher saturation. It also tends to apply less saturation to skin tones.

> **Saturation:** The effect of this slider is similar to the Saturation slider in the Hue/Saturation dialog box. However, the same values in each command can have different effects. That's because the Vibrance command's Saturation slider's effect is combined with settings of the Vibrance slider.

PRO TIP

A slight downside to the Vibrance command is that there is no shortcut key for it. That's okay because you can create your own in the Keyboard Shortcuts menu (Edit⊄ Keyboard Shortcuts).

Here's a cool experiment to show the difference between the effects of the Vibrance and Saturation sliders:

1. Open the Hot_Air.tif file one last time or return it to its opening state if it's still open.

2. Choose Image⇨Adjustments⇨Vibrance. The Vibrance dialog box opens.

3. Increase the Vibrance value to its maximum of +100. Notice that the colors in the image barely change. (Use the Preview option to compare.) That's because the colors in this photo are already very saturated, especially the blue. The Vibrance slider prevents them from becoming oversaturated. Return the Vibrance value to 0.

4. Increase the value of the Saturation slider to its maximum of +100. Notice that the colors nearly glow as they all become oversaturated.

This new smart color-correction method enables you to work with saturation in two ways: You can boost overall saturation using the Saturation slider, or you can boost only less saturated colors by using the Vibrance slider. Sometimes a combination of these two sliders is just what the doctor ordered.

NOTE

Unfortunately, it isn't possible to work with specific color ranges using the Vibrance command, as you can with Hue/Saturation.

Is it important to calibrate and profile my monitor if I always do my own printing?

If you're working in a closed color management loop and you're getting results you like, then calibration and profiling aren't as important as when you use a lab for printing. Keep in mind though, that if you ever decide to step outside of your loop, all bets are off when it comes to predicting how color is reproduced. That's why it's best to calibrate and profile your monitor even if you don't think you need it. Then when you do send a file to someone else who's working on a calibrated and profiled system, you can be confident that the color he sees is very similar to the color you see.

You mentioned that you use the Color Balance command to adjust overall color. Is it possible to use the Hue/Saturation command to do this instead?

Yes. You can adjust a photo's overall color using the Hue/Saturation command. However, you don't have the same level of control that the Color Balance command provides. That's because the main color-correction slider in Hue/Saturation is the Hue slider. When you use it, you essentially shift all colors in one direction. This is useful when removing a colorcast from an image, but it makes it difficult to fine-tune overall color. With the Color Balance command you have control over each color channel and how it affects the entire image.

Additionally, you can work with a color's highlights, midtones, or shadows, providing a degree of finesse that's absent in Hue/Saturation. In effect, these two commands are best used in tandem. Color Balance is used to get the basic color of the image as close as possible and Hue/Saturation to increase saturation or to modify specific color ranges.

All of the color-correcting methods you demonstrated in this chapter affect colors throughout the image. What if I want to change the color of the sky, but not the color of someone's blue jeans? Is there a way to use one of these commands to do that?

All of the color adjustment commands shown in this chapter can be used to modify color locally. However, to do so it's necessary to isolate the area to be modified. The most common methods for adjusting local color are selections and masks. Part II of this book covers selections and masks in detail. Before you get to those chapters, though, it's a good idea to have a fundamental understanding of how to use the commands and tools discussed in this chapter.

Chapter 4

UNDERSTANDING THE
ADVANTAGES OF LAYERS

Photo by Mark Fitzgerald

The use of layers is one of the most important concepts you can learn in Photoshop. Layers are the key to building a nondestructive workflow because they enable you to isolate important image components so that you can edit each independently of the rest of the image.

Because the use of layers is central to many of the following chapters, this is one of the most important chapters in this book. I suggest you take time to read it and review each exercise so that when you encounter advanced projects later in this book you'll be prepared to get the most from them.

WHAT ARE LAYERS?

Think about music for a moment. When a band is in a studio recording a song, a sound engineer records each singer and instrument individually on separate sound tracks. In fact, vocals and instruments often are recorded at different times with different musicians in attendance.

Sometimes, multiple recordings of the same vocalist or instrument are overlaid to create the sound the album's producer wants to create. No one really knows what the song sounds like until all the pieces are blended together on a mixing board and played back as a single musical work.

All these separate tracks give the producer a tremendous amount of creative control. If he doesn't like the way a particular instrument sounds, he can modify it — or even toss it out and re-create it — without affecting all the other pieces.

If he had to work with a single track containing all vocals and instruments recorded at the same time, massaging the sound would be very difficult.

Photoshop has used layers since version 3.0. The concept is very similar to recording music in a studio. Just like the sound engineer in a recording studio, you control all the separate elements of an image.

If you don't like the way all these pieces fit together, you can modify some of them or throw them away without compromising the whole image. This ability creates a huge amount of flexibility when editing an image, especially when you invest hours of editing time into it.

Layers, in their most basic sense, are layers of image information that sit on top of each other. The best way to see this is to do a little experimenting with these steps:

1. Create a new file by choosing File➪New (⌘/Ctrl+N) and give it the following properties: width = 6, height = 4, resolution = 300, Color Mode = RGB Color, and Background Contents = White. These settings are shown in Figure 4-1.

   Be sure to choose inches from the drop-down list next to the Width and Height input boxes. When you click OK a new file opens with a white background.

2. Select the Rectangular Marquee tool (M) from the Tools panel. It's the second tool from the top on the single-column Tools panel. If you don't see the Rectangular Marquee tool, it's hidden beneath another marquee tool.

3. Use the Rectangular Marquee tool to draw a selection in the middle of the new file you created. Make it any size you want. You should see the *marching ants* that indicate something is selected.

X-REF

Selections are discussed at length in Chapter 5. For now, just be aware that a selection isolates part of an image so that you can affect it without affecting the rest of the image.

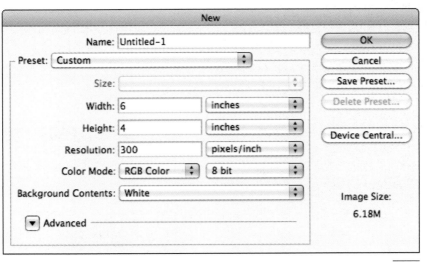

4-1

4. Press D to set the color swatches at the bottom of the Tools panel to their default colors — black as the foreground color and white as the background color.

You can also do this by clicking on the miniature swatches icon next to the color swatches at the bottom of the Tools panel, as shown in Figure 4-2.

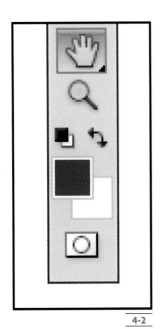

4-2

5. Select the Paint Bucket tool (G) from the Tools panel. It's the 12th tool from the top on the single-column Tools panel. If you don't see it, it's hidden beneath the Gradient tool, which is stacked with it. This tool is used to fill an area with the foreground color. Click inside the selection to fill it with black paint.

6. Deselect the rectangular selection by choosing Select⇨Deselect (⌘/Ctrl+D). You just created a black box in the middle of the white background, as shown in Figure 4-3. Cool, huh?

But what if you now decide to move the black box to a different part of the image? In this case that isn't easy to do because the black paint was applied directly to the white background.

Try again. This time, use a separate layer for your black box. Follow these steps:

1. Repeat Steps 1 through 4 in the previous exercise.

2. Choose Layer⇨New⇨Layer (Shift+⌘/Ctrl+N). Click OK when the New Layer dialog box appears. Notice that a new layer called Layer 1 appears above the Background layer in the Layers panel.

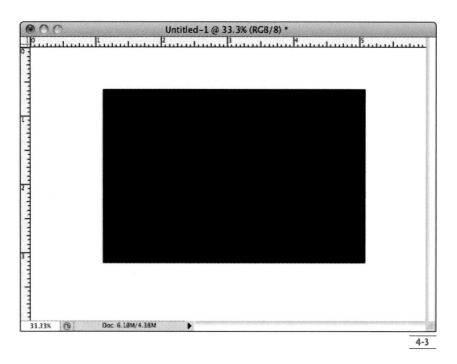

4-3

3. Select the Paint Bucket tool from the Tools panel and click inside the selection to fill it with black paint.

4. Deselect the selection to deactivate it and remove the marching ants. Your Layers panel should now look something like Figure 4-4. You get into the details of this panel in a moment.

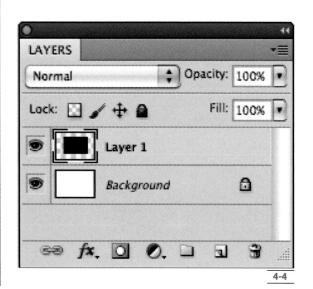

4-4

5. Select the Move tool (V) at the top of the Tools panel. The Move tool allows you to move a layer (other than the Background layer) to any position you desire. Click and drag the black box to move it to a new position. You don't have to actually click on the box itself to move it. You can click anywhere and drag because the entire layer is active.

6. Go to the Layers panel, and click the eyeball next to the thumbnail on Layer 1 to hide the layer. Notice that while the layer is hidden, it's still possible to move it with the Move tool even though you can't see it in the image.

That's because the layer is still the selected layer in the Layers panel. Click the eyeball again to make Layer 1 visible.

7. Click the eyeball icon on the Background layer. Now the Background layer is hidden, so none of the white is visible. Click the eyeball again to make the Background layer visible again.

8. Leave this practice file open for a moment longer so you can use it in the next exercise.

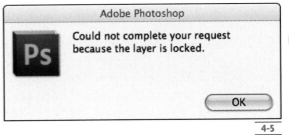

4-5

This ability to isolate image content to individual layers is important. It enables you to create a bulletproof workflow that keeps all options open so you can make future adjustments if you change your mind — or if you learn a new and improved technique sometime in the future.

UNDERSTANDING THE BACKGROUND LAYER

When a new document is opened or freshly created, it consists of a single layer. Photoshop gives this layer the special name of Background. A Background layer has certain properties that make it a bit different from most other layers.

This is indicated by a small lock icon that appears on the right side of the layer in the Layers panel indicating that the layer is locked. The locking property is designed to keep you from making inadvertent changes to the Background layer.

Sometimes, though, you may want to do something to a Background layer that's prohibited, such as move it.

Follow these steps to explore some of the differences in Background layer behavior:

1. Return to Step 7 in the previous exercise.

2. Using the Move tool, click on the Background layer and try to move it. Notice that when you do, the error message shown in Figure 4-5 appears.

3. Double-click on the Background layer in the Layers panel. When you do, the New Layer dialog box opens and Layer 0 is suggested as a new name. You can type a different name or just click OK. As soon as you do, the lock icon disappears.

   Now you can reposition the layer with the Move tool. Give it a try by dragging it to the right or left.

4. Undo the move of Layer 0 so that the bottom layer is back in position.

5. Click the thumbnail in Layer 1, and drag it so that it's below Layer 0. The two layers swap positions, and Layer 1 becomes hidden below Layer 0 because the white in Layer 0 fills the entire layer.

6. Go back to Step 2 before the Background layer was renamed by backing up three steps in the History panel. Try dragging Layer 1 below the Background layer. Now it won't work because a layer named Background has to be the bottom layer in the stack.

You need to be aware of the special nature of the Background layer mainly when you want to do something illegal to a Background layer, such as move it, transform it, change its stacking order, or delete part of it.

When one of these needs arises, just remember to rename the layer and you'll be in business.

MANAGING LAYERS

To take advantage of the flexibility that layers provide, you must be comfortable working with the Layers panel. You need to know how to move layers up and down in the panel's layer stack, how to create a new layer by cutting something from an existing layer, how to merge two layers, and how to flatten all layers. Let's explore each of these ideas one at a time.

MOVING LAYERS

Follow these steps to get some practice moving layers in the layer stack:

1. Open the Layers_Fun practice file from the downloadable practice files on the Web site (www.wiley.com/go/phoprestorationandretouching).

   Make sure that the green triangle layer is active. You should see something similar to Figure 4-6. Notice that the header of the file's dialog box displays the active layer.

2. Select the Move tool (V) from the Tools panel. Click and drag anywhere in the image to reposition the Green Triangle layer.

3. Click the Yellow Circle layer in the Layers panel to make it active. Move it to a new position with the Move tool. Notice that to reposition a single layer, it's necessary to first select it from the Layers panel.

4. With the Yellow Circle layer still active, choose Image⇨Adjustment⇨Hue/Saturation (⌘/Ctrl+U) and adjust the Hue on the Master channel to +143. Notice that only the yellow layer is affected by this change.

The main thing to take away from this exercise is that only the layer that's currently active is affected by a tool or command. That's almost always the case when you work with layers.

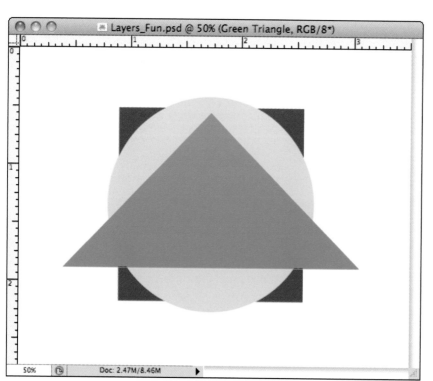

4-6

When a layered image is being edited, adjustments usually must be performed on a layer-by-layer basis. With that in mind, you can do some things to multiple layers at the same time. Repositioning with the Move tool is one of them. Here's how:

1. Open the Layers_Fun.psd file again. If it is already open from the preceding exercise, return it to its opening state by clicking the image's icon at the top of the History panel. The Green Triangle layer should already be active.

2. Hold down the Shift key and click the Red Square layer so that all three layers are active, as shown in Figure 4-7.

PRO TIP

To select *contiguous* layers — layers that are next to each other — click the first layer, and then Shift+click the last layer. To select noncontiguous layers, ⌘/Ctrl+click them individually. You also can use ⌘/Ctrl+click to deselect a selected layer.

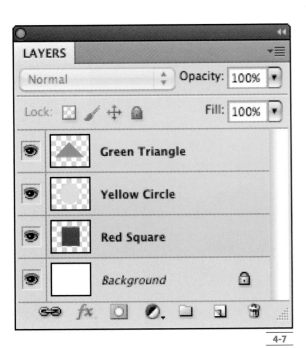

4-7

3. Use the Move tool to move all three layers at the same time. Experiment with different combinations of selected layers and the Move tool.

All the moving done here has been on an x-, y-axis — up and down, or side to side. You can also move layers forward and backward by changing their positions in the layer stack. Try this little exercise:

1. Open the Layer_Fun.psd file. If you already have it open from the preceding exercise, return it to its opening state by clicking the image's icon at the top of the Layers panel.

2. Click and drag the Red Square layer upward in the Layers panel until it's between the Green Triangle layer and the Yellow Circle layer. When you see a black line appear between them, release the mouse button. Now the Red Square layer is above the Yellow Circle layer, as shown in Figure 4-8.

3. Select two contiguous layers with the Shift key, and move them up or down together in the layer stack.

You can move layers together or by themselves. You can move them on an x-, y-axis and forward or backward in space by moving them up and down in the layer stack. Sometimes, though, you may want to move only part of a layer rather than the whole layer. To do this, you need to cut or copy sections of information from a layer before you can move it.

4-8

CREATING A NEW LAYER BY COPYING

Creating a layer from part of another layer works a little differently. To do this, a selection tool is used to isolate the part of the image to be copied to the new layer.

Selection tools haven't been discussed in detail yet, so I'll help you out on this one by supplying the selection. Follow these steps:

1. Open the Girls_Vette.tif practice file from the downloadable practice files on the Web site (www.wiley.com/go/phoprestorationandretouching). The goal here is to copy this young woman and place the new layer beside her so that you get the effect of twins.

2. Choose Select⇨Load Selection to load the selection that's provided. The Load Selection dialog box appears with the selection already chosen, so just click OK.

After the selection is loaded, the marching ants start moving around the young woman, indicating she is selected, as shown in Figure 4-9.

3. Choose Layer⇨New⇨Layer via Copy (⌘/Ctrl+ J+J). The marching ants go away, and the image looks the same as it did before. The clue that something has changed is in the Layer menu. A new layer called Layer 1 has been created above the Background layer.

4-9
Photo by Jerry Auker

4. Go to the Layers panel, and turn off the visibility of the Background layer by clicking the eyeball. Now the new layer is more obvious because you can see all the transparency around it, as shown in Figure 4-10.

5. Turn the visibility of Layer 1 back on. Select the Move tool (V). Click anywhere in the image, and drag the young woman's "twin" to her new spot. I moved her to the front, as shown in Figure 4-11.

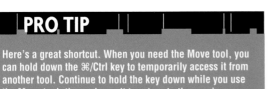

6. If you're up for more fun, duplicate Layer 1 to create another copy of the girl and move it somewhere else.

In reality, you probably won't be creating many images like this too often. However, copying information from one layer to another is a very common technique in restoration and retouching. Often, you may even need to copy something from one image and move it into another image — for example, when you're doing a head swap, as you do in Chapter 13.

MERGING AND FLATTENING LAYERS

One of the main reasons for creating layers is to have flexibility in the future. Consider the previous exercise with the young woman. As long as you keep Layer 1 around, you can continue to reposition the copy of her. When you go through the effort to create layers in an image, you usually intend to keep them intact by saving it as a PSD or layered TIFF master file.

4-10

Sometimes though, it is desirable to merge layers together. For example, when reconstructing someone's eye in a restoration job, you may need to copy information from a couple of different eyes and merge them together onto a single layer so that they can be worked on as one unit.

Also, not everyone is prepared to deal with layered files. Often, when sharing files with someone else, such as a graphic designer, you should supply a flattened file — all layers merged into a single layer — to avoid confusion.

If any modifications need to be made, they can be done on the saved layered master file. Then a new flattened file can be sent to the designer.

When you take a file to a photo lab, it almost always has to be flattened. Very few labs accept layered files because the file size is much larger. Every layer adds to the overall file size. If the Background layer on a single layer file is duplicated, the file's size instantly doubles. Smaller pieces copied to a layer add smaller amounts to the overall file size.

4-11

4

Understanding the Advantages of Layers

Follow these steps to get a quick look at how merging and flattening are done:

1. Open the Layer_Fun.psd file again. If you already have it open from the preceding exercise, return it to its opening state by clicking the image's icon at the top of the Layers panel. Make sure that the Green Triangle layer is active. Choose Layer➪Merge Down (⌘/Ctrl+E).

   Notice that the Green Triangle layer and the Yellow Circle layer are now combined into one layer called Yellow Circle. The Green Triangle was merged with the Yellow Circle; they are no longer independent, as shown in Figure 4-12.

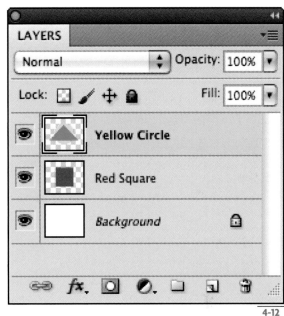

4-12

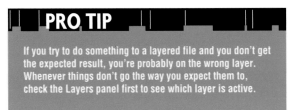

PRO TIP

If you try to do something to a layered file and you don't get the expected result, you're probably on the wrong layer. Whenever things don't go the way you expect them to, check the Layers panel first to see which layer is active.

2. Select the Move tool (V), and move the new combination. Notice that they move together because they are now one layer.

3. Merge the newly combined layer with the Red Square layer below by choosing Layer➪Merge Down (⌘/Ctrl+E). Now all three of the colored layers are combined into one layer called Red Square. Any movement with the Move tool affects all of the colored shapes because they are all part of the same layer.

4. Finally, merge the Red Square layer with the Background layer. Now try the Move tool. It won't work because all layers have been merged down to the Background layer, which is locked.

5. Go back to the opening state of the image by clicking the thumbnail at the top of the History panel. If the goal is to merge all layers into one, there's a faster way. This time, instead of merging one layer at a time, choose Layer➪Flatten Image.

Here's one more wrinkle that's quite useful. Suppose you want to merge all the layers except the Background layer. The fastest way to do this is to turn off the visibility of the Background layer and choose Layer➪Merge Visible. Only the layers that are currently visible are merged.

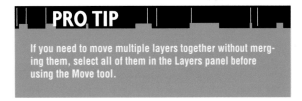

PRO TIP

If you need to move multiple layers together without merging them, select all of them in the Layers panel before using the Move tool.

So that's the scoop on merging and flattening layers. When you use layers to separate image elements, you have to know how to bring them back together when it's appropriate. You'll see some of those instances in use later in this book.

Using Adjustment Layers

In Chapter 2, when exploring the Levels and Curves commands, you may have noticed something peculiar. Whenever you made a tonal adjustment to a photo and then updated the histogram, you noticed odd behavior in the Histogram's graph.

Figure 4-13 shows an example of what I'm referring to. It's the histogram of the Snow_Dog.tif file after a Levels adjustment.

The odd things about this histogram are the gaps and spikes in the data that appear after a simple tonal adjustment. The gaps are called *combing*, because they cause the histogram to look like a comb.

These gaps represent empty tonal ranges caused by the loss of pixels during adjustment. The tall columns that appear are called *spiking*, or *spikes*. They represent data that was compressed during adjustment.

Combing and spiking, and the data loss they represent, are a byproduct of the editing process. If you think about it, this makes sense. For example, when you modify the black and white points in Levels, you're stretching and/or compressing the histogram. When you stretch it, gaps appear; when you compress it, spiking occurs.

4-13

This data loss is one of the reasons that Photoshop is considered destructive to the image. If this loss isn't controlled, it can eventually become visible in the image as necessary tones are removed or compressed.

X-REF

This data loss isn't as severe when working with 16-bit files. See Chapter 8 to learn more about 16-bit files.

The easiest way to control data loss during tonal and color adjustment is to limit cumulative changes. For example, if you want to adjust the tones in a photo, use Levels or Curves only one time. The problem with this is that you might change your mind at a later date and want to further modify the photo, adding to the previous data loss.

Fortunately, Photoshop offers a simple solution to this problem. It uses adjustment layers to place tonal and color adjustments on separate layers. Because these layers store data rather than pixels, they don't affect any pixels in the image.

The only time they act destructively is when they are flattened into the pixels of the image. This means that you can infinitely modify an adjustment layer, but the destructive nature of the adjustment happens only one time.

Working with the Adjustments panel

Adjustment layers have been a part of Photoshop for many years. However, finding and using them wasn't always intuitive. Adobe changed this with the release of Photoshop CS4 by introducing the Adjustments panel, as shown in Figure 4-14.

This panel is designed to take the guesswork out of creating and using adjustment layers.

The upper portion of the panel is populated with buttons that are used to create specific types of adjustment layers. When you click one of these buttons, a new adjustment layer is created and the panel changes to display the controls for that layer.

> **The first row contains the common tonal adjustment tools.** From left to right they are: Brightness and Contrast, Levels, Curves, and Exposure.

> **The second row contains the most common color adjustment tools.** They are Vibrance, Hue/Saturation, Color Balance, Black & White, Photo Filter, and Channel Mixer.

> **The third row has the more esoteric adjustment tools.** They are Invert, Posterize, Threshold, Gradient Map, and Selective Color.

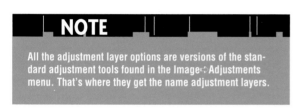

NOTE

All the adjustment layer options are versions of the standard adjustment tools found in the Image↔Adjustments menu. That's where they get the name adjustment layers.

The lower half of the panel contains groups of common presets for many types of adjustment layers. Click the triangular twirly next to a heading to uncollapse it and see the presets for that adjustment. Specific presets are also available when a particular adjustment layer is in use.

CREATING AN ADJUSTMENT LAYER

The best way to understand adjustment layers is to use one. Follow these steps:

1. Open the Snow_Dog.tif practice file from the downloadable practice files on the Web site (www.wiley.com/go/phoprestorationandretouching).

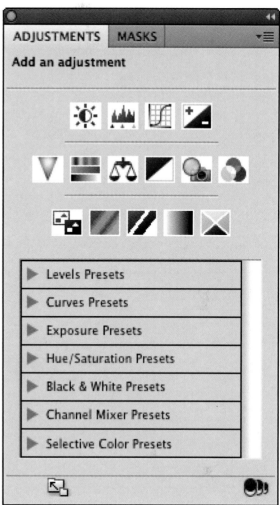

4-14

PRO TIP

If you recently opened the Snow_Dog.tif file while working on the exercises in Chapter 2, you can find it quickly by choosing File↔Open Recent. The last ten files you opened are listed here. You can increase this number in Photoshop's File Handling preferences.

2. Be sure that the Adjustments panel is visible. If you don't see it, choose Window⇨Adjustments. It's usually grouped with the Masks panel.

3. Click the Create a New Curves Adjustment Layer button on the top row of buttons in the Adjustments panel (it's the one with the small Curves icon). When you do, the panel changes to display a version of the Curves dialog box, as shown in Figure 4-15.

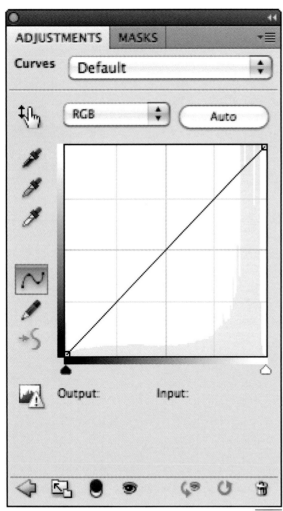

4-15

This version has most of the important features of the Curves dialog box, including the On-image adjustment tool. The only obvious exception is there's no Show Clipping option. That's okay because you can display it by pressing the Alt key while dragging the black and white Input sliders, just as you did when working with Levels in Chapter 2.

4. Use the sliders to adjust the black point and white point, and then adjust the midtones by placing a point on the diagonal line and dragging it upward or downward — just like you did when working with the Curves command in Chapter 2.

You can also try using the On-image adjustment tool to place points on the line.

Now look at the Layers panel shown in Figure 4-16. A new layer named Curves 1 is above the Background layer, which is the original image layer. Click the eyeball icon next to the Curves 1 layer to hide the layer and its adjustment. Turn the layer's visibility back on by clicking the eyeball again.

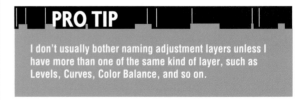

PRO TIP

I don't usually bother naming adjustment layers unless I have more than one of the same kind of layer, such as Levels, Curves, Color Balance, and so on.

You can modify the layer's settings any time you want to by clicking it in the Layers panel to make the layer active and then adjusting the settings in the Adjustments panel. (If you click the Create a New Curves Adjustment Layer button again, a second Curves layer is created.)

You can test this by making cumulative adjustments to the Curves 1 layer while monitoring the Histogram panel. Notice that data loss in the histogram stays about the same every time you make a new adjustment because the adjustments are only being calculated one time.

The only time the image suffers data loss is when the layers are flattened or merged and the adjustments become a permanent part of the image. Ideally, this happens at the end of the workflow.

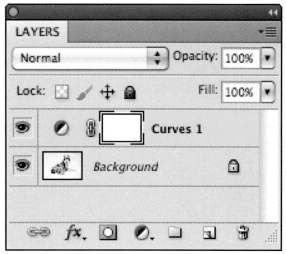

4-16

When a specific adjustment layer tool is in use, a set of buttons appears along the bottom of the Adjustments panel. These buttons, shown in Figure 4-17, allow you to manage the layer and your adjustments to it. Here's a quick description of what each button is used for:

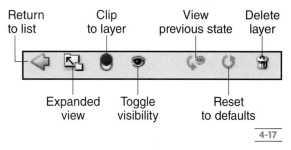

4-17

> **Return to Adjustment List.** Use this to go back to the display shown in Figure 4-14. It allows you to add an additional adjustment layer, such as a Color Balance layer on top of a Curves layer.

> **Switch Panel to Expanded View.** Use this to make the panel larger, more like the standard Curves dialog box.

> **Clip to Layer.** Sometimes you want an adjustment layer to only affect the layer directly below it. Say, for example, that you have a project where you need to cut someone's head from one image and add it to another.

If the tone or color on the head layer is different than the rest of the image, you can add an adjustment layer and click the Clip to Layer button to make the adjustment layer affect only the layer directly below it.

> **Toggle Layer Visibility.** This is the same as clicking the eyeball icon in the Layers panel. It simply turns the adjustment layer's visibility off and on.

> **View Previous State.** Use this button to undo individual changes.

> **Reset to Adjustment Defaults.** Use this to reset the adjustment layer to its default settings.

> **Delete Adjustment Layer.** Click this button to delete the currently active layer.

There's one more thing about adjustment layers you should know before you move on: You can have more than one of a particular type.

It's quite common to have one Levels or Curves adjustment layer for overall image adjustment and another Levels or Curves adjustment layer that's used only for a particular printer. This way the second adjustment layer is used to compensate for any variations with that printer. It's only made visible when you're ready to print. This is a very common use of Levels, Curves, and Color Balance adjustment layers.

This flexibility you learned about here is only the beginning of what you can do with adjustment layers. You encounter them again as you move through some of the future chapters in this book.

WORKING WITH THE LAYERS PANEL

So far, you've used the Layers menu to access commands that are used with layers. It's good to remember that any time you work with layers, the things you need are found under this menu. For example, you use commands in the Layers menu to create a new layer and to merge layers. You can also use it to create an adjustment layer (Layer⇨New Adjustment Layer).

However, when you work with layers there are faster ways to get things done that help to speed up your workflow.

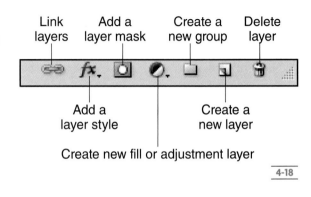

4-18

Figure 4-18 shows the strip of buttons along the bottom of the Layers panel. These buttons provide you with quick access to several items that are in the Layers menu. Using these buttons to accomplish common tasks saves you time because you don't need to dig through menus to access them. Here's what these buttons do, from left to right:

> **Link Layers.** Use this button to link two layers together so that when one layer is moved, the other moves, too. To link layers, select them in the Layers menu and click this button.

> **Add a Layer Style.** Add special effect styles to a layer. For example you can use these styles to add a drop shadow or a stroke to a layer.

> **Add Layer Mask.** This is one of the fastest ways to add a Reveal all layer mask.

Masks are covered in detail in Chapter 6.

> **Create a New Fill or Adjustment Layer.** This provides you with another way to add an adjustment layer. When you click this button a menu of all adjustment layers is displayed. When you choose one, the layers controls open in the Adjustments panel.

> **Create a New Group.** This is used to group layers together. This is useful for organizing complex images that have lots of layers.

> **Create a New Layer.** Click here to quickly create a new, empty layer.

> **Delete Layer.** This button is used to delete the selected layer(s). You can click the button to delete them, or simply drag and drop them onto the button.

Another set of shortcuts used with layers is the Layers panel's Panel menu, as shown in Figure 4-19.

This menu contains many other options from the Layers menu, such as Duplicate Layer and Merge Visible. The availability of specific options varies with the type of layer that's chosen.

If you learn to use this menu when working with Layers, as well as the buttons on the bottom of the Layers panel, you'll save mouse clicks and save time, which both help to improve the speed and efficiency of your workflow.

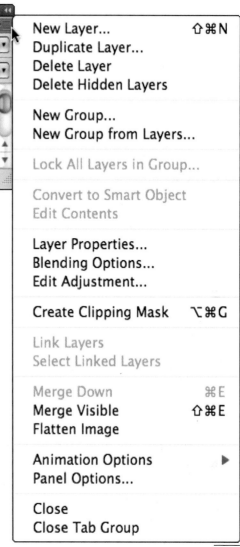

4-19

■ **Can a photo have more than one Background layer?**

A Photoshop document can only have one official Background layer. You can rename a second layer Background, but it won't automatically be locked like a true Background layer. If you have a document with no Background layer and you want to convert an ordinary layer to a Background layer, select the layer and choose Layer⇨New⇨Background From Layer. The layer is automatically placed at the bottom of the layer stack. Additionally, any transparency in the layer is replaced by the current background color, shown in the swatches at the bottom of the Tools panel.

If I'm working on a quick project, is it necessary to use an adjustment layer for tonal or color correction?

If I'm working quickly with an image, spending only a few minutes or even seconds with it, I don't use adjustment layers. In those cases, I don't need the flexibility of an adjustment layer because I'm not making cumulative adjustments. However, when I spend lots of time editing an image or if I know I'll be editing it again later, I'm sure to use adjustment layers to do all tonal and color adjustment. If I'm working with an image that already contains layers that I plan to preserve when saving the file, I go ahead and use adjustment layers to keep all options open.

At the end of this chapter you showed some panel features that are used to provide quick access to several tools and commands. Are these kinds of features available in other panels?

Nearly every panel is loaded with options in the form of buttons and commands in the panel's Panel menu. It's a good idea to hover your cursor over the icons on the strip at the bottom of a panel to learn what they are. Then investigate the Panel menu and its options and commands to become familiar with them. These shortcuts are placed here to make the workflow more intuitive and efficient. They save you from locating commands buried in some of the main menus and from needing to remember specific keyboard shortcuts.

Chapter 5

USING SELECTIONS TO ISOLATE CONTENT

Photo by Doreen Wynja

In the last chapter you used a selection in one of the exercises. Though I don't like to mention an important concept without explaining it, sometimes it's necessary. The reason I was able to get away with asking you to use selections earlier without going into detail is because selections is one of the few Photoshop concepts that seems to be familiar to new users. By that I mean that most people have seen the *marching ants* that define a selection, and they understand that selections are usually created around objects in an image. If that doesn't apply to you, fear not. By the end of this chapter, you'll not only know what a selection is, you'll also know when to use one selection tool rather than another and how to combine and refine selections to create complex selections.

What Is a Selection?

The concept behind selections in Photoshop is quite simple. They provide a system for isolating pixel information in an image so that adjustments are applied only to the selected area. This is very useful when it's necessary to darken something or adjust its color independently of the rest of the image. Selections also are useful for isolating part of an image that you want to duplicate and copy or move to another layer or image. You saw this in Chapter 4 when you copied the young lady in front of the Corvette to a different layer. In that example, the selection was provided for you.

Using Photoshop's Main Selection Tools

Like most things in Photoshop, there's more than one way to create a selection. The most common methods involve three selection toolsets that are located in the Tools panel. They are: the Marquee, Lasso, and the Magic Wand and Quick Selection tools. The following sections explain all of the tools in these toolsets so that you'll know which is best for a particular selection job.

The Marquee tools

You'll find the Marquee tools stacked together in the second toolset from the top in the single-column Tools panel (see Figure 5-1). The toolset consists of the four tools:

> **Rectangular Marquee:** Used for making rectangular selections

> **Elliptical Marquee:** Used for making elliptical selections

> **Single Row Marquee:** Used for selecting a row that's only 1 pixel high

> **Single Column Marquee:** Used for selecting a column that's only 1 pixel wide

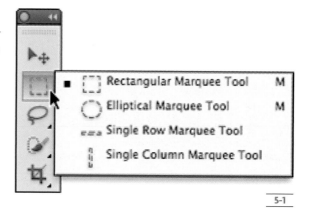

5-1

In many years of using Photoshop, I don't think I've ever used the Single Row Marquee or Single Column Marquee. However, I use both the Rectangular and Elliptical Marquees often. They both work in pretty much the same way. Explore that system using the Rectangular Marquee by following these steps:

1. Choose File➪New to create a new file, and give it the following properties: Width = 6 inches, Height = 4 inches, Resolution = 300, Color Mode = RGB Color/8-bit, and Background = White. Click OK.

2. Select the Rectangular Marquee tool (M) from the Tools panel. Go to the top-left area of the new file. Click and drag downward to the lower right. As you do, you see a rectangular shape outlined by

the marching ants and anchored at the spot where you first clicked. When you let go of the mouse button, the selection floats on the image. This selection isn't technically on a layer, but it can be repositioned by moving the cursor inside of it and clicking and dragging.

3. Remove the selection by going to the Select menu and choosing Deselect (⌘/Ctrl+D).

4. Hold down the Shift key and draw another selection. Notice that now the *aspect ratio,* the ratio of the height and width of the shape, is locked to a perfect square with a 1:1 aspect ratio.

5. Deselect again. Sometimes you need to draw a rectangle with an aspect ratio that's fixed to a different ratio than 1:1.

6. Go to the Options bar, click the drop-down list next to Style, and choose Fixed Aspect Ratio. Type a value of **1** in the Width box and **2** in the Height box. Now draw a selection with a 1:2 aspect ratio.

7. Deselect one more time and draw a new rectangular selection like the one you drew in Step 2.

8. Select the Brush tool (B) from the Tools panel. Set the brush's properties to any settings you want while choosing a fairly large brush. Now use the Brush to draw a stroke across the entire image that begins and ends outside the boundaries of the selection. Notice that the stroke appears only within the selection, as shown in Figure 5-2.

This is what selections are all about. When a selection is active, any action taken affects only pixels within the boundaries of the selection. All the pixels outside the selection are protected from any changes. Undo the paint stroke you just made by choosing Edit⇨Undo Brush Tool (⌘/Ctrl+Z).

9. Choose Select⇨Inverse (Shift+⌘/Crtl+I) to invert the selection. Now the pixels outside the original box are selected and the pixels inside the box are protected (unselected). The only change you'll notice is that the marching ants begin to march around the perimeter of the image.

10. Use the Brush tool to draw another stroke across the image. This time the paint is applied only outside the box, as shown in Figure 5-3. The ability to invert any selection is very useful. It allows you to alternately isolate opposite areas of an image. It also allows you to make a difficult selection by selecting something easier and then inverting it.

As you've seen so far, the Select menu is the main place to go to modify the properties of a selection after it's been created. Another way to access some of the commands in the Select menu is to right-click with your mouse anytime a selection is active and a selection tool is chosen.

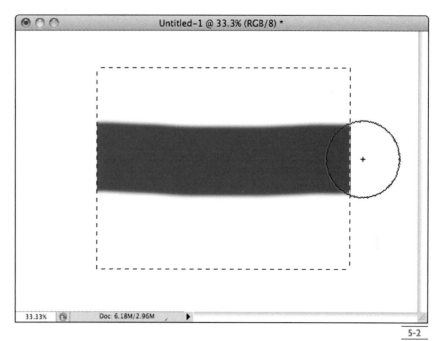

5-2

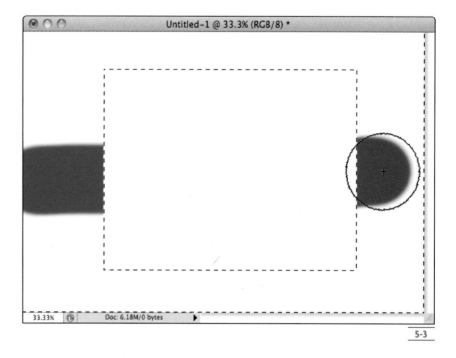

5-3

Figure 5-4 shows the options in this context-sensitive menu. If you compare them to the Select menu, you see that the right-click menu has some options that aren't even in the Select menu.

Also, be aware that if you right-click when no selection is active, you get a different context-sensitive menu.

The Elliptical Marquee tool works much the same way as the Rectangular Marquee. Click and drag to draw an ellipse of any shape. Hold down the Shift key to lock it to a perfect circle.

PRO TIP

You can open one of these context-sensitive menus by right-clicking with almost any tool. Because right-clicking enables you to work more efficiently, it's mentioned throughout this book. If you're a Mac user, your right-click option may be disabled. Go to the Mouse section of your System Preferences to enable it. It may take a bit of getting used to, but after you get comfortable with it you'll wonder how you got by with only one mouse button.

The Marquee tools are quite handy when you need to select an ellipse or a rectangle. But quite often you need to make selections that are more organic — free-form shapes. Most of the rest of the selection tools in Photoshop are used for those kinds of selections.

THE LASSO TOOLS

The Lasso toolset is the third toolset from the top on the single-column Tools panel. The three Lasso tools are stacked together (see Figure 5-5). They are:

> **Lasso tool:** A true free-form tool. You can create a selection with just about any type of organic shape by drawing it. This tool is not very well suited to creating selections with straight edges; for example, selecting an area along the side of a building.

> **Polygonal Lasso tool:** Used to create selections with straight lines. Every time you click with this tool, a straight line is drawn between your current click and the most pervious click. This tool is useful for drawing a selection along the edge of a building.

Deselect
Select Inverse
Feather...
Refine Edge...

Save Selection...
Make Work Path...

Layer via Copy
Layer via Cut
New Layer...

Free Transform
Transform Selection

Fill...
Stroke...

Last Filter
Fade Brush Tool...

5-4

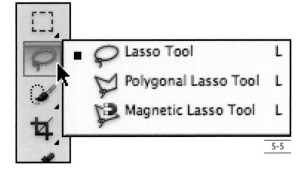

	Lasso Tool	L
Polygonal Lasso Tool	L
Magnetic Lasso Tool	L

5-5

97

> **Magnetic Lasso tool:** This is a *smart* selection tool. It's designed to see the lines that divide regions of differing tonal contrast to help you draw detailed shapes that may be difficult to draw accurately with the standard Lasso tool.

The Polygonal Lasso tool is useful when straight lines are needed. Most of the time, though, I need a selection that follows the contours unique to a specific situation in a specific image — which is rarely a straight line. For that reason, the focus here is on the two other Lasso tools: the Lasso and Magnetic Lasso tools.

Following are some exercises to compare and contrast these two tools:

1. Open the Snow_Dog.tif practice file from the downloadable practice files on the Web site (www.wiley.com/go/phoprestorationandretouching). Make a Levels adjustment (⌘/Ctrl+L) similar to the one you did in Chapter 2. I used 23, 1.08, 226. In this exercise, the goal is to enhance Ruby's colors so that they're richer against the neutrality of the snow without intensifying the cool, cyan/blue tint of the snow.

2. If you can't see the entire dog on your screen, Zoom out until you can using the Zoom tool (Z) with its zoom out option selected from the Tool options bar. (You can also temporarily switch the Zoom tool to zoom out by holding down Alt while clicking.)

3. Select the Lasso tool (L), and draw a selection around the dog. Stay as close to the edges of the dog as you can. Go all the way around until you get back to the place where you started drawing.

When you connect the beginning and endpoints, the selection is complete. If you release the mouse button before completing the shape, it automatically connects the starting point with the place where you released.

As you can see, drawing a selection like this is easier said than done. The Lasso tool is great for creating free-form selections that are loose, as you see in later chapters. It just isn't the right selection tool for this job.

4. Remove the selection you just created by choosing Select➪Deselect (⌘/Ctrl+D), or just click somewhere outside the selection with the Lasso tool.

5. Switch to the Magnetic Lasso tool (L), which is stacked under the Lasso tool. Using the options bar, set the tool's options to the following settings: Feather = 0px, Anti-alias = checked, Width = 5px, Contrast = 40, and Frequency = 40. (You look closer at these settings in a moment.)

6. Click near the tip of one of the ears to get the tool started. After you click, release the mouse button. Begin outlining the dog again, staying as close to her edges as possible. Notice how much easier you can follow the edge of the contrast between the dog's dark fur and the snow with the Magnetic Lasso because it is automatically attaching a selection along the edge of the dog. Carefully trace her entire outline until you get back to where you started.

If you have your cursor preferences set to Standard under Preferences ⇨ Cursors ⇨ Other Cursors, your cursor will look like the icon of the Magnetic Lasso tool. If you want to see the actual width of the tool, press the Caps Lock key. Just remember to press the key again when you finish, because it modifies the way many cursors look. You can also permanently change your cursor using the Cursor Preferences Photoshop ⇨ Preferences ⇨ Cursors (Edit ⇨ Preferences ⇨ Cursors).

As you trace, notice that fastening points are being laid down by the Magnetic Lasso. These points anchor the selection to the lines and points that separate areas of contrast. If the tool won't place a point where you want one — maybe near the tip of Ruby's white tail or paw or along her back — click to manually insert a fastening point. If a point is placed in a place where you don't want one, press

Delete to remove it. Successive points are removed every time you press Delete, so you can back up several points in a row if you need to. If you want to bail and start over, press Esc.

7. When you complete the selection and get back to the starting point, a small circle appears next to the cursor. This indicates that a click will connect the beginning point with the endpoint, completing the selection. If you have problems closing the selection, try a gentle double-click. Your selection should now look something like Figure 5-6.

NOTE

If your gentle double-click is too strong, or not in the right place, the tool thinks you want to start a new selection. If this happens and the selection you just drew disappears, press Esc to make your selection reappear.

Notice that the selection in Figure 5-6 isn't perfect. I missed the tip of one of her ears, as well as the edge of her fur in a couple of places. I'll show you how to fine-tune selections in a moment. For now, work with what you have.

8. Choose Image ⇨ Adjustments ⇨ Hue/Saturation (⌘/Ctrl+U) to enhance the color of the dog's fur. Adjust the Master Saturation value to 55. Notice that the colors intensify, especially Ruby's blue eyes. The white fur begins to look more yellow, which is accurate to true life. Make any other adjustment you want to make, and click OK. Now Ruby stands out from the background because her colors are so much richer. Now you can do something about the color of the snow.

9. Invert the selection by choosing Select ⇨ Inverse. Now the marching ants are moving around the outside perimeter of the image.

10. Choose Image ⇨ Adjustments ⇨ Hue/Saturation. Select Cyans in the Edit drop-down list, and use the eyedropper to sample the snow color in the top-right corner of the image. Lower the Saturation value to -100, and click OK. This removes much of the cool color of the snow, causing a subtle change because the colors aren't too intense. If you make this adjustment to the entire image, without any selections, Ruby's eyes lose most of their blue color.

11. Before deselecting, Choose Filter ⇨ Blur ⇨ Gaussian Blur. When the Gaussian Blur dialog box appears, type a value of **5** and click OK. This blurs the snow around the dog a bit, making her pop out of the background a bit more.

As you can see, the Magnetic Lasso tool is powerful, especially in a scenario with edges between regions of contrasting tones like this one. When edges aren't so well defined, it becomes necessary to modify the tool's properties in the options bar, as shown in Figure 5-7, so that it accurately follows the edge.

5-7

The following list highlights some of these settings:

> **Feather:** Used to blur the edge of the selection, creating softer selections. This is discussed in detail in a moment.

> **Anti-alias:** Used to smooth jagged edge transitions. This should be turned on and left on. It's available for the Lasso tools, the Elliptical Marquee, and the Magic Wand.

> **Width:** This controls the size of the area where edge detection occurs by specifying the maximum distance from the cursor where an edge will be seen by the Magnetic Lasso tool.

> **Contrast:** Used to modify the Lasso's sensitivity to edge contrast. Higher settings limit the tool to working along edges with higher contrast only.

> **Frequency:** Specifies the rate at which fastening points are attached to the edge. Higher settings tend to anchor the selection more quickly because more points are attached.

> **Use tablet pressure to change pen width button:** If you're using a graphics tablet, discussed in Chapter 6, you can click this to quickly turn the pen pressure setting on and off.

> **Refine Edge:** This feature enables you to make a number of modifications to the edge of a selection, which is the most important part of a selection. It's discussed in detail in a moment.

Experiment with each of these settings individually on the Snow_Dog.tif file. Get a feel for how each affects the Magnetic Lasso's selection process. When used properly, this tool creates a selection that's 90 percent complete in just a few moments. Areas that are missed can quickly be added to the selection with more appropriate selection tools.

THE MAGIC WAND TOOL

The Magic Wand tool — as you probably can tell by its name — is another automated selection tool. It's best suited for selecting colors that are similar to one another. In fact, in the right scenario, few selection tools can match its speed.

This tool has two important settings on its options bar:

> **Tolerance:** This affects the range of similar colors that the tool selects. Low settings restrict the selection to colors that are very similar. High values allow the tool to select a broader range of colors that are less similar. Settings range on a scale of 0 to 255.

> **Contiguous:** When this is checked, only similar pixels that are touching are selected. (Contiguous means that two things are touching or sharing a common border.) This is a great way to control the Magnetic Lasso's power. Using Contiguous allows you to do things like select a single pink flower out of a field of similarly colored flowers, as long as their pink petals aren't touching one another.

Follow these steps to explore the Magic Wand:

1. Open the Bird_2.tif practice file from the downloadable practice files on the Web site (www.wiley.com/go/phoprestorationandretouching). The goal in this exercise is to select the bird as quickly as possible. After the last exercise, you could probably select it with the Magnetic Lasso in under a minute, but there's a faster way.

2. Choose the Magic Wand tool (W) from the Tools panel. It's fourth from the top on the single-column Tools panel. It might be stacked under the Quick Selection tool. Set the tool options to the following values: Tolerance = 30, Anti-alias = on, Contiguous = on, and Sample All Layers = off.

3. Click the sky. When you do, everything but the bird is selected due to the uniformity of the sky's tone and contrast. Invert the selection by choosing Select⇨Inverse, and the job's done. The bird is selected, as shown in Figure 5-8, with two clicks.

5-8

It's pretty rare for an automated tool to work this flaw-lessly. When it doesn't, it's quite common to combine multiple selections to create the right selection. You learn to do this in a moment, but first look at the final selection tool.

THE QUICK SELECTION TOOL

The Quick Selection tool, introduced in Photoshop CS3, is the latest smart selection tool from Photoshop. This tool combines the smart technology behind the Magic Wand with the flexibility of a brush-style tool, enabling you to paint a selection into an image. The Quick Selection tool also does a nice job of creating boundaries around the selected area, sometimes pro-viding more refined selection boundaries than selec-tions with the Magic Wand.

1. Open the Spring_Tulips.tif file from the download-able practice files on the Web site (www.wiley.com/go/phoprestorationandretouching).

2. Choose the Quick Selection tool (W) from the Tools panel. It's stacked with the Magic Wand. Make sure that Auto-Enhance is selected in the tool options and that Sample All Layers is not selected.

PRO TIP

Selecting Auto-Enhance on the options bar creates selec-tions that have smoother boundaries. This setting also enables the selection to flow more easily toward the edges of the content being selected.

3. Adjust the size of the Quick Selection tool to 100px by clicking the Brush button on the options bar and adjusting the Diameter value from the pop-up menu. Set the Hardness value to 100 and the Spacing value to 0. Begin painting in the lower-right section of the image to select some of the orange and yellow flowers. As you paint, notice how the tool seeks similar colors, as shown in the lower-right area of Figure 5-9.

4. Continue painting until all of the flowers in front of the fence are selected. Notice that as you paint, more of the image is automatically added to the selection. That's because the default setting on this tool is Add to Selection. You can verify this by checking the buttons on the left side of the options bar, as shown in Figure 5-10.

Here's what these options do:

> **New selection:** This option is used to create a new selection. Every time you begin painting, the selection tool removes any previous selections and starts a new selection.

> **Add to selection:** This option is used to add to any existing selections. Every time you use the tool more of the image is selected. This is the default setting for this particular selection tool. The default for the other selection tools covered in this chapter is New selection.

> **Subtract from selection:** Use this option when you need to remove an area from the selection without starting over from scratch.

5-9

PRO TIP

Press the Shift key to temporarily access the Add to selection function and press the Alt key to temporarily access the Subtract from selection option. When you release either of these keys, the selection tool reverts to the selection mode it was at before using the keyboard shortcut. This is a good way to avoid forgetting that you left a selection tool in one of these special modes, causing unpredictable behavior.

New selection   Subtract from selection

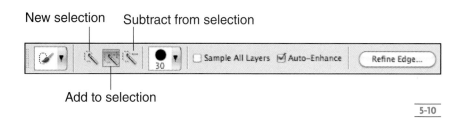

Add to selection

5-10

All of the selection tools have these buttons, though they look a bit different in the other selection tools. These other tools also have a fourth button, named Intersect with Selection. When this option is used, only the overlapping area of multiple selections is selected.

5. Decrease the size of your brush when you get to the edges where the flowers and the fence overlap. If some of the fence is accidentally selected, use the Subtract from selection option to remove it.

6. When you're happy with your selection, choose Image⇨Adjustments⇨Hue/Saturation and adjust the Saturation slider to 60 to increase the saturation of these selected flowers. This makes them stand out even better from the other flowers, as shown in Figure 5-11.

7. Deselect the selection to complete the process.

5-11

COMBINING TOOLS FOR SELECTION SUCCESS

Each of the selection tools you've looked at so far has strengths and weaknesses. One smart tool might be good at selecting similar colors, while another is good at finding edges. Other tools, like the Lasso, are great when you want complete control over the tool.

Knowing about these differences and choosing selection tools based on them is the foundation of successful selection strategies. After you're comfortable with these differences, you can take your selections to the next level by combining selection tools, based on their strengths, to quickly create perfect selections.

In the previous example, you still have a slight technical problem, which you can see in Figure 5-11. Background areas, showing between and behind the foreground flowers, were also selected when the flowers were selected.

You could use the Subtract Selection button on the tool options of the Quick Selection tool (or hold down the Alt key) so that you could go back and remove each of these areas from the selection, but you may need to fiddle with the tool's options to get it to accurately remove these areas.

There is a much faster approach that takes only one or two clicks on the image with the Magic Wand tool. Follow these steps:

1. Return to Step 5 in the previous exercise. Select the Magic Wand tool, and set its Tolerance value to 28. Make sure that the Contiguous check box is deselected so that all similar tones are selected.

2. Choose the Subtract from selection option (or hold down the Alt key). Click in the large dark area that's just left of the middle of the image. When you do, all the dark areas in the foreground are deselected. If too much is deselected, back up and try again with a slightly lower Tolerance value.

3. If by chance a couple of floating pixels are not deselected, switch to the Lasso tool and remove them by holding down the Alt key and drawing a loose shape around them.

This is the key to selection success. Begin by using one tool that's suited to quickly building 90 percent of the image. Then use other selection tools to add and remove the bits and pieces they're most suited for working with. This strategy is much more efficient than fiddling with a particular tool's settings, trying to set its preferences so it creates the perfect selection all by itself. Creating a superstar selection tool setup might feel rewarding, but teamwork is much more efficient.

FINE-TUNING SELECTIONS

Selecting the right information is the first part of creating a great selection. The second part is adjusting the edge of the selection so that adjustments made to selected pixels blend with the surrounding, unselected pixels.

FEATHERING A SELECTION'S EDGE TRANSITION

One of the most used methods of modifying a selection's edge boundary is the Feather command. You feather some selections in projects later in this book, so it's good to look at it here. Follow these steps:

1. Open a new file. Choose File⇨New, and give it the following properties: Width = 6 inches, Height = 4 inches, Resolution = 300, Color Mode = RGB Color/8-bit, and Background = White.

2. Select the Rectangular Marquee tool and use it to create a basic selection on the left side of the image. Make sure that the Feather value on the options bar is 0px.

3. Select the Paint Bucket tool (G) from the Tools panel. It's stacked with the Gradient tool, 12th from the top. Click inside the rectangular selection to fill it with the foreground color from the color swatches near the bottom of the Tools panel. (I used black, the default foreground color.)

4. Move to the right side of the image, and draw another selection with the Rectangular Marquee similar in size to the selection on the left.

5. Choose Select⇨Modify⇨Feather, and type a value of 30 when the Feather Selection dialog box appears. Click OK.

6. Use the Paint Bucket to fill the new selection with the foreground color. Your image should look something like Figure 5-12.

This exercise demonstrates the edge softening effect of feathering a selection. Notice that the tone of the paint transitions from full intensity to zero intensity as it's feathered. Also notice that the feathering takes place on both sides of the selection boundary. That means the feathering effect is feathering outward and inward, with respect to the marching ants. The higher the value used, the farther the effect extends from the selection's boundary.

Feathering a selection allows changes in a selected area to transition into unselected areas so that adjustments to selected areas aren't as obvious. This is extremely useful. You could have used it earlier when you were working on the photo of Ruby in the snow (Snow_Dog.tif). You may not have noticed it, but if you had zoomed in to the edges of the selection, you could have seen abrupt changes where the focus goes from sharp to blurred. You can see this in a close-up of the area along the edge of her head in Figure 5-13.

5-12

5-13

A feather of about 20 pixels before blurring the background would have helped to minimize the abruptness of the change from blur to nonblur.

The amount of feathering for a particular job depends on the size of the file. Thirty pixels is a lot for a small file like the 4 x 6 300 ppi file you just used. On a larger file, like a 16 x 20 or 20 x 30, a feather of 30 pixels would have much less of an effect. Fortunately, there's an easy way to evaluate the amount of feathering before adjusting or modifying a selected area.

Using the Refine Edge

When any selection is active and a selection tool is in use, the Refine Edge button is displayed on the tool's options bar. The command is also found by choosing Select⇨Refine Edge. Choosing either option opens the dialog box shown in Figure 5-14.

There's a lot going on in the Refine Edge dialog box so it's best to break it down into smaller parts to get the best understanding of how this powerful feature is used. The dialog box consists of four pods. The following sections describe the use of each.

View Mode

These settings are used to control the way other adjustments are displayed on the image. When you

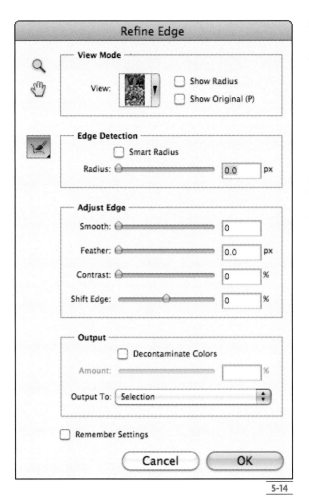

5-14

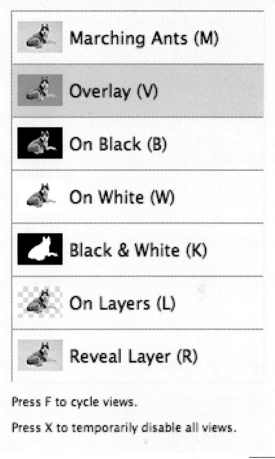

Press F to cycle views.

Press X to temporarily disable all views.

5-15

click on the View drop-down list, the list in Figure 5-15 is displayed.

Each of these options changes the way a selection is previewed, allowing you to choose the preview method that you prefer. When you hover over each of these options, a tooltip informs you about how it affects the preview on the main image.

NOTE

Press F while the Refine Edge dialog box is open to cycle through the five preview modes. While in those modes, press X to temporarily hide the preview. Press X again to reinstate it.

This pod also contains two other options:

> **Show Radius:** Displays the selection border where edge refinement is taking place.

> **Show Original:** Displays a preview of the image without any Refine Edge adjustments. It works like the Preview button does in most other dialog boxes.

Edge Detection

The Edge Detection pod features three options. They are:

> **Smart Radius:** Choosing this automatically adjusts the radius for either hard or soft edges along the selection boundary.

107

> **Radius:** This slider is used to designate the size of the area around the selection's boundary in which changes are allowed.

You can create more precise selections around soft detail, such as hair and fur, by increasing the value. It would have been useful on the Snow_Dog.tif project you did earlier.

> **Refine Radius/Erase Refinements tools:** To the left of the Edge Detection pod is a button for activating either of these tools. They enable you to use a brush to precisely modify the border area of a selection. Click and hold on the button to switch between them. You can also choose between them and modify the brush's diameter using the settings on the options bar.

Adjust Edges

The Adjust Edge pod is where the most important action happens. These sliders are used to modify the selection boundary in four ways:

> **Smooth:** This slider is used to remove the hills and valleys in a selection's boundary. Higher settings create a smoother edge.

> **Feather:** This slider is used to soften edge transitions on either side of a selection.

> **Contrast:** This slider removes any fuzziness in a selection's edge. It's often used to remove any *noise* that's picked up by increasing the Radius setting. (Noise is caused by random fluctuations in pixel values. In its purest sense, it usually looks like film grain.)

> **Shift Edge:** This slider is used to enlarge or shrink the selection border. Positive values expand and negative values decrease the size of the selection. These adjustments allow you to make subtle changes to soft-edged selections. A small amount of shrinking often helps to remove unwanted colors from a selection boundary.

Output

The Output pod is used to fine-tune the selection that's created using the previous settings. Here's what its settings are used for:

> **Decontaminate Colors:** Sometimes the edge of a selection is affected by color fringing due to partially selected, unwanted colors. Selecting this option decreases color contamination by replacing pixel colors. Because of that, it's necessary to output the refined selection to another layer or document to avoid affecting the main image.

> **Output To:** Clicking here opens a drop-down list that lets you output the refined selection as a selection or a mask. You can also choose to place it on a different layer and/or into a new document.

You may have noticed that the Select menu has a submenu named Modify that contains many of these controls. Using them from this menu is anything but intuitive because the effects of changes to these settings can't be seen until after the selection process is complete. When these settings are combined, the results become even harder to predict.

The preview feature in the Refine Edge dialog box is extremely helpful. It allows you to create the selection you need without lots of trial and error. It also lets you see how one setting can be used to tweak the modifications of other settings.

The biggest drawback I see is that I end up playing with this tool more than I need to because it's so much fun to compare and contrast different edge refinement scenarios.

PRO TIP

When you get down to business with this tool, zoom in to take a closer look at the selection's edge. You can use the Zoom tool in the dialog box to click on the image or use the standard keyboard shortcuts for zooming. If you use the Zoom tool and you need to zoom back out, press and hold the Alt key and click on the image. This changes the Zoom tool to zoom-out mode.

5-16

I used the settings shown in Figure 5-15 to modify the selection on the Snow_Dog.tif project. Notice that now the hair sticking up along Ruby's back is even selected, as shown in Figure 5-16, using the Overlay View mode.

Consider taking a few minutes to revisit that project to see how well you can refine your selection.

SAVING AND LOADING SELECTIONS

Sometimes, it takes lots of work to build a complex selection. Several selection tools and techniques might have to be combined to get it just right. You usually don't want to have to redo one of these selections after all that work is done.

If you are about to make permanent changes to a complex selection with the tools in Refine Edge, or if you are going to deselect a complex selection, then save the selection in case you want to go back and try a different editing direction. My rule is that I save a selection if it takes longer than 5 minutes to create. That way, if I need the selection again, I don't have to re-create it — or even try to remember how I created it in the first place.

To save a selection, choose Select➪Save Selection. When you do this, the Save Selection dialog box appears (see Figure 5-17). You have three options in the Document pop-up menu as to the location of where the selection will be saved:

> **Document:** Choosing the current filename allows you to save the selection as part of the current file so you can access the selection later. This is the usual place to save a selection. Choosing New allows you to create a new file that contains only the selection. This is a good way to store a selection by itself. I rarely do this, but it's nice to know it's possible.

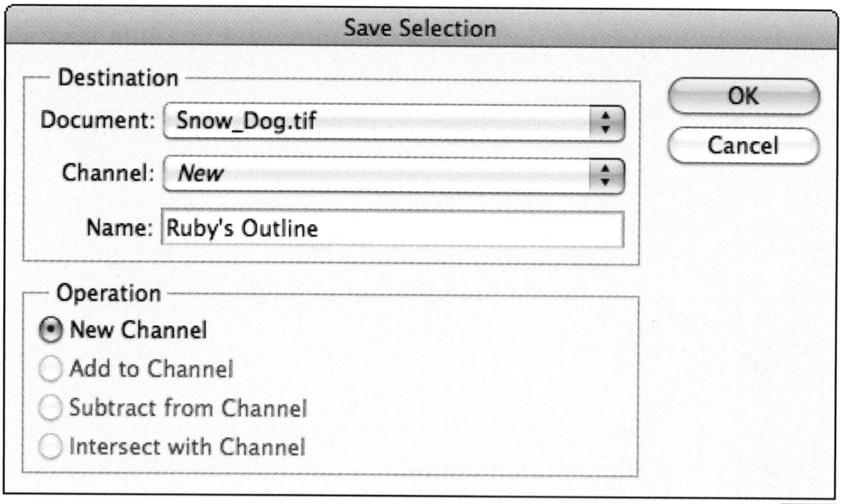

Save Selection

Destination
Document: Snow_Dog.tif
Channel: *New*
Name: Ruby's Outline

Operation
◉ New Channel
○ Add to Channel
○ Subtract from Channel
○ Intersect with Channel

OK
Cancel

5-17

If there are other files open and they have the same *pixel dimensions* of the current file, their names appear in the list. You can save the selection to one of those files to transfer it. This is useful when the second document contains the same area that needs to be selected.

> **Channel:** Because selections are saved as channels, you need to specify a channel to save it to. If no other selection-type channels are available, New is the only option.

> **Name:** Use the textbox to type a descriptive name for the selection. Otherwise it is named Alpha 1 if no *alpha channels* exist. Alpha channels are used to store masks, which, as you see in Chapter 6, are closely related to selections.

Loading a selection works pretty much the same way, except in reverse. Choose Select↪Load Selection to display the Load Selection dialog box. When the Load Selection dialog box opens, choose the saved selection from the Channel menu (see Figure 5-18).

The Document pop-up menu allows you to choose which image you want to work with. The same rule applies. Only images with the same pixel dimensions as the current document appear in the pop-up menu. You can invert the selection as it's loaded by selecting the Invert option.

Saving a selection not only enables you to make a copy of any detailed selection so you have it in the future in case you need it, it also allows you to share a selection with another, similar file, which can be handy indeed.

5-18

CUTTING AND PASTING WITH SELECTIONS

You've seen how useful selections are for isolating parts of an image so that local changes can be made to them. Selections are also used to isolate something in an image and then copy it somewhere. In Chapter 4 you used a selection to copy the young woman by the car to a new layer. Then you positioned this "twin" elsewhere in the image.

Here's a project that let's you explore this process from start to finish:

1. Open the Bird_2.tif practice file from the downloadable practice files on the Web site (www.wiley.com/go/phoprestorationandretouching).

2. Select the Magic Wand from the Tools panel. Set the Tolerance to 30, and select the Contiguous option. Click the sky to select it. Use the Add to selection option if you don't get it all in one click.

3. When the entire sky is selected, invert the selection by choosing Select⇨Inverse (⌘/Ctrl+I). Now only the bird is selected. You have two options here for creating a duplicate of the bird: copy the original information, or you can cut it. The difference is that cutting leaves a hole behind in the original layer. Copying doesn't affect the original layer.

4. Choose Layer⇨New⇨Layer via Copy (⌘/Ctrl+J) to copy the selected material to a new layer. The first clue that a new layer has been created is that the marching ants disappear. The second clue it that a new layer, called Layer 1, appears in the Layers panel.

5. Select the Move tool (V) from the Tools panel, and move the bird to the right so that it looks something like Figure 5-19 with two birds visible.

PRO TIP

If you want to move the duplicate bird straight to the right, hold down the Shift key as you click and drag. The Shift modifier key restricts the movement of the Move tool to straight lines: up, down, and sideways.

This would be more interesting if the bird were moved to a different photo, so try that.

6. Open the Bird_1.tif practice file from the downloadable practice files on the Web site (www.wiley.com/go/phoprestorationandretouching). You should now have two files open. If you're working in Photoshop's tabbed mode you many only see one of the photos.

5-19

To see both files at the same time, choose Window➪Arrange➪Float All in Windows. This places each photo in a separate window. You also can match all files to the current file's zoom and location by selecting Match Zoom and Match Location from the Arrange submenu.

PRO TIP

If you don't like having your photos open in tabs, go to Photoshop's Interface preferences and deselect Open Documents as Tabs. Consider also deselecting Enable Floating Document Window Docking to turn off the automatic tabbing that can occur when you drag a file too close to another file's header.

7. Click the header of the Bird_2.tif file to make it active. (The header is the top of the image that displays the name of the file.) When the Bird_2 file is active, you can see both Background and Layer 1 in the Layers panel.

To transfer the duplicate bird to the Bird_1 file, click and drag the duplicate bird's thumbnail in the Layers panel from its original file and simply drop it on top of the main image in the Bird_1 file, as shown in Figure 5-20. It's that easy. (You don't have to use any particular tool when doing this.) Go ahead and give it a try.

By the way, when you drag a layer from one image into another, the first layer stays behind and a duplicate is created in the second image's Layers panel.

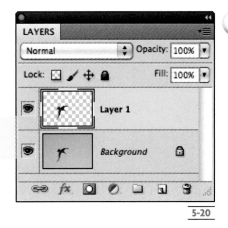

5-20

I use this technique when I need the same adjustment layer on two files. Suppose I have two photos that were shot of the same subject at the same time with the same exposure. If I create a Color Balance adjustment layer for one, I can drag it onto the other image instead of building one from scratch for the second image.

The cool thing about an adjustment layer is that it isn't fixed to specific pixel dimensions so you can copy an adjustment layer from a file with small dimensions to a file with larger dimensions without noticing any difference in the effect of the layer.

8. After the duplicate bird is in the new image, use the Move tool to fine-tune its positioning.

The two images in this example happen to have the same pixel dimensions. In practice, they don't have to be the same. However, be aware that if the dimensions are different, the incoming layer changes size relative to the difference in sizes between the two files.

If you drag a layer from an image with pixel dimensions of 1200 x 800 into an image with pixel dimensions of 2400 x 1600, the incoming layer — the bird in the previous example — will look much smaller in the new image than it did in its original image.

The general idea when using the technique shown earlier is to add a visual element to an image. However, the same technique also can be used to hide a visual element by copying background information and placing it on top of the thing you want to hide.

For example, you may want to hide an annoying light switch on a wall in the background of an image. Yes, you can do a job like that with a retouching tool, such as the Clone Stamp, but sometimes it's faster to copy a section of nearby wall and drop it on top of the light switch.

Here's an example of using this method to hide something. The photographer who shot the portrait in Figure 5-21 wanted me to remove the long drawstring hanging down on the right side of the sweater. Follow these steps to see how I do it with only a few clicks:

1. I draw a loose selection around the area, as shown in the first frame of Figure 5-22. This selection is used to get the shape I need when I create a copy. The area where the selection touches the edge of the sweater is the most critical part of this selection.

2. I drag the selection to the side so that none of the white drawstring is inside of it, as shown in the second frame of Figure 5-22. With the selection repositioned, you can use its shape to precisely select material to be pasted over the area originally selected.

3. I use Refine Edge to feather the selection 1 pixel to soften the edge of the background area I'm about to copy.

5-21
Photo by Dan Christopher

PRO TIP

I almost always feather a selection by 1 or 2 pixels when copying and pasting. Otherwise, the hard edge of the selection may show on the edges of the copied information.

4. I copy the selected area to a new layer by choosing Layer⇨New⇨Layer via Copy (⌘/Ctrl+J). A new layer, Layer 1, is created with the exact shape of the selection, as shown in the third frame of Figure 5-22. You can see that the 1px feather softened the edges just a bit.

5. I drag Layer 1 to the left with the Move tool so that it's back in the spot where the original selection was created, as shown in the final frame of Figure 5-22.

The entire process took less than a minute and is much cleaner than trying to do this with one of the standard retouching tools because of the large area being covered. This technique won't always work, but when it does, it's hard to beat for speed.

NOTE

Quite often it's necessary to do a bit of cleanup with a retouching tool, such as the Clone Stamp or Patch tool to blend any uneven edges in a patch job like this one.

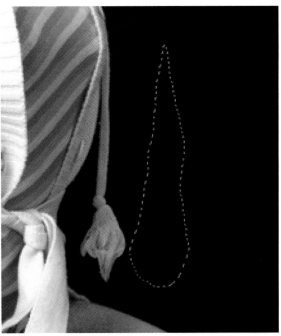

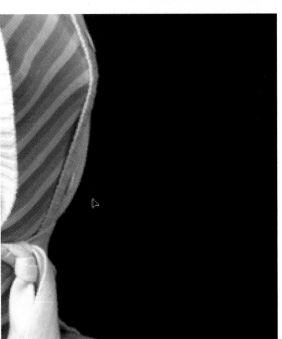

5-22

Earlier in this chapter, you selected the snow around the husky and used the Gaussian Blur filter to blur it without blurring her. Is this a common procedure, and is it used with any other filters?

This was a common technique in the days of film photography. Photographers would smear petroleum jelly around the edges of a clear filter to blur the background around someone. With digital capture, most filtering takes place after the image is photographed or scanned. Thank goodness petroleum jelly never has to come near our cameras again!

This effect is much easier to create in the digital age. That's good because digital SLRs tend to have a greater depth of field than their film counterparts, particularly those with smaller image sensors. When everything's in focus, the viewer may not know what to look at. By selectively adjusting areas of sharpness (or blurriness), you can guide the viewer through the image. Another use of this technique is to help a photo that has marginal focus. By blurring everything around the main subject, the subject looks comparatively sharper.

It's also common to use selections with other filters. For example, you can select someone's eyes and then sharpen them without adding sharpness to the skin — which could detract from its smoothness.

In the chapter on layers you mentioned that layers provide you with lots of options because you can save different sets of information on layers. However, from what you say here, when a selection is saved, it isn't saved to a layer, it's saved to a channel. Why can't I save it to a layer?

Because a selection may or may not have pixels within its boundaries, it doesn't always make sense to save a selection as a layer. Also, due to the nature of the way a selection is saved, saving it to a layer doesn't work too well. That's because a saved selection is more like a mask. Masks are covered in the next chapter, but you can get a preview of what a mask looks like by saving a selection and then clicking on it in the Channels panel to load it onto the image. Keep this relationship in mind as you work through the next chapter.

Chapter 6

TAKING CONTROL WITH LAYER MASKS

Photo by Mark Wilson

Several years ago, when I first began my journey with Photoshop, the concept that seemed hardest to grasp was layer masking. I don't know how many times I read about it before the proverbial light turned on.

When that light did go on, it illuminated not only a style of editing files, but also a philosophy of using a nondestructive Photoshop workflow based on the flexibility of layers and masks. My goal here is to turn that light on for you so you learn to master one of Photoshop's most powerful features — masking.

UNDERSTANDING LAYER MASKS

My neighbors recently had their house painted. Before the painter began spraying the house with paint, he used masking tape and paper to cover all the windows so they wouldn't be painted. This is very much the way selections work in Photoshop. You select only the things you want to paint before you start painting. Everything outside the selection is covered with virtual masking tape and paper. Masking in Photoshop works in a similar way, except that the tape and paper don't have to be applied before changes are made.

Layer masking is just what it sounds like. When one layer sits on top of another, part of it can be selectively hidden with a mask. When layer information is hidden, that part of the layer becomes transparent. It would be the same as using the Eraser tool to remove part of the upper layer, except that the Eraser is a destructive tool; when something is erased and the file is closed, it's gone forever. When image information is masked, it can be unmasked at any point in the future, providing all layers are preserved in the saved file.

As they say, "A picture is worth a thousand words." Figure 6-1 shows two completely different photos: a young woman by a car and a photo of a Japanese garden. In this example I want to combine them into a single image with the young woman in front of the garden instead of the car.

From what you've learned so far, you might think that the best course of action is to use a smart selection tool, such as the Magnetic lasso or the Magic Wand to select the young woman, copy her to a new layer, and then drag that layer into the garden image. That would work okay, if the selection were perfect.

6-1
Photos by Jerry Auker

However, if you noticed a problem with the original selection later on — for example, part of the subject that wasn't completely selected — you'd have to back up and start all over again with the original source image. (If this is what you were thinking, you're actually on the right track regarding the use of a selection because a selection can be used to quickly create a mask. I show you how to do that in a moment.)

Here's what I decide to do instead: Combine the two images into a single file with the young woman as the top layer. I then create a mask and use the Brush tool with black paint to hide everything I don't want to see on the young woman's layer. When I finish painting the mask, the images are combined, as shown in Figure 6-2.

Look at the layer stack in the second image in Figure 6-2. Notice that a new black-and-white thumbnail is now beside the thumbnail of the young woman on Layer 1. This black-and-white thumbnail is the layer mask I created with the Brush tool.

Everywhere I painted around the young woman with black is now hidden from view, which leads to the basic rule of layer masks: black conceals and white reveals. The beauty of this is that anytime I want to unhide something, I just come back with the Brush tool and apply some white paint to the area I want to reveal again.

This concept is simple and powerful. With a layer mask, you can hide and reveal layer information at will. This is the ultimate in workflow flexibility because layer masks are completely nondestructive. Any application of paint on a layer mask can always be undone, as long as the layer is never merged or flattened with other layers.

As with most things in Photoshop, there's more than one way to create a mask. With that said, the Brush tool is the simplest method. Because of that, it's a good idea to take a close look at this tool and how it's used with a mask before learning advanced masking techniques.

WORKING WITH THE BRUSH TOOL

The Brush tool is one of the most ubiquitous tools in Photoshop. That's because so many tools use a form of it. For example, when using the Quick Selection tool in Chapter 5 you used a brush to paint a selection onto the image.

When working with layer masks, you use the brush in its purest form — the Brush tool. If you understand this basic tool, you'll understand how a brush is used in any of the other brush-based tools.

6-2

Setting up Painting Cursor preferences

Photoshop has a set of preferences that are used to control the way cursors are displayed. Taking a moment to evaluate these settings, especially for tools that use brushes, is well worth the effort.

To open the Cursors preferences, choose Photoshop➪ Preferences➪Cursors (Edit➪Preferences➪Cursors). Figure 6-3 shows the list of options in the Painting Cursors area of these preferences. Here's how they're used:

> **Standard:** The selected tool's icon is displayed as the cursor. Though this seems useful, it isn't the best option because it doesn't give you any indication regarding the current state of the tool; including an indicator of which part of the cursor is the exact application point of the tool.

> **Precise:** Changes the cursor icon to a crosshair. This solves the second problem of the Standard view because it lets you know exactly where the action is centered when using the tool.

> **Normal Brush Tip:** This changes the cursor to a preview that's in the size and shape of the brush. However, the size of the tip in the preview is restricted to areas that are affected by 50 percent or more of the tool. This can be a bit disorienting when working with a brush with a low hardness value because much of its effect falls outside this indicator.

> **Full Sized Brush Tip:** Sizes the cursor to the full area that's affected by a brush stroke.

> **Show Crosshair in Brush Tip:** Adds the crosshair to the brush tip preview for a complete painting cursor.

> **Show only Crosshair While Painting:** Causes the brush tip preview to be hidden when painting.

I like to see an accurate preview of a brush-based tool, so I set my brush preferences as shown in Figure 6-3. This provides me with a full-size preview and crosshair. Feel free to experiment with the various options until you find the combination that works for you.

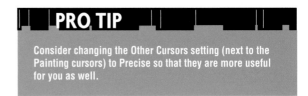

PRO TIP

Consider changing the Other Cursors setting (next to the Painting cursors) to Precise so that they are more useful for you as well.

Changing Brush settings
with the options bar

Like most tools, the easiest way to make adjustments to the Brush tool is by modifying its options on the options bar. Figure 6-4 shows the Brush tool's options. Here's what each setting is used for:

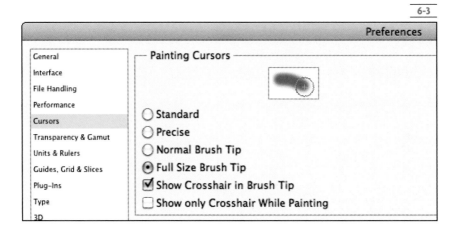

6-3

Taking Control with Layer Masks

> **Tool Preset Picker:** This preset picker is the first button on almost every tool's options bar. You can use it to pick a tool preset for the current tool, or any other tool by deselecting Current Tool Only.

> **Brush Preset Picker:** This dialog box features sliders for controlling the brush's master size and hardness. Below these sliders are several brush presets. These are saved brush diameter, hardness, and shape settings that you can load by clicking on them. The first set of presets features standard shapes, while some of the lower choices are a bit more exotic. Every brush-based tool has some form of this menu on its options bar.

> **Painting Mode:** Clicking here opens a drop-down list with different blending options. Each option has a different effect on how a brush stroke blends with the tone and color below it. Nearly every example in this book uses the Normal blending mode.

> **Stroke Opacity:** This value controls the opacity of the stroke. A value of 100 percent is full opacity.

> **Tablet Pressure controls opacity:** When you work with a graphics tablet, this button is used to override the main tablet settings that are configured using the Brush panel. When this override is in effect, the opacity of the stroke is controlled by the pen's pressure against the tablet.

PRO TIP

The Brush Preset Picker can also be accessed by right-clicking on the image when a brush-based tool is active.

X-REF

Graphics tablets are covered later in this chapter.

> **Toggle Brush panel:** This button toggles the more advanced Brush panel on and off. Click it once to open the panel and click it a second time to close it. The Brush panel is covered in more detail in a moment.

> **Flow:** Another adjustment on the options bar is the Flow setting. Flow controls the rate at which a color is applied as a stroke is drawn. The lower the value, the more spread out the color's application

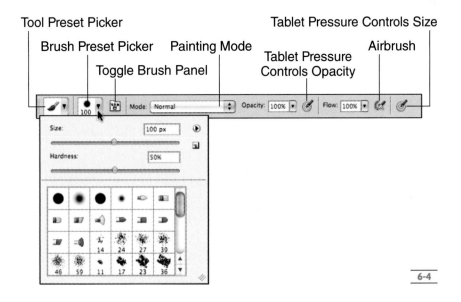

Tool Preset Picker
Brush Preset Picker   Painting Mode
Toggle Brush Panel
Tablet Pressure Controls Size
Airbrush
Tablet Pressure Controls Opacity

6-4

is. With a hard brush, this manifests as overlapping circles. I have to tell you that I rarely change the Flow value from 100 percent. I mention it here because students often ask what the Flow setting does.

> **Airbrush mode:** When this setting is enabled by clicking on it, paint is continually applied while the mouse button is held down, much like holding a can of spray paint in one place while spraying. The results of painting with the Airbrush vary depending on the other settings on the brush. Because of that, I suggest leaving it turned off for now while you familiarize yourself with the Brush tool.

> **Tablet Pressure controls size:** Use a graphics tablet's stylus pressure to vary the size of a stroke. This enables you to change the size of a stroke as you draw it by changing how hard you press the pen tip against the tablet.

Naturally, these options are used in countless ways, making the Brush tool a versatile tool. Here's an exercise that will familiarize you with the Brush tool and some of its most important settings.

1. Choose File⇨New to create a new file, and give it the following properties: Width = 6 inches, Height = 4 inches, Resolution = 300, Color Mode = RGB Color/8-bit, and Background = White. Click OK.

> **PRO TIP**
>
> If you want to speed up the creation of this special practice file in the future, click the Save Preset button in the New File dialog box to save it as a custom preset. This adds it to the dialog box's Preset menu.

2. Select the Brush tool (B) from the Tools panel, eighth from the top on the single-column Tools panel.

3. Press D to set the foreground and background colors to black and white, respectively. You can verify this by checking the two color swatches at the bottom of the Tools panel. This shortcut is the same as clicking on the small swatch button to the upper left of the swatches near the bottom of the Tools panel.

4. Use the Brush Preset Picker pop-up menu shown to set the Master Diameter to 100px and the Hardness to 100%.

5. Click and drag on one side of the new file you opened in Step 1 and drag across the upper part of the white background. You should see a heavy, black line appear on the white background, similar to the top line in Figure 6-5.

> **PRO TIP**
>
> If you want a perfectly straight horizontal or vertical line, hold down the Shift key while drawing.

6. Use the Brush Preset Picker to change the Hardness value to 0 and then paint a second line below the first one. Notice that the edges of the line are much softer. Notice also that the line isn't as thick as the first line. The softness of the edge fades in toward the middle of the stroke. (The effect is similar to the selection feathering concept you learned about in Chapter 5.)

7. Change the Opacity to 50% in the options bar, and draw a third line below the second line. The new line is just like the previous line except that it's much lighter in tone.

8. Draw another line from top to bottom, as shown in Figure 6-5. Notice that when this line crosses the bottom line, the two strokes combine to create a tone that's twice as dark. If you want to verify this, use the Eyedropper tool to measure the bottom line where the lines cross and where they don't cross.

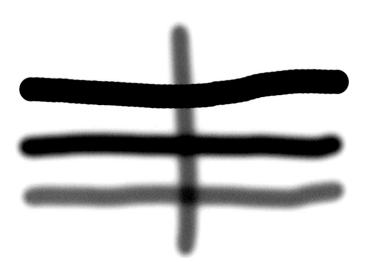

6-5

Your values should be close to 64 and 128, respectively. Recall that you have 256 tones at your disposal (black = 0 and white = 255). The vertical stroke darkened the horizontal stroke by 50 percent, lowering it from 128 to 64.

9. Continue to explore the various Brush tool settings to familiarize yourself with these basic settings. If you want to erase your canvas, click on the file's thumbnail at the top of the History panel to begin again.

You may be wondering why two 50 percent opacity strokes that cross each other don't combine to create 100 percent opacity. That's because each of the 50 percent strokes is simply making the current darkness of the stroke 50 percent darker.

Even ten 50 percent strokes on top of each other don't combine to equal 0 (black). Instead, they equal 1 because no matter how many times you reduce the brightness of the strokes by 50 percent, you can never halve the density to 0.

SHORTCUTS FOR MANAGING THE BRUSH TOOL

There are some useful shortcuts that make life easier when working with the Brush and other brush-based tools. The primary keyboard shortcuts are:

> **To change the brush size, use the bracket [ ] keys on your keyboard.** The right bracket makes the brush larger, and the left bracket makes it smaller.

> **To change the hardness in 25 percent increments, press the Shift key and the right or left bracket.** The left bracket reduces the hardness, and the right bracket increases it. If you are set at 100 percent, pressing Shift+[four times reduces the hardness to 0 percent.

> **To change opacity, use the numbers on the keyboard.** Press 3 to set it to 30 percent or 5 to set it to 50 percent. If you want 55 percent, press 5 twice quickly. If the Airbrush feature is active, pressing numbers on the keyboard changes Flow instead of Opacity. To change the brush's opacity when using the Airbrush, use Shift plus the number.

123

You can resize and change the hardness of a brush by dragging it while holding modifier keys. Press and hold Ctrl+Alt+left-click/Alt+right-click) and drag right or left to resize. Drag up and down to change hardness. You see a bright orange preview of both size and hardness as you drag.

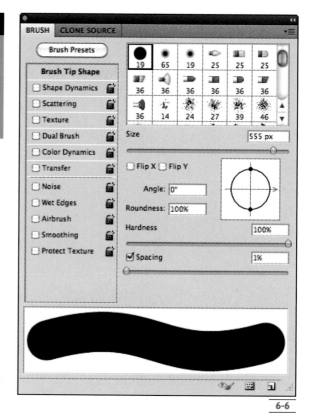

6-6

Exploring advanced options in the Brush panel

With the Tool options bar and a handful of shortcuts, you can quickly change the main settings on a brush. Sometimes, though, those quick settings aren't enough to create the type of brush you need. When this happens, it's time to go to the main control center for the Brush tool — the Brush panel.

You open the Brush panel, as shown in Figure 6-6, by clicking the Toggle Brush panel button on the options bar. Selecting a menu on the left of the panel opens its options on the right, allowing for a huge amount of control over the Brush tool. In Figure 6-6, the Brush Tip Shape menu is shown.

The options in the Brush Tip Shape menu offer a more comprehensive version of the Brush Preset Picker. This expanded panel not only provides you greater control, it also has a preview window at the bottom that displays the effects the current settings are having on the brush stroke.

Each of the menus on the left gives you access to different brush controls, allowing you to create highly stylized brushes. Selecting the check box next to the menu title activates the settings in that menu. Clicking on the menu's name loads its settings into the pod on the right. You can combine most of these settings to create some truly exotic brushes. If you create one you like and want to use again, click the Create new brush button at the bottom right of the Brush panel.

The Brush panel is where Brush power users come to create their special tools. These people usually are illustrators and painters who use Photoshop in very creative ways, especially now that Photoshop CS5 has new wet brush features that are accessed using the Wet Edges menu.

Even though I use Photoshop tools that use brushes almost every day, I rarely go to the Brush panel because I don't often need such sophisticated brushes. I point it out here in case you decide to explore some of the custom settings — and maybe become a brush power user yourself.

USING A GRAPHICS TABLET

Most people I know can't draw very well with a mouse. This is easy to demonstrate by trying to write your name with a mouse. It's really hard for most people. Mice just aren't designed for detail and articulated work. They're better for quick clicking and dragging. When you need real control, it's difficult to get it with a mouse.

A graphics tablet consists of a special pen called a stylus and a sensitive tablet that senses when and where the pen touches the tablet. The action of holding a pen and drawing with it is more natural than using a mouse. This natural motion also lends itself to fine articulation and detail work with less strain on the body. I often work with mine in my lap if I want to give my arm a rest.

Wacom tablets are currently the industry standard for graphics tablets. Wacom makes a variety of tablets with different features and sizes under two main lines: Intuos 4 for professionals and Bamboo for lower-priced consumer-oriented tablets. It also has a more sophisticated line called Cintiq with an LCD monitor embedded into the tablet.

The tablet shown in Figure 6-7 is an Intuos 4. It features a handy set of programmable buttons on the side that can be mapped for right-handed or left-handed users.

Considering Ergonomics

Because it can be difficult to control a mouse when working precisely, using a mouse for extended periods tends to be hard on the body. Even though there are ergonomic mice on the market, the whole concept of a mouse isn't exactly ergonomic. When you use a mouse in a very controlling way, it tends to tense the muscles in your hand, and sometimes even muscles all the way up into your arms and neck.

When I really got serious about Photoshop several years ago, I began developing pain in my wrist and neck because I was spending so much time editing. The pain began to diminish the pleasure I was getting from Photoshop. After I bought a graphics tablet, my Photoshop life changed. I can now work long hours with much less stress to my body.

When you spend a lot of time in front of a computer, you have to be conscious of your working environment. I've met many digital photographers who pour lots of money into their equipment, but never consider the health consequences of working in a nonergonomic environment. To learn more about ergonomics, see the U.S. Department of Labor's Safety and Health Topics Web site at www.osha.gov/SLTC/ergonomics/.

6-7
Photo courtesy of Wacom

Tablets range in size from small to large. Keep in mind, though, that this is one case where bigger isn't necessarily better. For one thing, a large tablet takes up lots of room on your desk. Also, when navigating the stylus around the tablet, you have to cover more distance on a large tablet, requiring more hand and arm movement.

I have used medium-sized tablets for many years and am completely satisfied with that form factor.

Be aware that beginning to use a graphics tablet can be a little disorienting. For one thing, the tablet is mapped to the screen. That is, if the pen is touching the tablet in the lower-left corner, the cursor is in the lower left of the screen. To move the cursor to the top right of the screen, move the pen to the top right of the tablet. This learning curve can take a little time, but it's well worth the effort.

WORKING WITH THE MASKS PANEL

When Photoshop CS4 was released, it contained a new panel that has greatly improved the way masks are created and modified. This Masks panel, shown in Figure 6-8, enables users to quickly access everything they need when working with masks.

There are lots of great features packed onto this small panel:

> **Add Pixel Mask:** Click this target-like button to create an empty mask. The button to its right with a pen icon on it, the Add Vector Mask button, is used for adding vector masks when working with vector images such as logos. You won't be using it in this book.

> **Density:** This slider controls the opacity of the mask. A value of 100 percent is full intensity. A value of 50 percent reduces the hiding ability of a mask to 50 percent.

> **Feather:** This slider is used to soften the edge of a mask, much the same as the feathering that's applied to a selection's edge.

Add Pixel Mask

Apply Mask — Disable/Enable Mask   Delete Mask
Load Selection from Mask

6-8

> **Mask Edge:** Click this button to open the Refine Mask dialog box, which is identical to the Refine Edge dialog box used with selections. It provides you with the same kind of control over a mask's edge.

> **Color Range:** Click this button to open the Color Range dialog box, which is used to generate a mask by clicking on specific colors in the image. It works much like the Magic Wand selection tool, though a Fuzziness slider is included for expanding or reducing the range of masked colors.

> **Invert:** Click this button to invert the colors on a mask. White becomes black and black becomes white. This works much like the Select menu's Inverse command.

> **Load Selection from Mask:** Click this button at the bottom left of the panel to create a selection that matches the mask and its edge quality.

> **Apply Mask:** Clicking this button permanently merges the mask with its layer and cannot be undone after the file is closed. It's best to not do this unless you need to, which in most cases is rare.

> **Disable/Enable Mask:** Click this button to hide and reveal the mask, which is a good way to check your work.

> **Delete Mask:** Click this button to delete the currently selected mask.

Before the introduction of the Masks panel, much of these features were hidden in the Layers menu and the Layers panel. If you've worked with that old system in previous versions of Photoshop, be prepared for your life to become easier as you become familiar with this panel.

CREATING A MASK

Now that you understand the general idea and the primary tools involved, do the following masking project to get a real feel for layer masking:

1. Open the 78_Vet.tif and the Garden.tif files from the downloadable practice files on the Web site at www.wiley.com/go/phoprestorationandretouching. Position them on the screen so that you can see some of both images at once. If you're working in the tabbed document mode, the easiest way to do this is to choose Float All in Windows from the Arrange Documents menu on the Application bar.

2. Click the 78_Vet file to make it active. Then go to the Layers panel and drag the background layer into the Garden file. Hold down the Shift key as you drag so the layer is dropped into the center of the image.

3. Now that both images are in the same file, you don't need the 78_Vet file, so close it. The Layers panel of the Garden.tif document should now show both documents as layers.

4. Click the Pixel Mask button on the Masks panel to add a mask. Now your Layers panel should look like Figure 6-9 with a white box beside the image thumbnail on Layer 1. This white box represents the mask, just as the image icon next to it represents the image pixels on the layer.

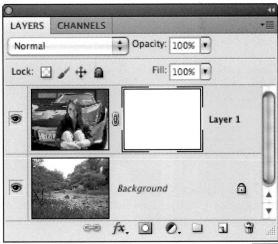

6-9

The link icon that appears between the two thumbnails signifies that the mask is linked with the layer's image content. If you use the Move tool to move the layer's image content, the mask moves too, staying in alignment with the image, which is what is generally desired.

5. Select the Brush tool (B), and set its Master Diameter to 300px, Hardness to 0%, and Opacity to 100%. Make sure that black is the foreground color. If it isn't, press D to reset the color swatches to white over black, then press X to exchange the colors so that black is over white.

6. Start painting around the outer edges of the image. Don't go too close to the young woman just yet. Notice that as you paint, you begin to see the garden layer below. Keep painting until most of the detail around the young woman is hidden. The mask should look like the layer mask in Figure 6-10.

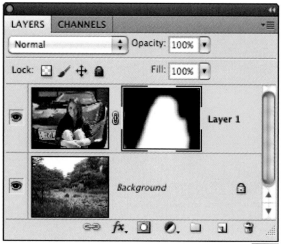

6-10

7. Reduce the size of your brush, and move in closer to the young woman. When you get right next to her, you find that the soft brush doesn't work very well because you can't get right next to her without getting paint on her, too. Increase the Brush tool's Hardness value to 75 or 80.

8. If you accidentally hide part of the young woman instead of the background, switch your foreground color to white (using the X key or the curved arrow by the swatches) and paint the detail back in and then switch back to black (X) and continue masking. It's that easy.

9. Keep painting until your image is close to what appears in Figure 6-2. Don't push yourself too hard to create a perfect mask just yet. When you like the mask you have, press the backslash key (\) to switch the image into Quick Mask mode, as shown in Figure 6-11.

This viewing mode allows you to see all your masking strokes as a red overlay. This is a great way to see exactly where your brushstrokes are. In Figure 6-11, you can see where a spot is missed below her elbow on the left. It wasn't noticeable in the image preview until Quick Mask mode was turned on. Now I can continue painting in this mode until all missing spots are covered.

6-11

10. When your mask is fine-tuned to your liking, press the backslash (\) key again to go back to normal viewing mode.

Click the Disable/Enable Mask button on the bottom of the Masks panel to temporarily hide the mask so you can check your work. Notice that a big red X appears on the mask's thumbnails in the Layers and Masks panels. This signifies that the mask is hidden. Click the button again to unhide the mask.

Another useful viewing option with a mask is to Alt+click the mask icon in the Layers panel. This makes the actual mask appear in the image preview, as shown in Figure 6-12. This mask viewing mode is extremely revealing.

Now in my example you can see other areas missed when painting the mask that weren't completely obvious in Quick Mask viewing mode. I can quickly fix them by adding a bit more black paint to the small areas that need to be masked. Alt+click again on the mask to go back to the normal view.

Be aware of one more thing when working with masks. When you're painting — or retouching for that matter — you can choose to work on the mask or on the image. This makes sense. Sometimes you want to paint the mask, and other times you may want to paint on the image itself. You can tell which area will be painted on by looking at the thumbnails in the Layers panel.

6-12

Click the image thumbnail for Layer 1 in the previous example. When you do this, notice that a small black box appears around the thumbnail. By default, this box is automatically placed around the mask thumbnail when the mask is created. Moving it to the image thumbnail like this enables you to paint on the image instead of the mask.

Now you can paint on the image itself, or you can use a retouching tool on it. Click the mask thumbnail if you need to adjust the mask, and watch the box move back its icon.

> ## PRO TIP
>
> If you're using a brush or retouching tool on a layer that has a mask and nothing is happening, it probably means that you're retouching the mask instead of the image. To solve this, click the image thumbnail in the Layers panel to make it active instead of the mask.

Now that you see how easy and powerful layer masking is, try this concept in with some of the other things you've learned in earlier chapters so you can see how they all fit together.

USING MASKS WITH SELECTIONS

When I first introduced the preceding exercise, I suggested an alternate way of handling the project, which involved a selection and a layer copy of the selected area. If you recall, the main drawback to that strategy was that it limits your options down the road because it doesn't incorporate a mask.

Creating a mask with the Brush tool is nondestructive, but it can be time consuming. Also, the edge of the brush isn't always as exact as a selection tool's edge. Fortunately, Photoshop makes it easy to combine the speed and accuracy of a selection with the nondestructive nature of a mask to create accurate masks quickly. Follow these steps to see how it's done:

1. If you still have the file from the previous exercise open, click and drag the mask thumbnail to the trashcan icon at the bottom of the Layers panel. When the Apply Mask dialog box appears asking if you want to apply or delete the mask, click Delete. (If the image is not open, open it and complete Steps 1 through 3 from the preceding steps.) Your Layers panel should look like the Layers panel in Figure 6-9 again.

2. Use the Magnetic Lasso to draw a quick selection outlining the young woman. If necessary, use the Lasso tool to fine-tune the selection by adding and subtracting any areas that weren't quite picked up by the Magnetic Lasso. Keep in mind that it isn't necessary to make this selection absolutely perfect. Just get it close to perfect as quickly as you can.

3. After your selection is in place click the Add Pixel Mask button on the Masks panel. A mask is created as soon as you click it, hiding everything on Layer 1 that is outside of the selection. The effect on the mask is just like filling all of the unselected area with black paint.

4. Use the Brush tool to touch up the mask in any of the spots where the selection wasn't perfect.

5. Click the Mask Edge button in the Masks panel so you can use the Refine Mask dialog box to fine-tune the edge of the mask to get the best blending possible. Figure 6-13 shows the settings I used to improve my mask.

6-13

In this case, using a selection was much faster than manually masking out everything with the Brush tool. It also provided an accurate edge boundary along the outer edges of the young woman. The selection could have been modified using Refine Selection before converting it to a mask with similar results as those achieved in Step 5.

This ability to convert a selection into a mask works both ways. In this case, a selection was converted to a mask. You can create a selection from a mask using the Load Selection from Mask button on the bottom left of the Masks panel. This is useful when you want to copy a masked area for another layer that needs similar masking. Simply load the mask as a selection, choose the new layer to be masked, and click the Add Pixel Mask button to convert the selection into a new mask.

Here's one more interesting thing regarding the kinship of selections and masks. In Chapter 5, when discussing saving and loading selections, I noted that a saved selection is saved as a channel in the Channels panel. Well, look at your Channels panel from the preceding exercise. It should look much like the Channels panel in Figure 6-14.

This is the same channel that would be created if the selection was saved, rather than converted to a mask. Now you know the secret: A mask is really a special channel that you can paint on. Dealing with these channels as masks creates a much more intuitive method for creating and interacting with them.

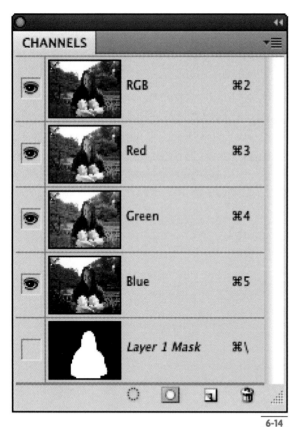

As you can see here, selections and masks have a special relationship. This is a great thing to be aware of as you begin to use masks in your retouching workflow. Sometimes it's easier to create a mask from a selection, and sometimes it's easier to create one using the Brush tool.

The specific job in front of you usually determines the most efficient route. Because of this, it's good to be comfortable using the main selection tools and the Brush tool.

USING MASKS WITH ADJUSTMENT LAYERS

Adjustment layers also have a special relationship with layer masks. You may have already noticed it. Whenever you create an adjustment layer, a layer mask is automatically created at the same time. The mask is ready to go; you just have to choose the Brush tool and start painting. The reason masks are automatically created with adjustment layers is because the two are used together extensively.

The image in Figure 6-15 is a portrait of a young man and his musical instrument.

A technique that's popular with a portrait like this is to convert everything in the image to black and white, except for the musical instrument. It's reminiscent of a hand-toning effect that film photographers have used since the earliest days of photography. Fortunately, creating this effect with Photoshop is much easier than hand-toning a black-and-white print.

X-REF

Manually adding color to a black-and-white image is covered in Chapter 10.

To learn how I handle this project, follow these steps:

1. Create a Black & White adjustment layer, which is similar to the Black & White command, making the image look black and white. The difference is that its effects are on an adjustment layer. Because it's an adjustment layer, a mask is automatically created.

X-REF

Creating black-and-white photos is discussed in Chapter 10.

2. Paint the saxophone with black paint to hide the black-and-white effect of the adjustment layer, allowing the full color of the saxophone to show. (If the musical instrument was a bright color such as green, you could save time by using the Magic Wand to select it before creating the mask instead of painting it in afterward.)

The whole process takes about two minutes to create, and it can be removed in a moment by turning off the visibility of the Black & White adjustment layer. Figure 6-16 shows the mask I painted and the Layers panel with the Black & White adjustment layer.

NOTE

Because there is no image thumbnail on an adjustment layer, you don't need to make sure you're on the mask when painting. If the adjustment layer is the active layer, then you're on the mask.

6-15
Photo by Denyce Weiler

This hand-toning effect is popular in wedding photography. You see it most often in portraits of the bride with her bouquet. Everything in the image is black and white, except for the flowers. The effect causes the flowers to almost jump out of the image.

COMBINING SELECTIONS, ADJUSTMENT LAYERS, AND MASKS

Now that you have a clear idea of how all of these elements work together, I want to show you one of the ways I most commonly combine the three of them. I always like to darken the corners of an image a bit to draw the eye away from its edges. This subtle vignetting is something that custom printers have been doing for years in wet darkrooms.

Follow these steps to darken all of the corners of the photo of Ruby:

1. Open the Snow_Dog.tif practice file from the downloadable practice files on the Web site at www.wiley.com/go/phoprestorationandretouching. Adjust the Levels, and make any other adjustments to tone and color that you feel like doing.

2. Select the Elliptical Marquee tool from the Tools panel. Make sure the Feather value is 0px, the Anti-alias option is selected, and Style is set to Normal. Create an elliptical selection that covers most of the central area of the image, as shown in Figure 6-17.

Remember that you can reposition the selection after it's drawn by placing the cursor inside the selection and then clicking and dragging into position. This way, you don't have to draw it perfectly the first time.

3. After the selection is in place, choose Select⇨ Inverse (⌘/Ctrl+Shift+I) to invert it so that the area outside of the ellipse is selected instead of the inner area.

6-17

4. Create a Levels adjustment layer using the Adjustments panel. Change only the middle gray slider. Set it to a value of .60, and click OK. Your image should now look like Figure 6-18. The hard edges along the selection boundary created an abrupt change that doesn't work. It needs to be softened.

5. Go to the Masks panel and adjust the Feather slider to a value of somewhere around 75. Then use the Density slider to decrease the brightness of vignetting if necessary, or revisit the Levels adjustment layer settings to modify the tonality.

6. If you need to make any other modifications to the selection, such as expanding or contracting it, click the Mask Edge button to open the Mask Edge dialog box. Now your photo should look something like Figure 6-19.

This simple effect combines three of the main Photoshop concepts covered so far: selections, adjustment layers, and masks. This is a good exercise to review whenever you need to refresh your memory about how these three important concepts interact to give you a huge amount of flexibility and control over your editing workflow.

NOTE

Because the Adjustments and Masks panels are used together so often, they are stacked together by default.

COMPARING REVEAL ALL AND HIDE ALL MASKS

Up to this point, all of the masks discussed have been reveal all masks. That means they are designed to show everything on the layer when they're created. Then you use the Brush tool or a selection to selectively hide what you don't want to see. Sometimes, though, it's faster to create a hide all layer and reveal what you want to see.

For example, if you want to lighten someone's teeth a bit with an adjustment layer you don't want to have to manually mask out everything in the image except for the teeth. It's easier to apply the adjustment, hide its effects, and then come back and reveal only what you need.

When you create a new layer mask using the Add pixel mask button in the Masks panel, a reveal all mask is created. The same is true when a mask is automatically created alongside an adjustment layer. If you remember the basic rule of masking — black hides and white reveals — you can tell that these masks are reveal all masks because they are white. You also understand that for a mask to be a hide all mask, it must be completely black.

> **PRO TIP**
>
> When you think about masks and the information they reveal and hide, always remember that we're talking about information on the layer that the mask is on, not information that is being seen on layers that are below the masked layer.

There are a few ways to create a hide all mask:

> **Create a reveal all mask and then use the Paint Bucket tool (G) to fill it with black.** This method is most useful when dealing with the reveal all masks that are automatically created with adjustment layers.

> **PRO TIP**
>
> Keep the Paint Bucket in mind whenever you want to change a mask from reveal all to hide all, or vice versa.

> **Hold down the Alt key while clicking the Add Pixel Mask button in the Masks panel.**

> **Choose Layer⇨Layer Mask⇨Hide All, as shown in Figure 6-20.** Notice that this menu also has some other useful masking options. When a selection is active both Reveal Selection and Hide Selection become options. These allow you to choose how a mask is applied to a selection. In the previous exercise, after you created the elliptical marquee it was necessary to invert it before creating the mask. That's because the mask was automatically a hide selection mask. When you have a selection in place and you want to reveal the selection, choose the Reveal Selection from the Layer Masks submenu.

When a full hide all mask is applied to a layer, everything on the layer is hidden. You then use the Brush tool to paint areas you want to see with white paint. You can also use a selection to select an area and then use either the Brush tool or the Paint Bucket to quickly fill it with white paint.

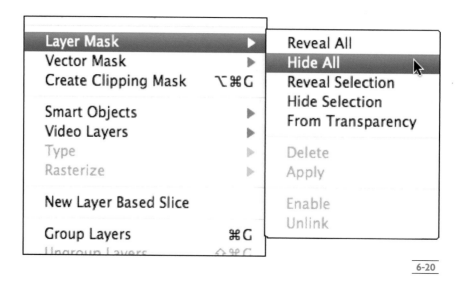

Layer Mask ▶	Reveal All
Vector Mask ▶	Hide All ⬉
Create Clipping Mask ⌥⌘G	Reveal Selection
	Hide Selection
Smart Objects ▶	From Transparency
Video Layers ▶	
Type ▶	Delete
Rasterize ▶	Apply
New Layer Based Slice	Enable
	Unlink
Group Layers ⌘G	
Ungroup Layers ⇧⌘G	

6-20

APPLYING A GRADIENT TO A MASK

As you know, black on a mask hides and white reveals. But what about gray? If you look at the mask created in the last exercise, shown in Figure 6-21, you can see that because of feather on the mask, it fades from black in the center to white around the edges.

The transitional area, created by the feathering, has lots of tones that aren't white or black; they're varying shades of gray. If you compare the mask to the image, you notice that as the gray gets lighter toward the edges of the mask, the effect of the adjustment layer on the image is more revealed.

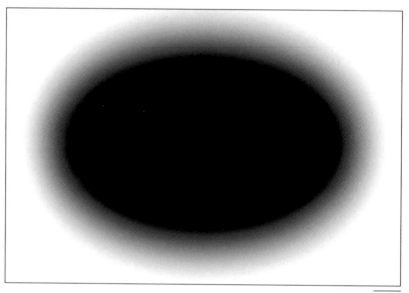

6-21

The first point to make here is that you can paint on a mask with any shade of gray. The darker the shade, the more hidden the layer's information is. This is useful for toning down something without completely hiding it. If you were to create a white Reveal All mask and paint it with 50 percent gray — or better yet, use the Paint Bucket to fill it with 50 percent gray (128, 128, 128) — the layer would be 50 percent hidden.

The result is the same as reducing the opacity of a layer filled with 100 percent black to 50 percent. (Reducing the Density value of a black mask to 50 percent using the Masks panel has the same effect.)

The second point is that a gradient can be used on a mask to fade it from white to black. The effect is similar to feathering a selection, but it gives you a different kind of control over the mask you create. Here's how that works:

1. Open the Snow_Dog.tif practice file one last time. (This is the last time you'll see Ruby in this book.) Make any levels or color adjustments you want to make. (If you still have the file open from the preceding exercise, return it to its opening state using the History panel.)

2. Apply basic tonal adjustment using either Levels or Curves. It would be nice to darken the foreground of the photo without being too obvious about it.

3. Create a Levels adjustment layer like the one you used in the previous exercise, changing only the gray slider to a value of .60.

4. Select the Gradient tool (G), which is stacked with the Paint Bucket tool, 12th from the top on the single-column Tools panel. This tool is used for drawing an assortment of gradients using different shapes and colors.

5. Press D to set your color swatches to their default colors of white over black. Press X to exchange these colors so that the color swatch on top is black (the foreground color) and white is on the bottom (the background color).

6. Go to the options bar to set up the Gradient tool. Click the Gradient Picker pop-up menu, as shown in Figure 6-22, and select the first gradient option: Foreground to Background. Now the Gradient tool will draw a gradient that begins with the foreground color and ends with the background color. As the stroke you draw gets longer, the gradient becomes more gradual.

7. Make sure that the Linear Gradient style is selected from the thumbnail buttons to the right of the Gradient Picker, as in Figure 6-22. This style creates a gradient that transitions tonally in a straight line.

8. Click at the bottom of the image and drag upward until you get even with Ruby's nose. When you let go of the mouse button, a black and white gradient is added to the layer mask. This mask enables the adjustments on the Levels adjustment layer to gradually transition through the lower portion of the photo without affecting the rest of it. Figure 6-23 shows the final image and its mask.

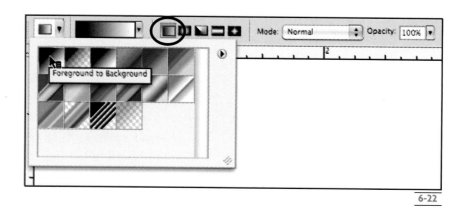

6-22

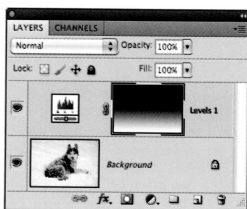

6-23

PRO TIP

Hold the Shift key while dragging to make the gradient go straight up, down, or sideways.

PRO TIP

When you use the Gradient tool on a mask, you don't need to undo one gradient before trying another. Each time you draw a new gradient, it replaces the previous one.

9. Experiment with shorter and longer strokes so you can see how they affect the image and the mask. Notice that every time you draw a new gradient, it replaces the previous one instead of combining with it. Also try adjusting the gray slider value on the Levels adjustment layer to vary the amount of darkening.

As you can see, a mask can be created very quickly with the Gradient tool. Keep it in mind whenever you have a scene where you need to quickly mask the top, bottom, or sides on an image — for example, when you have a section of sky that you want to darken. You can even use a second layer with the same mask to also adjust the color of the sky.

Q & A

The Brush tool appears to be one of the most flexible tools in Photoshop, yet you mentioned that you don't often use it to its full potential. Why is this?

Almost all of the brushwork I do in Photoshop can be accomplished without using a sophisticated brush. In fact some of the more exotic settings, such as Dual-Brush and Jitter can get in the way when using a brush to paint a mask or to retouch with the Clone Stamp. Because of that I tend to neutralize these settings by unchecking them from the Brush panel so it's only necessary for me to work with the brush size and the hardness of its edge while I work.

The people I see using the more exotic brush controls are illustrators who use Photoshop to create artworks from scratch. When doing this it's necessary to have more control over the brush, much like when working with a real paintbrush. It's like comparing a professional house painter to a fine art painter. The person who's painting a house mostly needs to be concerned with the size of the brush and how much paint is being applied by it. Someone who's painting a scenic landscape needs much more control over a brush because each stroke is distinctive. The house painter could use the same brushes and techniques as the fine art painter. However, it would take a long time to get the house painted and finished job wouldn't be much better than the traditional house painting approach.

In one masking exercise you used an elliptical selection to darken all corners. In the final exercise you used a gradient to darken only the foreground. Which is the best technique to use?

Naturally, the tonal content of the image dictates which method to use. If all corners need to be darkened equally, an elliptical vignette works quite well. If different parts of the image require different treatments, you may find it easier to use individual masks so you can control them individually. For example, in the photo of Ruby you could use an adjustment layer with a straight gradient to darken the foreground a bit. Then use a second adjustment layer with an elliptical marquee to darken all corners at the same time. The net result is that all corners are darkened, with the lower corners and the foreground being a bit darker than the upper corners.

Chapter 7

USING PHOTOSHOP'S MAIN RETOUCHING TOOLS

Photo by Mark Fitzgerald

When you hear the word *retouching,* the first thing that often comes to mind is high-end fashion and beauty retouching seen in magazines. This kind of retouching is used to perfect an image of someone so that she appears flawless.

Though retouching is used on a wide range of images beyond just fashion, the objective remains the same: to perfect the image so that weaknesses are eliminated and strengths are enhanced. Some of the techniques you've learned about in other chapters involving selections and masking are technically considered retouching.

However, Photoshop has several tools that are collectively referred to as retouching tools because of the way they're used. In this chapter, you learn about these tools and how they are commonly used.

BASIC RETOUCHING WITH THE CLONE STAMP TOOL

The Clone Stamp tool has been part of Photoshop since the earliest days. It opened the door to digital retouching as we know it. In essence, the Clone Stamp tool is used to sample information from one part of an image so that it can be painted (cloned) into another part of the image.

REMOVING DISTRACTIONS

Figure 7-1 is a section of a photo I shot early one morning at a dahlia farm. I like the photo, but I don't like the sign on the left, below the tractor. It's visually distracting because it pulls the viewers eye away from the tractor, which is where I want it to be.

In addition to the sign, there are three other things that compete for the viewer's eye in this image: The bright orange vertical marker near the middle of the road that runs above the tractor, the bright vertical line just below it at the far end of the flowers, and a light cream-colored flower in the foreground on the right that's in with a group of dark red flowers.

When I look at Figure 7-1, my eye bounces around the image looking at these things and the tractor instead of focusing on the person in the tractor. My job as a retoucher is to eliminate these distractions so that the viewer's eye goes where it's supposed to go.

Begin your exploration of this tool by retouching your own version of the photo in Figure 7-1:

1. Open the Dahlia_Farm.tif file from the downloadable practice files on the Web site (www.wiley. com/go/phoprestorationandretouching).

2. Zoom in to 100 percent and pan the image using the Hand tool (H) so that you can see the white sign. The goal is to use the greenery in the group of flowers to the left to cover the sign.

3. Duplicate the Background layer by choosing Layer⇨Duplicate Layer. When the Duplicate Layer dialog box opens, name the layer Retouching and click OK. The new layer is added to the top of the layer stack and becomes the active layer. All retouching is done on this duplicate layer.

PRO TIP

It's always a good idea to apply retouching to a separate layer. Doing so enables you to modify or even throw away the retouching layer and try again if you don't like your work. It also gives you the option to turn off the visibility of the retouching layer to check your work against the unretouched layer(s).

4. Select the Clone Stamp tool (S) from the Tools panel. It's ninth from the top on the single-column panel. Make sure that you're not selecting the Pattern Stamp tool that's stacked with the Clone Stamp tool. The Clone Stamp tool has the same brush controls on the options bar as the Brush tool.

7-1

That's because it works in the same way. The difference is that instead of using paint, the Clone Stamp tool applies sampled portions of the image as you paint.

5. Set your Brush size to about 75px and the Hardness to about 50 percent and make sure Opacity and Flow are set to 100. Also be sure the Aligned option is selected. This insures that the sample point and the application point stay in alignment as you paint.

When this option is deselected, only the initial sample point is used as a source for the brush. I almost always work with this option on and all of the exercises in this book assume that it's on.

NOTE

When the Aligned option is selected, the two Clone Stamp cursors stay in alignment each time you stop and resume painting. When the option is not checked, the sampled pixels from the initial sample area are used for every stroke.

6. Move the cursor over the upper part of the greenery of the group of flowers directly to the left of the group with the sign and press the Alt key. Notice that as soon as you press Alt, the cursor changes, indicating that wherever you click will become the clone source point used for sampling. Try to make sure that your sample point is level with the center of the sign.

7. Release the Alt key, and move you cursor over the upper part of the sign. Notice that a preview appears on the cursor, to indicate what the cloned bush will look like when you begin to paint. This preview feature is called the *Clipped Clone preview.* It was introduced in Photoshop CS4.

This preview can be quite useful for critical alignment because it allows you to evaluate placement before you paint. However, it can be a bit disorienting when you're working on a complicated project, so I show you how to turn it off later.

8. Click and drag downward to begin cloning detail from the bush on the left onto the sign on the right. Stop before you get to the bottom of the sign. Notice that a crosshair-style cursor appears on the cloned greenery to the left and follows the painting cursor in perfect alignment as you move the mouse, as shown in Figure 7-2.

This is the effect of having the Alignment option selected on the Options bar. It allows you to sample the length of the bush as you cover the length of the sign.

7-2

PRO TIP

When using any brush-based tool, be sure to use a stroking motion when painting even if the strokes are very short. This prevents you from getting what are called cloning-tracks. These circular tracks come from individual clicks with the mouse and they are sure signs that retouching has taken place.

9. Reduce the size of your brush and make a second stroke to complete the process by covering the bottom of the sign. If necessary, go back to the greenery on the left and sample it again to clone the lower part of it so that your work is convincing. That's it. The sign is gone in two strokes.

PRO TIP

It's often a good idea to cover an area by sampling different areas. This prevents the cloning from being too obvious by painting an exact duplicate of the cloned area.

10. Use the same technique to remove the orange marker, the tall bright flower below it — the bright cream-colored flower in the foreground. Figure 7-3 shows the finished image.

11. Hide the Retouching layer's visibility by clicking the eyeball next to it on the Layers menu to check your work. Notice how much better this image looks after a few minutes of work with the Clone Stamp tool.

This is retouching in its most basic form. It was used to make a nice image more presentable. Whenever you work on an important image, look for ways to fine-tune it by removing small distractions that have a big impact.

7-3

ADDING VISUAL ELEMENTS WITH RETOUCHING

In the last exercise, you learned to hide problem areas by cloning other areas over them. Sometimes though, the goal is to add additional elements to the image by cloning them.

Follow these steps to use the Clone Stamp tool to add an element to a photo rather than remove one:

1. Open the Pink_Flowers.tif file from the download-able practice files on the Web site (www.wiley.com/go/phoprestorationandretouching). Figure 7-4 shows that there are a couple of empty areas in this photo that would look better if there were more flowers. The goal with this project is to add a flower to the empty area on the right by cloning one of the other flowers.

2. Duplicate the Background layer by choosing Layer⇨Duplicate Layer so that all retouching is done on this duplicate layer. When the Duplicate Layer dialog box opens, name the layer Retouching and click OK.

PRO TIP

A faster way to duplicate a layer is to drag the layer onto the New Layer icon at the bottom of the Layers panel. This skips the Duplicate Layer dialog box so if you want to rename the layer, you'll need to double-click its name to highlight it in the Layers panel and then type a new name.

147

7-4

3. Select the Clone Stamp tool (S) and set the brush diameter to about 300px and the Hardness to about 75 percent using the options bar. These initial settings can be varied as needed after you begin working on the flower.

4. Set a sample point by Alt+clicking the center of the flower that's in the center of the photo.

PRO TIP

When making an exact copy of something, it's best to make one sample of the cloned material. This makes cloning easier because the sample cursor stays aligned with the brush cursor throughout the process.

5. Click and begin painting in a circular motion, working your way outward to begin adding the new flower. If you don't like the placement of the duplicate flower, use the Undo command to back up so you can resample and try again.

PRO TIP

When painting with the Clone Stamp, let go of the mouse button once in a while to break up the process into more than one step. That way if you make a mistake near the end of the process, you only have to undo the last step, rather than the entire process.

7-5

6. As you get closer to the outer edges of the flower, reduce the size of your brush and continue painting until you've added a duplicate flower. Don't worry if it isn't perfect around the edges. I show you how to clean it up in a moment. Figure 7-5 shows the results I had with a couple of cloning strokes. Leave this file open so you can continue with it in the next exercise.

Undoing with the History Brush Tool

The background in this project is quite forgiving so the lower part of the new flower blends in quite well. The main problem in Figure 7-5 is that I accidentally cloned part of the flower that's behind the main flower I was sampling. Parts of it now show behind the duplicate flower. Fortunately, there's an easy way to selectively paint out some of the cloning.

Directly below the Clone Stamp tool is another tool called the History Brush. The History Brush enables you to pick a previous history state from the timeline on the History panel by clicking in the box to the left of that state. This places a small icon of the History Brush into the box to indicate it's the state you're working from. After you select a history state, you can use it to paint that state back into the image. It's like using a paintbrush that samples a previous point in time. In this case, you want to pick any history state that is previous to the addition of the duplicate flower.

By default, the History Brush is set to the opening thumbnail at the top of the History panel, shown in Figure 7-6, which is exactly what you want for this exercise.

Here's how you use the History Brush to clean up the cloning job from the previous exercise:

1. Go back to Step 7 in the preceding exercise. Select the History Brush (Y) from the Tools panel. It's tenth from the top on the single-column Tools panel. Make sure you aren't selecting the Art History Brush that's stacked with the History Brush.

2. Select a small brush with a medium hardness and paint out anything that you don't want to show around the outside of the duplicate flower, replacing it with the way the area looked when the file was first opened. Zoom in to make it easier to see what you're doing. If your brush is too soft, you'll have a hard time getting a nice edge along the edges of the petals because the brush affects the edge of the flower. If this happens, increase the Hardness value until you get the kind of edge that you want.

3. Leave this image open because you use it again in the next exercise.

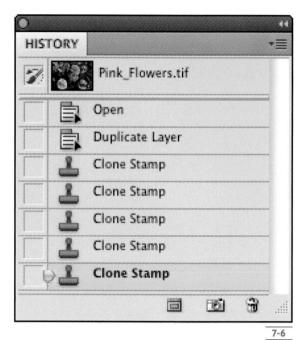

7-6

ADVANCED CLONING TECHNIQUES

As you can see, the Clone Stamp tool is extremely useful. Sometimes, though, its default settings aren't enough for the cloning job at hand. In this section I show you some of the advanced settings that really open up the power of this core tool.

CLONING TO A DIFFERENT LAYER

Photoshop's retouching tools are destructive by their very nature. That's because the things you do with them permanently change pixels in the image. In the earlier exercises in this chapter I had you duplicate the Background layer to isolate your retouching to its own layer. This was useful for making comparisons, and it protected the Background layer from having permanent changes made to it. The problem with this technique is that it doubles the file size on a single layer file. It also limits what you can do with the cloned information because it's not isolated by itself.

You may have noticed a menu on the Clone Source tools options bar that's called Sample. This menu is used to control which layer(s) is sampled when you Alt+click with the Clone Stamp tool. (This menu is also available for the Healing Brush and the Spot Healing Brush.) You have these three options in this menu, as shown in Figure 7-7:

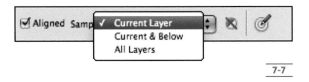

7-7

> **Current Layer:** Only pixels from the current layer are sampled. With this default option, all cloning must be done on the same layer that samples are taken from.

> **Current & Below:** Only pixels from the current layer and layers below it are sampled. This option allows you to arrange the layers you're working with by dragging them into place so you sample only the layers you're interested in. After the retouching is done, the layers can be rearranged if needed.

> **All Layers:** All layers are sampled.

One of the most popular ways of using this multilayer sampling ability is to create an empty layer above the layer to be retouched so that all new retouching is isolated to this layer. That way, if you need to make changes to the retouching later, you can work with it on its own layer. Here's how:

1. Open the Pink_Flower.tif practice file again. If it's still open from the previous exercise, click the image icon at the top of the History panel to return the image to its opening state.

2. Choose Layer⇨New⇨Layer to create an empty layer above the Background layer. When the New Layer dialog box opens, name the layer Retouching and click OK.

3. Select the Clone Stamp tool (S) from the Tools panel, and choose All Layers from the Sample menu in the options bar.

4. Set the brush's Diameter and Hardness to the settings of your choice.

5. Alt+click to sample the flower you cloned in the earlier exercise and begin painting it into the empty area to the right. When you finish, the image should look similar to the finished image in the preceding exercise, with the duplicate flower added to the right. The difference is that the cloned flower is on Layer 1 in the Layers panel.

6. To see Layer 1 by itself, click the eyeball icon next to the Background layer to hide the layer. Now the cloned flower should look something like Figure 7-8.

7-8

The important thing is that the Background layer is undisturbed. If you need to fine-tune your cloning job and it's too late to use the History Brush, you can use a mask to refine the retouching on the retouching layer. In this case, you could quickly create a mask by using one of the smart selection tools to create a selection based on color. Then convert it to a mask.

IGNORING ADJUSTMENT LAYERS WHEN CLONING

Just to the right of the Sample menu is an important button that allows you to ignore adjustment layers when using the Clone Stamp or Healing Brush tools. When All Layers is selected in the Sample menu and an adjustment layer is present, the effect of the adjustment layers is duplicated — even if it's above the layer being cloned. This effect is easy to see by doing a simple experiment:

1. Choose File⇨New to create a new file, and give it the following properties: Width = 6 inches, Height = 4 inches, Resolution = 300, Color Mode = RGB Color/8-bit, and Background = White. Click OK.

2. Choose Edit⇨Fill, and select 50% Gray from the Contents drop-down list. At this point, your new file is 50 percent gray (red = 128, green = 128, blue = 128).

3. Use the Adjustments panel to create a Levels adjustment layer. Change the middle, gray slider to 1.50 to lighten the image. Don't change the white-point or black-point sliders.

4. Click the Background layer in the Layers panel to make it active again.

5. Select the Clone Stamp tool (S) from the Tools panel, change the brush diameter to 200px, and use the Hardness setting of your choice. Make sure that Opacity is 100%.

6. Choose All Layers from the Sample menu on the options bar, and make sure the Ignore Adjustment Layers button has not been clicked.

7. Choose any location and Alt+click to sample it, then scoot the cursor to the side a bit and paint a circle. When you do this, notice that the circle you just painted is lighter than the gray you sampled, as shown in Figure 7-9. That's because the lightening effect of the Levels adjustment layer was doubled when it was sampled along with the gray background.

8. Now click the Ignore Adjustment Layers button and paint again. The painted gray is the same tone as the sampled gray, making the retouching impossible to see.

The inadvertent sampling of adjustment layers when all layers are selected for sampling has thrown many a novice retoucher for a loop. If it happens to you, you'll not only recognize the problem, but you'll also know how to solve it by clicking a little button.

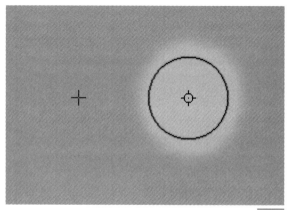

7-9

Cloning from One Image to Another

Sometimes the information you want to clone is in a different image. For example: say you want to add a flower to the Pink_Flowers.tif image by cloning a flower that's in a different photo. The steps to doing this are quite straightforward:

1. Open both files.

2. Select the image you want to sample from by clicking its header and use the Clone Stamp to Alt+click on the area you want to sample.

3. Select the target image by clicking its header and begin painting the sampled information from the first image into the second image.

Be aware that when working with different images, if one is larger than the other, this size differential is reflected in the cloned material. For example, if the image you're sampling from is a 4 x 5 and the target image is an 8 x 10, the cloned material will look smaller in the 8 x 10.

Using the Clone Source panel

The Clone Source panel, shown in Figure 7-10, provides a number of features that enhance the performance of the Clone Stamp tool (as well as the Healing Brush tool).

If you don't see it, choose Window⇨Clone Source. Like the Brush panel, it can also be toggled on and off using the toggle button near the left of the options bar.

Here are some of the things you can do with this panel:

> **You can save up to five sample sources.** Click a different Clone Source button at the top before sampling with the Alt key. That way you can revisit a sample point in the image that was previously sampled.

> **Rotate or scale source material using the settings in the Offset area.**

> **Customize the overlay.** This helps you with positioning cloned data as it's applied. Several options give you a great deal of control over the look of the preview.

7-10

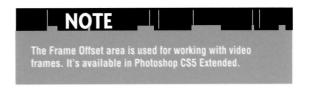

> **NOTE**
>
> The Frame Offset area is used for working with video frames. It's available in Photoshop CS5 Extended.

Because saving multiple Clone Source points is fairly straightforward, the focus here is on the Overlay and Offset settings and how they're used to control the Clone Stamp tool. Look at the Overlay settings first so you can modify them before working with the Offset settings.

MODIFYING THE CLONE OVERLAY PREVIEW

Earlier I mentioned that the clone overlay can be very useful depending on how it's configured. Follow these steps to learn to set it up the way you like to use it:

1. Open the Pink_Flowers.tif practice file. If it's still open, return it to its opening state.

2. Select the Clone Stamp tool, and open the Clone Source panel. If you don't see it, choose Window⇨Clone Source.

3. Sample the flower in the middle using the Alt key, just as you did in the earlier exercise. After the sample is made, the clone overlay appears, just as it did before, indicating where cloned information will be pasted when you paint.

4. Deselect the Clipped option at the bottom of the Clone Source panel, and notice what happens. Instead of a small preview of the size of the Clone Stamp's brush you get a preview of the entire image. Lower the Opacity value to 50 percent so that you can see through the preview. This helps when you're trying to place the cloned data in a particular spot in relation to the rest of the image.

5. Select the Auto Hide option to temporarily hide the preview whenever you're painting. This is the way I like to set up the clone preview, whether I'm working with the clipped preview or the full pre-view. (You can also use the Alt key to temporarily hide the preview at any time instead of setting it to Auto Hide.)

PRO TIP

The Clone Source overlay is extremely useful. However, not everyone likes to use it. You can turn it off completely by deselecting the Show Overlay option. You can tempo-rarily display it if you need it by pressing Shift+Alt.

The blending mode menu at the bottom of the panel is used to change the way the clone preview blends with the image. The options are Normal, Darken, Lighten, and Difference. The settings are most useful when your sample and target areas are very similar — for example, when you're cloning someone's face from one photo into another photo where he has a bad expression.

ADJUSTING GEOMETRY AS YOU CLONE

The settings in the Offset area of the Clone Source panel are used to change the geometric relationship between the sampled pixels and the pixels that are applied with the Clone Stamp tool. There are a number of options. Explore some of them so that you get a feel for when offsetting the clone tool is useful. Follow these steps:

1. Open the Cargo_Bike.tif file from the download-able practice files on the Web site (www.wiley.com/go/phoprestorationandretouching). Figure 7-11 shows this photo. The goal in this exercise is to move the logo from the lower right of the cargo bin and place it sideways on the left side.

2. Hover your cursor over the Rotate clone source icon to the left of the text box, as shown in Figure 7-12. The cursor changes to a small hand icon with two arrows. This is called a scrubby slider. It enables you to click and drag to change a value instead of typing a value into the box.

PRO TIP

Photoshop is loaded with scrubby sliders. You find them almost anywhere there's a box for typing a value. Use them when you want to make fine adjustments without having to type exact numbers into a number box.

3. Click and drag to the right to increase the value. (Dragging to the left decreases the value.) Notice that as the value changes, the overlay displays a preview of the changes enabling you to see the effects of the change. Stop when you like the alignment. I chose 50 percent.

7-11

4. Set the brush Diameter to about 15px and the Hardness value to 0. Alt+click on the left side of the logo to set the clone source sample point.

5. Begin painting on the left side of the cargo bin, as shown in Figure 7-13 until the copy of the logo is in place.

6. Click the circular Reset Transform button to the right of the rotate box to reset the rotation angle. Then go back to the original logo and remove it by cloning the surrounding orange color of the cargo carrier on top of it.

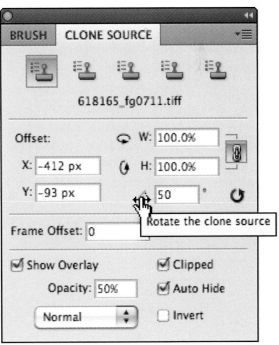

7-12

PRO TIP

It's a good workflow habit to reset any transformations when you finish using the Clone Source panel. Otherwise, it's easy to forget you applied special settings, which can be confusing the next time you use the Clone Stamp or the Healing Brush tools.

155

7-13

As you can see, the Clone Source panel gives you lots of control over the Clone Stamp tool. You can use the Width and Height boxes to scale the cloned material vertically or horizontally as you clone. By default these two values are linked. When you change one, the other changes proportionally, preserving the original aspect ratio. If you want to scale it on one axis only, click the small link icon to unlink them.

Using the Healing Brush Tool

The Healing Brush tool (J) is very similar to the Clone Stamp tool. Targeted information is sampled by Alt+clicking and then painting it into other parts of the image. The big difference is that the Healing Brush tool attempts to make the sampled data match the lighting and shading of the area to which it's being applied. In other words, it looks at the area where the sampled data is being applied and tries to make the sampled information match the target area. This is extremely useful when you're more interested in blending your retouching than getting a literal copy.

1. Open Portrait.tif from the downloadable practice files on the Web site (www.wiley.com/go/phoprestorationandretouching).

2. Select the Clone Stamp tool and try to remove the black dot I placed on the woman's cheek, as shown in Figure 7-14. Notice that if you don't sample skin that is exactly the same tone and color of the target area, your strokes are noticeable. This has always been one of the issues with using the Clone Stamp tool for retouching.

3. Undo any work you did with the Clone Stamp tool, and then switch to the Healing Brush tool (J). It's seventh from the top on the single-column Tools panel and is stacked with the Spot Healing Brush tool, the Patch tool, and the Red Eye tool. (Be sure not to choose the Spot Healing brush.)

4. Set the brush to similar size and hardness settings for your attempt at using the Clone Stamp tool in Step 2.

7-14
Photo by Dave Hutt

5. Alt+click to sample some skin and then paint over one of the dots. Notice that as you paint, the sampled information looks similar to the way it did in Step 1. However, when you release the mouse button the Healing Brush tool takes over and intelligently blends the tone and color of the sample so that it matches the target area.

6. Alt+click on the background to the left of the woman to sample the gray background tones and use the Healing Brush tool to paint the other dark spot. Notice that the Healing Brush is able to blend these tones even though they are very different. That's because there isn't much of a difference in the texture of the two tones. This simple step reveals the power of this retouching tool.

7-15

Though the Healing Brush tool is powerful, there are situations where it totally fails. It fails when it's used to retouch areas that are near an edge with strong contrast; for example, if you try to remove the woman's flyaway hair by sampling the background, as shown in Figure 7-15. That's because the tool doesn't know how to blend the tones because it sees light and dark.

There are two ways to deal with this scenario. The first is to switch to the Clone Stamp tool. The other is to use a selection to isolate the area so that tones outside of the selection are not used in the Healing Brush's calculations.

Even though the Healing Brush is a brush tool, the options for setting it up are a little different than the Clone Stamp tool or the Brush tool. The first thing you notice is that it doesn't have an Opacity setting. Another big difference is that the Brush pop-up menu on the options bar isn't the same. Figure 7-16 shows what it looks like.

PRO TIP

The Clone Source panel can also be used with the Healing Brush.

7-16

Something else you might have noticed is that when the Healing Brush tool is selected, all the options on the Brushes panel are grayed out. That means that you can't use the Brushes panel with this tool. The few features that are available have been moved to the Brush pop-up menu in Figure 7-16.

There are two other settings on the options bar that affect how this tool functions:

> **Source:** This option determines where source data comes from. When set to Sampled, the Alt key is used to sample image information. When set to Pattern, a pattern from the Pattern pop-up menu (which is activated when this option is selected) next to the pattern is used. I always leave this set at Sampled.

> **Aligned:** This is the same as the Aligned setting in the Clone Stamp options. When this option is selected, sample points are aligned with the brush as it moves. When it is deselected, the original selection is used for every new stroke.

The main difference between the Clone Stamp and the Healing Brush tools is that the Clone Stamp tool makes a literal copy of the sampled information. The Healing Brush, on the other hand, attempts to blend sampled data into the target area.

BUSTING DUST WITH THE SPOT HEALING BRUSH

The Spot Healing Brush is a close cousin to the Healing Brush. They're both stacked together, along with the Patch tool and the Red Eye tool. The Spot Healing Brush has the same smart blending abilities as the Healing Brush. The main difference is that sampling isn't done with the Alt key. This tool automatically creates a sample from around the area that's being retouched.

This lack of control can cause problems when detail you don't want to sample is inadvertently sampled. The Spot Healing Brush works best in areas that are low in detail, such as backgrounds. This tool is most useful when cleaning up dust on scans or removing dSLR sensor dirt from a background that doesn't have a lot of detail in it.

The Spot Healing Brush has three tool options of note:

> **Proximity Match:** Uses pixels around the selection to generate the sampled data.

> **Create Texture:** Uses the pixels in the selection to create a texture that is used to fill the area being painted.

> **Content-Aware:** This powerful new feature enables the Spot Healing Brush to synthesize image content from the surrounding area so that it blends more seamlessly as you paint. It can do an amazing job of removing large spots in complex scenes.

When using this tool to remove dust, you may have to try each of these settings to find the one that best suits your needs for that particular image.

USING THE PATCH TOOL

As useful as the Healing Brush tool is, I find I use the Patch tool for a large percentage of my retouching. The Patch tool is stacked with the Healing Brush tool and the Spot Healing Brush tool, and it works in a similarly intelligent manner. The main difference is in the way image information is sampled and applied.

This tool uses a selection instead of a brush. You draw a selection and then drag it to the area to be sampled. When you release the mouse button, the sampled information fills the original target selection and blends in the same way as when you use the Healing Brush tool. To see how this tool works, follow these steps:

1. Open the Portrait.tif file from the downloadable practice files from the Web site (www.wiley.com/go/phoprestorationandretouching). If it's already open from the last exercise, you may continue working with it.

2. Select the Patch tool (J) from the Tools panel and make sure that Source is selected on the options bar next to Patch. In this example, you want to tone down the lines under the woman's eyes.

PRO TIP

To quickly select a tool that's stacked underneath another tool, press Shift along with the tool's shortcut key to cycle through the stacked tools. In this case, press Shift+J. (To make this work, be sure to select the Use Shift for Tool Switch option in Photoshop's General preferences; it is already selected by default.)

3. Click and drag your cursor to draw a selection around the lines under the left eye. Keep the selection a little loose around the outside so it's not too close to the detail that's being removed.

4. Click inside of the selection and drag it to a clean area of skin that has a similar texture so you can sample it. In Figure 7-17, you can see that I used the cheek below. Notice that as you drag the selection, the originally selected area is updated with a preview of the information in the sample selection you're dragging.

5. When you like what you see in the preview, release the mouse button to replace the original selection with the information in the sample selection.

6. Choose Select⇨Deselect (⌘/Ctrl+D). This deselects the selection and completes the Patch tool's application. The only problem with what you just did is that the effect is too strong because it removed all of the lines and took away some of the definition around the woman's eye, making the retouching obvious.

Because the Patch tool, like the Clone Stamp tool, doesn't have an Opacity setting as an option, you have to use something else to reduce the effect of the tool.

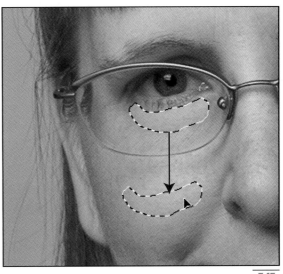

7-17

PRO TIP

You can create selections using any of the selection tools covered in Chapter 5. You just have to switch back to the Patch tool to use it after creating the selection.

7. Go back two steps in the History panel's timeline. You should now be at the point where the selection was first created with the lines showing under her eye.

8. Drag the selection to the skin on the cheek again, and release the mouse button — just as you did previously in Steps 4 and 5.

9. Choose Edit⇨Fade Patch Selection (⌘/Shift+Ctrl+F). The Fade dialog box opens.

10. Move the slider to the left until you see just enough of the lines reappear to give the eye socket some shape. You can use the Fade command after just about anything you do in Photoshop, which is extremely useful. It allows you to overdo something and then fade it back to the point where you like it.

The key to using Fade is that it must be the very next thing you do. For example, if you deselect the selection first, the Fade command under the Edit menu is grayed out.

11. Back up again to Step 3 using the History panel. This time, drag the selection to the dark background to the left of the woman and release the mouse button. Notice that the background tones are blended in to match the skin tones. The effect is even softer than when you sampled the skin on the forehead because the background doesn't have as much texture as the skin you sampled earlier. Use the Fade command to tone it down. This is a useful technique for a situation like this when there isn't any clean skin to work with.

12. Follow the same procedures to retouch the lines under the left eye, giving it approximately the same amount of fade.

The tool options for the Patch tool on the options bar, as shown in Figure 7-18, are fairly simple. On the left, just to the right of the Tool Presets, are four small buttons. These allow you to modify your selection by adding or subtracting to it, just like the tool options for the main selection tools. To the right of these buttons are two radio buttons that control how the patch is applied.

Three settings that do the following when clicked:

> **Source:** The originally selected area is patched with the sampled pixels.

> **Destination:** The information from the original selection is dragged and dropped when you move the selection — sort of the opposite of the effect of clicking the Source button.

> **Transparent option:** Only the texture of the sample area is used as a sample. None of the color and tone information is sampled. (I have to say that I never use this option on an actual retouching job.)

You should be aware of a couple of other things when using the Patch tool. Quite often, you need to do a little cleanup around the edges of the patched area, using the Healing Brush tool or the Patch tool itself, so that the edges blend a little better — especially when patching large areas.

Another issue with the Patch tool is that it suffers from the same smudging problem as the Spot Healing Brush tool when patching areas that are near edges of high contrast or the edge of the image frame. When working in areas like this, try to create the original selection away from these edges.

One other thing to be aware of with this tool is that it doesn't have the Source menu on the options bar that allows you to sample one layer and patch onto another layer.

I get around this by duplicating the layer (Layer➪ Duplicate Layer) I want to work with and doing all retouching on it. This allows me to keep the original layer intact so that I can occasionally hide the retouching layer to make a before and after comparison. It also allows me to trash the retouching layer and begin again if I want to without affecting the rest of the image.

7-18

Body Sculpting with the Liquify Filter

Y ou began this chapter by learning about Photoshop's most fundamental retouching tool, the Clone Stamp tool. You wrap this chapter up by learning about one of Photoshop's most exotic retouching tools, the Liquify filter (see Figure 7-19).

This tool is so specialized that I rarely use it. However, it's a powerful tool, so I want to make you aware of it so that you can take a closer look at it as your Photoshop skills improve.

The Liquify filter works by distorting the image with tools like Warp, Pucker, and Bloat. To access the Liquify filter, go to the top section of the Filters menu and choose Filter⇨Liquify. Figure 7-19 shows the Liquify dialog box.

As you can see, the options in this dialog box are quite comprehensive. On the left side is a set of tools that affect the filter's distortion in different ways. On the right side are a number of options for fine-tuning the effects of those tools.

The woman in Figure 7-19 didn't like the way her bottom looked because the camera angle distorted it. This is the sort of problem that the Liquify filter is well suited for solving. The goal here is to distort the image so that the protruding bottom is minimized.

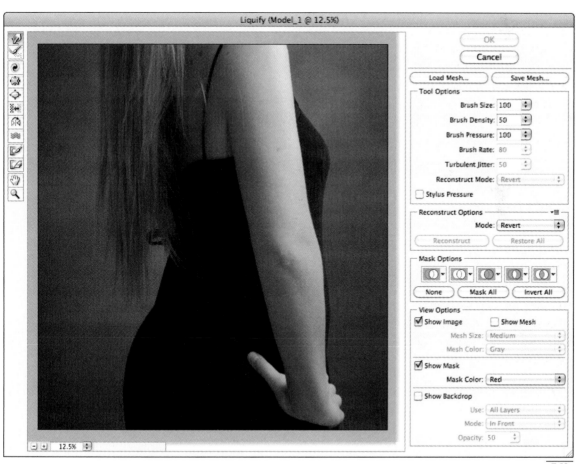

7-19

For this job, I selected the Push Left tool from the Tools panel on the left, sixth from the top. The Push Left tool moves pixels to the left when you click and drag straight up. When the cursor is dragged downward, the tool moves pixels to the right.

Here, I want to move the pixels around her bottom to the right, so I drag the tool downward while holding down the mouse button.

The left image in Figure 7-20 shows the effect of dragging and moving pixels to the right. The right image shows what the girl looks like after the application is completed. This was all done with a single stroke.

PRO TIP

Use Liquify's Freeze tool to paint a mask onto areas you don't want to affect. An existing layer mask can also be used.

This filter works so well here because the background is simple. If the background contained lots of detail — like an outdoor portrait in a garden — adjustments like this would require more work. As it is, the only area that needs to be cleaned up with the Clone Stamp tool or Healing Brush is where the bottom tips of her hair were also distorted to the right. This kind of cleanup is quite common when using the Liquify filter.

7-20

NOTE

The Liquify filter is a resource hog. If you're working on a large file, it can take quite a while to load and execute. When working with a large file, use a selection to isolate the area being worked on before opening the Liquify filter. That way, only the selected area is loaded into the Liquify filter's dialog box, which speeds up the process quite a bit.

Again, I'm barely scratching the surface of what this filter is capable of. I encourage you to spend time exploring it in more depth. When you get playful with it, you can also create some really interesting visual effects, but it's most powerful when you simply need a little nip-and-tuck.

Photoshop Tools and Techniques

As you pointed out, when the Healing Brush tool or Patch tool is used near areas of contrast, it often fails. I find that I run into this kind of situation often, requiring me to use the Clone Stamp tool. Is there a way to get this tool to work more intelligently?

Before the introduction of the Healing Brush and Patch tools we were limited to doing most retouching with the Clone Stamp tool. Because this tool is so literal in transferring sampled material to the target area, it is helpful to find a way to get the tool to behave in special cases. For example, when removing dark flyaway hair by sampling the background and painting over the hair, it's important to sample background area that's very close in tone to the background surrounding the hair. This can be difficult when working with a complex background that has dark and light tones.

When you run into a scenario like this one, you can change the tool's blending mode by using the Mode menu on the Options bar. This modifies the way sampled material is blended. In the case where you need to remove dark hair from a background that has lots of variation, set the Mode to Lighten. Then the tool only affects tones that are darker than the sampled area and leaves others untouched. If the hair is light against a dark background, the solution is to choose Darken to affect only tones that are lighter than the sampled area.

In the early days of Photoshop it was common for me to work with the Clone Stamp in either the Lighten or Darken mode. Ever since the introduction of the Healing Brush and Patch tools I find that I rarely resort to this strategy. However it's a good trick to have up your sleeve for the special occasions where it can help.

When retouching the lines under the woman's eyes using the Patch tool, you suggested fading the effect of the Patch tool to lessen it. I thought it looked pretty good without fading. Why did you recommend fading it?

The object when retouching someone is to tone down any imperfections without drawing attention to the retouching. In the case you mentioned, the full effect of the tool was so strong it completely removed all lines under the woman's eye. If this were done to every wrinkle on her face, the skin would begin to look plastic and fake because many of the lines that describe the shape of her face would be gone. Even if it didn't look completely fake, it would still change the appearance of the woman by making her look much younger than she is. Though many people would like to look younger in reality, they often find it objectionable when the retouching of their portrait is taken too far.

RESTORATION: RESCUING DAMAGED PHOTOS

Part III

Chapter 8

STARTING WITH THE SCAN

Because the starting point for most restoration projects is an old print, it's necessary to scan the images before your primary work can begin. In the early days of digital imaging, scanners were expensive and difficult to master. Today, quality scanners are affordable and straightforward to use — especially when you know how to set up the scanner software and prepare scans for editing in Photoshop.

CONSIDERING COPYRIGHT

In today's digital world, you can easily copy just about anything: photos, music, software, and so on. Because of this, it's easy to lose sight of the rights of the person who created the thing being copied. Just as musicians and record companies own the rights to music, photographers own the rights to their creations.

You may not be aware of this, but unless it is specifically spelled out, you don't own the photos of your wedding or any portraits shot by a professional photographer. Many people are shocked when they hear this because they think that they own the photos since they paid for their creation.

When a professional photographer takes a photograph, she owns the copyright to it from the moment she clicks the shutter. Someone may buy a tangible copy of the photograph, but she still owns the intangible aspect of the work as *intellectual property* because she is its creator.

Ownership can be transferred, but the transfer must be in writing and signed by the owner. When the original owner of the copyright is no longer living, the image may still be covered by copyright if the copyright was passed on in a will or trust.

If you have an image you want to scan, but you think it may be covered by a copyright, try to find the creator of the image and ask for written permission to scan and reproduce it for your own uses. Unless the image is recent or famous, most photographers will gladly comply.

Quite often, if you bring a scan of a professional-looking photo for printing, the lab may require you to have written permission. So many of these small businesses have been sued for printing copyrighted materials that now they're quite careful about what they print. In some cases, if it looks like a professional created it, the lab won't touch it without a release — even if you're the one who shot it.

SCANNING PRINTS AND FILM

To begin scanning, you need to get a handle on two things: the scanner and the software the scanner uses. To create high-quality scans, you need a clear understanding of these two elements.

SCANNER HARDWARE

The most common style of scanner is the *flatbed print scanner*. These scanners have a lid that lifts to reveal a glass-covered copying bed where you place prints for scanning. These flatbed scanners are useful for scanning documents and photos up to legal size. This style of scanner starts at less than $100.

More advanced *hybrid flatbed scanners* are capable of scanning prints and film. These range in capabilities as well as price. Hybrid scanners start at about $150 and rise quickly to almost $1,000. A decent hybrid scanner costs about $250 to $400.

The Epson V600, shown in Figure 8-1, is an example of a hybrid scanner. It costs about $250 and does a good job of scanning 35mm to 4×5 film. If you want to scan film, but you're on a limited budget, a hybrid scanner like this one is a good place to start.

If you're serious about scanning film, you'll want a *dedicated film scanner*. The quality on these is far superior to the film scans from hybrid scanners. These dedicated film scanners start at about $500 for one that will scan only 35mm film.

A scanner that will scan medium format 120/220 film costs more. These begin at about $2,000. High-end scanners used by film labs and other digital image processors can easily cost ten times that. My film scanner is from the $2,000 range. I've used it to scan a wide variety of negatives and slides with excellent results.

SCANNER SOFTWARE

Just as scanner hardware varies, so does scanner software. Most scanners come with software ranging from basic operational software to advanced scanning software. Because software is part of the package, it's a good idea to find out what software comes with any scanners you're considering purchasing.

Scanner software usually comes in two parts. The first part is the *scanner driver*, which allows the scanner to talk to the computer. This conversation is often referred to as a *digital handshake*. Driver software works behind the scenes. If it's doing its job, you won't even be aware of it.

The other piece of scanner software is the *user interface* (UI) that pops up when the scanner is activated. You can set up this software to make scanning decisions automatically, or you can turn on advanced settings to activate additional options.

In the Epson scanner software shown in Figure 8-2, the advanced settings are named Professional Mode, which you can see at the top right of the dialog box. I recommend that you find the advanced settings on your scanner software so that you have more control over your scanner when you need it.

Some third-party *plug-in* software works within the scanning software. The most popular of these is Digital ICE, a product of Applied Science Fiction Inc,

8-1
Photo courtesy of Epson

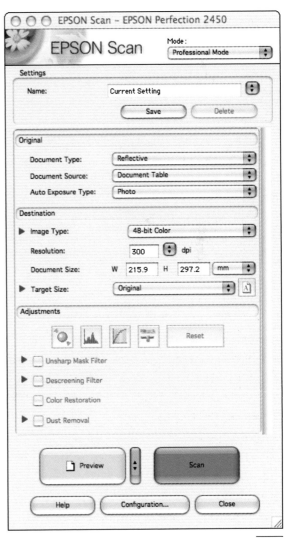

8-2

which is now owned by Kodak. This amazing software goes through the file after the scan and tries to remove dust spots. It's a must when scanning film because it eliminates the need for most dust spotting after the scan.

Digital ICE is activated from within the main scanner window. Figure 8-3 shows this dialog box in the Nikon film scanner software.

8-3

Applied Science Fiction also makes other scanner plug-ins, including Digital ROC for automatically correcting and restoring color, and Digital GEM for reducing and managing digital noise and film grain. Sometimes these products come with the scanning software, and sometimes they have to be purchased individually.

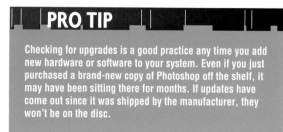

PRO TIP

To learn more about these products, visit http://asf.com/products.

After you purchase a scanner, check the manufacturer's Web site to see if any updates to the software are available. This insures that you have the latest and greatest software updates. Look for updates to the driver as well as to the scanning software. Also check for *firmware* updates.

Firmware is software that is coded into the hardware. It controls the various programmable chips inside the scanner on a hardware level. When upgrading firmware, be sure to follow the manufacturer's instructions exactly.

PRO TIP

Checking for upgrades is a good practice any time you add new hardware or software to your system. Even if you just purchased a brand-new copy of Photoshop off the shelf, it may have been sitting there for months. If updates have come out since it was shipped by the manufacturer, they won't be on the disc.

Using your scanner

With some scanners, you can scan directly into Photoshop. To do so, turn on the scanner, choose File⇨Import, and look for your scanner in the pop-out menu.

In Figure 8-4, you can see Epson Perfection 2450 in the list on my system. When I choose it, the scanner wakes up and prepares itself for use. The TWAIN software shakes hands with the computer, and the two agree to do business together.

With so many scanners and so much associated scanning software available, I can't offer a comprehensive set of scanning instructions here. I'll point out the highlights to help you get a handle on the important settings. Just keep in mind that some of this varies from manufacturer to manufacturer, as well as model to model.

Here are some of the settings to check:

> Make sure your scanner is set to scan the type of media you're scanning — photos rather than documents, negatives rather than slides, and so on.

> Choose RGB for the color mode.

> Set the color setting to 8-bit/24-bit or 16-bit/48-bit. This is where you choose to create a high-bit file.

X-REF

Bit depth is discussed in the following section.

> Choose your output resolution.

> Look at any color and tone adjustments to see if you can fine-tune the preview that your scanner displays.

> If you're scanning film, look for a Dust Removal setting or Digital ICE.

Also make sure the glass is clean and that any dust has been blown off the print or film with compressed air. If you don't have a compressor, use the canned variety of compressed air.

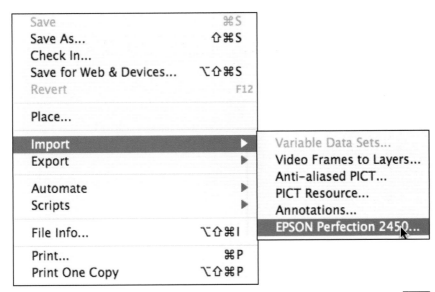

8-4

If you don't see a preview of your original, click the Preview button in the software to generate a preview. In the preview window, click and drag a marquee around the area you want to scan.

After you're satisfied with your selection, click the Scan button.

COMPARING 8-BIT AND 16-BIT FILES

In Chapter 4, you learned about how common adjustments are destructive to the pixels in an image. In that discussion, you saw how spiking and combing in the histogram are manifestations of this data loss.

Figure 8-5 shows the histogram that demonstrated this point from that chapter. The spiking and combing in this histogram are the result of a limited amount of data being compressed and stretched by a simple Levels adjustment.

In that discussion, you learned that an adjustment layer is often used to mitigate this loss when multiple adjustments are made to an image. However, not every adjustment you do can be applied to an adjustment layer.

Additionally, even if changes are isolated to an adjustment layer, when massive changes are made, they still have a destructive effect on the pixels because of the limited amount of data in the file. Because of that, many people prefer to work with files that have more data, giving them a greater operating overhead.

Figure 8-6 shows a histogram from a 16-bit version of the same file after the same Levels adjustment. Notice that there is no combing and that the spiking is barely noticeable. That's because this 16-bit file has much more data to work with.

Here's how 8-bit and 16-bit files differ in the amount of data contained in them:

> An 8-bit file has 256 tonal values per color channel. A 16-bit file has over 65,000 tonal values per channel.

> An 8-bit file contains a possible 16.7 million colors. A 16-bit file contains more than 281 trillion colors.

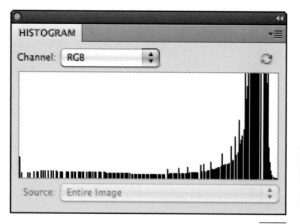

8-5

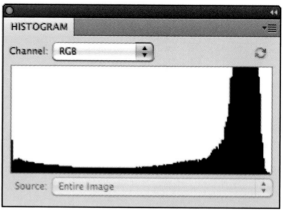

8-6

This may seem like overkill, and quite often it is. Humans can't even see 281 trillion individual colors. But if you're going to be making cumulative or massive adjustments in Photoshop, it's good to have lots of extra editing headroom.

Here are a couple of things to remember about 16-bit files: 16-bit files contain much more information than 8-bit files, so they are larger in size. In fact, they're twice as big as 8-bit files. Because they're bigger, they consume more hard drive space and other computer resources like RAM. Also be aware that some commands in Photoshop CS5 don't work with 16-bit files.

For example, the Variations command is grayed out when working with 16-bit files. Because of these issues it's best to save 16-bit files for difficult images that need massive adjustments or lots of retouching and other editing — what I call *heavy lifting*.

Not all file formats support 16-bit. For example, saving a 16-bit file as a JPEG is impossible. If you try to do it, you won't see a JPEG option under Format in the Save As dialog box. If you need a JPEG, you can convert the file to 8-bit. Choose Image⇨Mode⇨8 Bits/Channel. Now you can save it as JPEG, as well as all other common file formats.

So now that you know about 16-bit files, I imagine you're wondering how to create one? If you're using a scanner to make a color scan, select 16-bit in the color mode. Some scanner software calls 16-bit 48-bit instead because it is adding all of the bits in each channel —16-bits multiplied by 3 channels equals 48-bits. If you're working with RAW format files captured with a dSLR, you can choose 16-bit when converting the file using the RAW conversion software (Adobe Camera Raw in the case of Photoshop).

If you're not doing heavy editing to a file, the difference between 8-bit and 16-bit can be hard to see. For that reason it's usually best to stick with 8-bit files because of the size difference and some tool limitations in Photoshop.

DEMYSTIFYING RESOLUTION

One of the things that can be hard to get your head around when you work with digital images is resolution. Any confusion is compounded by the fact that there are two kinds of resolution to be considered. One is *dots per inch* and the other is *pixels per inch*.

Dots per inch (dpi) refers to the number of dots per inch that an inkjet printer is capable of applying to the paper surface. It typically ranges from 150 to 2,800. The closer these dots are to each other, the more they blend together forming continuous tones on the print. Naturally, this depends on the paper that is being printed on.

If the paper is porous watercolor paper, the dots will soak in and blend just fine at lower dpi settings like 720. On glossy photo papers, a higher setting — such as 1,440 — is needed because the ink dries on the surface. About the only time people discuss dpi is when they are talking about a printer.

When a file's resolution is discussed, *pixels per inch* (ppi) is used. This describes the distance between the pixels that make up a digital image. Similar to the effect of ink dots when printing, if the pixels themselves are too far apart, it becomes possible to see the space between them, causing jagged lines on edges that should be smooth.

A photo's resolution is important to consider when printing or when resizing the file. When a file is prepared for printing, the goal is to get the pixels close enough together so that these single dots form continuous tones and lines.

If you are printing on an inkjet printer, the sweet spot for matte and glossy papers is 360 ppi, though 300 ppi often works just as well. If you plan to take files to a commercial photo lab for printing, you'll need files that are 250 or 300 ppi, depending on the lab. It's best to check ahead of time to see what's best for it.

When resizing a photo, resolution becomes important because the distance between pixels has a direct relationship to the photo's dimensions in inches. For example, if I have a file that's 150 ppi and I convert it to 300 ppi for printing, the image is reduced to half its size when I convert it. An 8 × 10 becomes a 4 × 5.

DOING THE SIMPLE MATH

I know I just said the dreaded *M* word, but please keep reading. In the next few paragraphs, I'll show you how to use simple math to understand what Photoshop is doing when you resize your photo files. Let's start off by getting a better handle on how resolution works:

1. Choose File⇨New, and create a new file with the following attributes: Width = 2 inches, Height = 2 inches, Resolution = 300 pixels/inch, Color Mode = RGB Color, 8-bit, and Background Contents = White. The New dialog box shown in Figure 8-7 shows these settings.

2. When the file opens in Photoshop, choose Image⇨Image Size (⌘/Ctrl+I). Notice that the dimensions are the same as what you specified with the New File command.

3. For the first part of the experiment, deselect the Resample check box. Notice that the Pixel Dimensions area at the top of the Image Size window is grayed out when Resample is turned off. This means that the number of pixels being used in this image is fixed at 600 × 600 pixels.

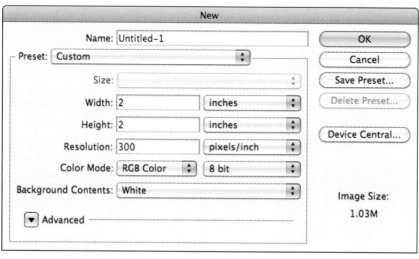

8-7

4. Change the resolution setting to 150. Notice that the size of the image goes from 2 × 2 inches to 4 × 4 inches, as shown in Figure 8-8. That's because as the distance between pixels increases, the document size has to expand to include all pixels.

Here's how the math works: The file has fixed overall pixel dimensions of 600 × 600. When the resolution is set to 300 pixels per inch, the math dictates that the image is 2 × 2 inches (2 inches x 300 ppi = 600 pixels).

When the resolution is changed to 150 ppi, then the image must become 4 × 4 inches in size (4 inches x 150 ppi = 600 pixels).

RESIZING AND RESAMPLING

In the previous example, I asked you to turn off Resample because Resample has a special function that affects the math involved in resizing an image.

With Resample turned off, the Pixel Dimensions remain fixed. Any change to Resolution affects Document Size, and vice versa.

Here's another exercise that demonstrates the role of resampling when adjusting resolution.

1. Create the same sample file again using the settings in Step 1 of the previous exercise.

2. This time, leave the Resample check box selected. Click it if it isn't already checked.

3. Change the Resolution to 150. Notice that the Image Size remains at 2 × 2 inches. What did change was the Pixel Dimensions at the top of the window. They went from 600 × 600 to 300 × 300.

4. Change the Resolution to 600. Now the Pixel Dimensions changes to 1200 × 1200, but the Document Size remains fixed, as shown in Figure 8-9.

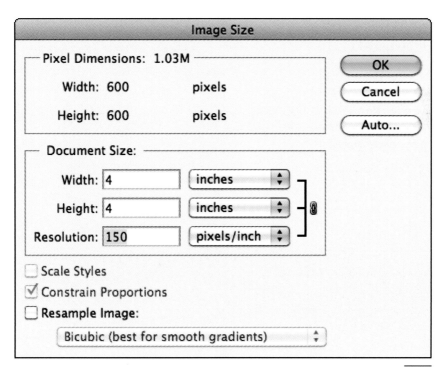

8-8

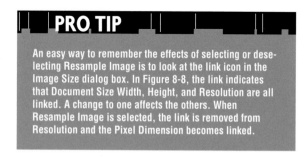

Image Size

Pixel Dimensions: 263.7K (was 1.03M)

Width: 300   pixels

Height: 300   pixels

Document Size:

Width: 2   inches

Height: 2   inches

Resolution: 150   pixels/inch

☑ Scale Styles
☑ Constrain Proportions
☑ Resample Image:

Bicubic Sharper (best for reduction)

OK
Cancel
Auto...

8-9

When Resample is turned on, modifications to Resolution or Document Size affect only the Pixel Dimensions. What's happening is that as the document is made smaller or its resolution is reduced, resampling removes pixels from the image to make it smaller. This is called *downsampling*.

If the Document Size or resolution is increased, resampling adds pixels to the image. This is called *upsampling*. The color and tone of the new pixels are based on the existing pixels that surround it.

Keep in mind that adding lots of pixels to an image through resampling can affect the image's quality. Photoshop is pretty good at upsampling, but only so much can be done. Lots of guesses need to be made on Photoshop's part when deciding what color to make a new pixel. If you push it too far and try to upsample an image beyond Photoshop's capabilities, you can end up with a low-quality file.

So remember, if you only want to change the resolution of the file, deselect the Resample Image check box. If you need to make the image smaller or larger, then Resample Image must be selected.

PRO TIP

An easy way to remember the effects of selecting or deselecting Resample Image is to look at the link icon in the Image Size dialog box. In Figure 8-8, the link indicates that Document Size Width, Height, and Resolution are all linked. A change to one affects the others. When Resample Image is selected, the link is removed from Resolution and the Pixel Dimension becomes linked.

Sometimes it's necessary to change the document size and resolution at the same time. For example, suppose you have a file that is sized to 8×10 inches at 250 ppi, and you need to change it to a 4×5 inches at

300. Making this change with the Image Size command requires two steps. However, both steps can be carried out in one use of the Image Size command:

1. Create a new file by choosing File⇨New. Make the file measure 8 × 10 inches at 250 ppi.

2. Open the Image Size dialog box by choosing Image⇨Size (Alt+⌘/Ctrl+I).

3. Deselect Resample Image, and change the resolution to 300. Notice that the Document size changes to 6.67 × 8.33 because you're moving the pixels closer together.

4. Select Resample Image, and change the Document Size Width to 4 inches.

5. Click OK. Now you have a file that is 4 × 5 inches at 300 ppi.

USING THE CORRECT IMAGE INTERPOLATION METHOD

There's one more wrinkle to throw at you before moving on. In the previous examples, you probably noticed a menu box next to Resample Image in the Image Size dialog box. When you click it, the drop-down list shown in Figure 8-10 opens.

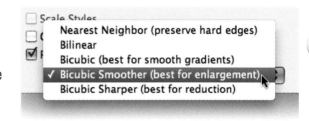

8-10

This box allows you to change the *image interpolation* that's used when you resample an image. Different interpolation settings affect the way new pixels are assigned color based on the pixels that surround it. There are five resampling methods:

> **Nearest Neighbor:** Fast, but not very precise; best for illustrations with distinct edges

> **Bilinear:** Produces medium quality results with most images

> **Bicubic:** Slower but more precise; produces smoother graduations with photo files than the two previous methods

> **Bicubic Smoother:** Based on Bicubic Interpolation, but designed for enlarging images

> **Bicubic Sharper:** Based on Bicubic Interpolation, but designed for reducing image size

What about the Ten Percent Method of Upsampling?

In early versions of Photoshop before Bicubic Smoother and Bicubic Sharper were introduced, many people used a special system to upsample photos. This system was commonly referred to as the Ten Percent Method because file size was upsampled in ten percent increments to get around the limitations of standard Bicubic resampling. The resizing process was repeated, ten percent at a time, until the image was close to the desired size. Now with Bicubic Smoother, the Ten Percent Method is no longer needed. Jumps of 100 percent and more can be done in one easy step. The reason I point it out here is that some Photoshop trainers are still teaching this time-consuming method, though it's no longer necessary.

Bicubic Smoother and Bicubic Sharper are used almost exclusively when resampling photos in Photoshop. When you're upsampling, increasing the number of pixels in an image, choose Bicubic Smoother. When you're downsampling, decreasing the number of pixels, choose Bicubic Sharper.

UNDERSTANDING HOW RESOLUTION RELATES TO SCANNING

So what does all this have to do with scanning? By understanding how resolution works, you can take advantage of it when scanning. Imagine that you're scanning a frame of 35mm film. A frame of 35mm film measures about 1.5 inches by 1 inch.

If you were to scan this frame of film at 300 ppi you would get a file that measures 1.5 × 1 inches at 300 ppi. If you wanted to make an 8 × 12 inches from this scan and plan to print it on a printer that requires a file resolution of 300 ppi, you would have to do some serious upsampling to make a 1.5 × 1 inches file into an 8 × 12 inches file.

I'll save you some time and tell you right now that it won't work very well.

There's a much better way to solve this problem. Scan the film at a higher resolution, and then change the resolution to 300 without resampling. Here's how it works: When you scan the 35mm slide at 2,400 ppi, you get sizes similar to those shown in the Image Size dialog box shown in Figure 8-11.

All you need to do is change the resolution to 300 with Resampling turned off to produce an 8 × 12 inches Document Size.

What this means is that a bit of planning before you scan can save time later and yield a higher-quality file.

If you're scanning a 4 × 5 inches original print and you need a file that you can use to print an 8 × 10 inches at 300 ppi, then you know that scanning the 4 × 5 inches at 600 ppi and then converting the file to 300 ppi without resampling gives you an 8 × 10 inches. It's all simple math.

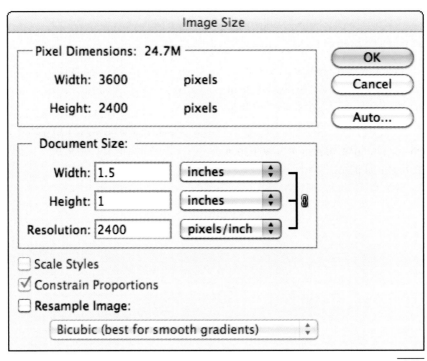

8-11

SCANNING LARGE ORIGINALS

Sometimes, you may need to scan something that's larger than the scanning area of your scanner. The solution to this is to make individual scans of the large original and then let Photoshop combine them.

A couple of years ago I ran across a large print of a photo I shot several years ago. It's a picture I took of my wife, Julia, the day after we were married. The film was severely damaged long ago and is unusable. I didn't think I had any copies of the print until I discovered this one in storage.

Now that I have the print, I can scan it and add it to my archives. The image area of the print measures 14 inches by 12.25 inches. My scanner is only able to scan an area of about 8 inches by 11. In order to scan it, I need to make four scans to cover the four different corners (top-left, top-right, bottom–left, and bottom–right) and then assemble them in Photoshop.

Here's how:

1. Turn off any auto color of tone correction in the scanner software. If it is left on, it can be harder to combine all of the pieces later because they may not all be the same color or tone.

2. Place the first area of the artwork to be scanned into the scanner, paying special attention to alignment to make it as straight as possible. This helps later when the parts are put together.

3. After the first scan is done, move the artwork over and scan the next quadrant.

4. When all the quadrants in that row are done, rotate the artwork 180 degrees so you can scan the bottom quadrants. The artwork must be rotated 180 degrees because of the way most scanner lids are hinged.

5. After all the scans are done, open them in Photoshop and rotate any that are upside down by choosing Image⇨Image Rotation⇨180°.

6. Use the Crop tool to trim any ragged edges from each file. They don't have to be exactly the same dimensions. Make sure that there is plenty of overlap in image content so that the files will line up correctly when combined. Figure 8-12 shows the four scans I made after cropping.

X-REF

Cropping is discussed in Chapter 9.

7. Save each file, otherwise you'll get an error warning when Photoshop tries to combine them in the following steps.

8. With the images open in Photoshop, choose File⇨Scripts⇨Load Files into Stack.

9. When the dialog box opens, click Add Open Files. Also select Attempt to Automatically Align Source Images. This is the key to getting Photoshop to automatically align the four images.

10. After all the layers have been stacked and aligned, evaluate the new file to be sure that you're happy with the alignment. If there are any differences in tone or color on any of the individual layers, adjust them on a layer-by-layer basis.

11. Make any global tone or color changes to the entire image using an adjustment layer at the top of the layer stack.

Figure 8-13 shows the stacked and aligned layers for the large print I scanned. It looks pretty good. Now I just need to flatten the layers so I can do a little retouching to blend areas where I can see some overlap.

After that's done, I use the Crop tool one more time to trim any ragged edges that are caused by differences in the individual file dimensions. (Or I could use the Clone Stamp to fill those empty areas instead of cropping them.)

PRO TIP

Sometimes, an original is so large that creating multiple scans is not practical. If you encounter one of these projects, think about using a digital camera on a tripod to photograph the artwork instead of scanning it.

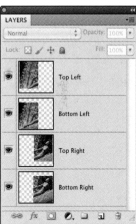

8-13

181

USING THE CROP AND STRAIGHTEN PHOTOS COMMAND

When scanning smaller prints, you can save time by scanning several at the same time by laying them side-by-side on the scanner glass and doing a *gang scan*.

After a gang scan is done, you must crop and remove each individual image from the scan. Figure 8-14 shows a scan that includes several images. Instead of cropping each of these images manually, you can let Photoshop do the work:

1. Open a file that contains several images that were scanned at the same time.

2. Choose File↪Automate↪Crop and Straighten Photos. When you do this, Photoshop examines the scan and extracts each image as a separate file. This saves lots of time by doing most of the work for you.

Be aware that if the command can't distinguish where the edge of an individual print is, uneven cropping can result. This occurs most often with old prints that have white borders around them. It's not a big problem; the white border gets cropped off. If you want the border, you'll have to crop the individual image out of the gang scan manually — which is still faster than doing individual scans.

3. Individually save each of the new files that are created.

PRO TIP

To help the Crop and Straighten Photos command do its job, be sure to leave some space between prints and the edges of the frame when gang scanning.

8-14

ADJUSTING GEOMETRY WITH THE TRANSFORM COMMAND

Sometimes, the originals you're scanning are not perfect rectangles, meaning that all corners are not perfect right angles. This can be caused by a few different things — maybe the print was trimmed and the person trimming it wasn't paying attention, or the print was printed crooked in the first place. When you're dealing with old prints, all kinds of things can affect the squareness of the corners.

When you encounter this, it's necessary to make some geometric adjustments after scanning. Otherwise, you may have problems when it's time to print the photo. Figure 8-15 shows a scan that's a little crooked at the top left and the bottom left.

You could crop in closer to square everything up, but you'd lose some of the intricate border around the image. Suppose you want to keep that border so you can clean it up later. Here's how you do it:

1. Open the file to be transformed, and duplicate the Background layer by choosing Layer⇨Duplicate Layer.

2. Choose Edit⇨Transform, and click Distort. A thin line appears around the boundary of the image. At the corners of this line are small boxes called handles.

   If you can't see these lines, a couple of things could be hiding them. You may be zoomed in too much so you can't see the boundaries of the image. Try zooming out to add some space around the document boundaries (⌘/Ctrl+-).

3. Click the handle of the corner that needs to be adjusted, and carefully drag it to the corner of the

8-15

document boundary. When it's square, let go of the mouse button and move to the next corner that needs to be adjusted.

4. After everything looks the way you want it to look, press Enter or click the Commit button on the options bar. It has a check mark icon on it. If you decide that you want to start over in the middle of a Transform operation, press Esc, or click the Cancel button, which is next to the Commit button, and begin again with Step 2.

Sometimes, all four corners are off by the same amount because the whole print was crooked when it was scanned. To solve this problem, use the Rotate option under the Transform command. When using Rotate, move the cursor outside the image area and look for a curved arrow. When you see it, click and drag up or down to rotate the layer.

I'm thinking about purchasing a scanner to scan some old family photos. What kinds of things should I consider to help me determine which scanner is the best fit for me?

It's a good idea to think about how you plan to use a scanner before making a purchase. Things to consider are: What are your current scanning needs and how might they change over time? Will you be scanning prints and film or just prints? If you're scanning film, what formats will you be scanning? What will the final use of your scan be — an Internet image or a large print? The answers to questions like these help to guide you to the type of scanner you require. You want a scanner that handles all of your needs, but if they aren't too great, there's no sense spending money on a piece of equipment that has capabilities beyond them.

If you determine that you need high-quality film scans for commercial purposes, then you'll need to go with a dedicated film scanner. However, if you're making scans of old negatives and slides for family archives, then a midrange hybrid scanner will do a great job — especially after you optimize the scan using what you've already learned in this book.

You mentioned the difference between dpi and ppi and explained that dpi is mostly related to inkjet printing. However, you also said that having the correct ppi is also important when printing. Can you compare how dpi and ppi each affect the printing process?

Dpi (dots per inch) describes how close the ink dots are when printing with an inkjet printer. The dpi value is set using the printer's driver software. These values are stated in two ways. Some printers use the actual values: 720dpi, 1440dpi, and 2880dpi. Other drivers use terms such as Draft, Photo, and Best Photo to describe the same values, respectively. When printing on matte or glossy paper, 1440dpi is often a good choice. One would think that 2880dpi would produce even better results because it delivers twice as much ink. But, in fact, only so much ink is needed to make a print and 2800 can be overkill. When printing on more absorbent papers, such as watercolor paper, 1440dpi can be overkill as well because the inks soak into the paper and tends to spread, reducing fine detail.

Ppi (pixels per inch) describes how tightly packed the actual pixels in an image file are — how closely they're squeezed together. The closer they are, the smaller the dimensions of the image. When they're too far apart, you can see the space between them when you make a print. The optimal resolution is often determined by the output process. The equipment used by most photolabs is designed to produce optimal results using 300ppi. When printing with an inkjet printer, there is some flexibility with ppi. Absorbent papers can hold only so much detail as inks soak into the paper. 150 ppi can be used with these papers because it's hard to hold fine detail on them.

Chapter 9

SOLVING TYPICAL REPAIR PROBLEMS

SEASON'S GREETINGS
A. V. FITZGERALD

When restoring old photos, you can be confronted with a wide range of problems ranging from mundane spots and scratches to exotic one-of-a-kind situations. Though the scale of problems is extremely wide, many of the solutions involve the same tools and techniques.

The goal of this chapter is to present you with a variety of restoration problems and the solutions for them. Because it's impossible to discuss the entire workflow for each project presented here, it's necessary to focus on the important highlights of how I would go about solving each of them.

X-REF

In Chapter 11, you get a chance to put many of these techniques into action when you work on a beginning-to-end, hands-on restoration project.

ASSESSING THE DAMAGE

You should always get a bird's-eye view of a restoration project before beginning it. This gives you the opportunity to identify problems and think about how to handle them. Those problems consist of physical damage such as rips and mold, faded tones and colors, and even extreme physical damage such as major tears and water damage.

These issues are often compounded by the fact that old photos tend to be small in size. This is probably because small photos have always been cheaper, so they are more abundant.

Also, smaller photos tend to have a higher survival rate because they're often stored in albums and boxes protected from the sun's damaging ultraviolet rays. When the intention is to make the restored photo larger than the original, all those problems are magnified.

PRO TIP

When possible you should scan at a resolution that's at least twice the resolution at which you plan to print. (If you're printing at 300 ppi, then scan at 600 ppi, or even 1200 ppi.) That way, you have the option of lowering the resolution and expanding the physical dimensions so that the new print is larger than the original. Just remember that scanning at a higher resolution creates bigger files.

Figure 9-1 shows some typical restoration jobs that range in difficulty. Each of these images has its own set of problems, requiring individual treatment. The first image has some spots and stains that are fairly easy to deal with.

This is especially true with the dark line on the man's beard. It will be much easier to remove than if it were on his skin because the texture of the beard is forgiving.

The second image is a bit more challenging because the damage is more extensive. The crease across the girl's face and the armrest of the chair are the most challenging aspects of this particular restoration job because of the intricate detail in those areas. Most restoration jobs fall into this realm. They need some basic work, with a few challenges thrown in here and there.

The third image is heavily damaged by water and neglect. It's amazing that the print still looks as good as it does. Some of the damage is in the neutral background, but much of it is in areas with important detail, such as faces and clothing. These require more finesse when retouching. This restoration job will require lots of time.

Figure 9-2 is about as bad as it can get. The print was damaged during a fire. The water used to extinguish the fire got the print wet, causing it to stick to the broken glass when it dried.

Removing the pieces of glass was impossible because they were stuck to the emulsion of the print when it was allowed to dry without removing the glass. The original had to be scanned with broken glass and all.

SEP   55

9-2

Though this project can seem overwhelming, it is doable, as you see later in this chapter. Before making a commitment to a project like this, you have to think about what's involved and how you can handle it with you're particular skill set. Don't be afraid to get in over your head; just allow yourself to walk away from the project if it's beyond your current skill set.

When I take on a difficult restoration job like this one, I tend to focus on the hardest parts of the job before addressing the small problems. This way, I get a feel for the problems that need to be solved. It also saves time if I decide that the project is more than I want to take on because I haven't invested lots of time on the small stuff yet.

With projects like the first two in Figure 9-1, where serious damage is limited, I follow a standard type of workflow. That workflow is explored in detail in Chapter 11. For now, I want to focus on dealing with specific restoration problems and solutions. As you explore these examples, notice how the tools and techniques you learned about earlier in this book are combined to solve real problems.

More than 50 percent of this image must be completely reconstructed. The regular pattern of the wall in the background complicates the process because it must be replicated so the background looks convincing.

Worst of all, one of the boy's eyes is completely obscured by the damage. This is exacerbated by the fact that the original is a very small print of limited original quality.

But you know what? None of this mattered to the photo's owner because this photo is the only photo of this boy.

WORKING WITH FADED PHOTOS

Photographic prints fade, especially if exposed to lots of ultraviolet light from the sun. When dealing with photos that are 100 years old, or older, fading is expected.

Figure 9-3 shows a photo that was taken almost 100 years ago. The print this scan came from probably looked great the day it was printed. However, the years have taken their toll, especially on the highlights.

A quick check of this photo's histogram shows that it doesn't contain any bright highlights or deep shadows. Most of the tones are in the middle range. To bring the tonality of this image into line it's necessary to use the Levels or Curves commands to expand the tonal range and then adjust the midtones. Here are the steps I follow to bring the tones of this image into line.

TIP

If you have to scan an original like this one with glass (or anything abrasive) stuck to it, use a sheet of high-quality clear acetate to protect the glass on your scanner from being scratched. Clear acetate can be purchased at art supply stores.

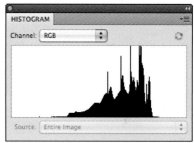

9-3

1. I create a Levels adjustment layer and use the Alt key while adjusting the black and white input sliders to insure that I get the most out of these tones without clipping them. I'm especially careful with the highlights because that's where most of the image's tonal problems are.

2. Then I adjust the gray input slider to darken the image overall. My final values are: 64, 0.89, 212.

These massive Levels adjustments work wonders on the tonal range, but they also oversaturate the sepia tones in the image. Now the color is too yellow, as shown in the detail in Figure 9-4.

This is a common side effect when making such large tonal adjustments, especially to the highlights. Fortunately there's an easy fix for it because I used an adjustment layer.

9-4

3. I go to the Levels panel and change the Levels adjustment layer's *blending mode* to Luminosity, as shown in Figure 9-5. This instantly solves the color shift problem.

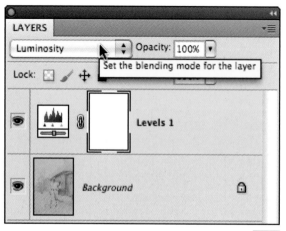

9-5

A layer's blending modes affect the way that layer interacts with the layers below it. The Luminosity blending mode changes the way the adjustment layer affects color of the Background layer. Only the hue and saturation of this base layer are used for the overall color of the image. In essence, what the Luminosity blending mode does is tell the adjustment layer to only affect the luminosity (the tonality) of the layer below it, not the color.

If I had used a Curves adjustment layer instead of a Levels adjustment layer, changing the layer's blending mode to Luminosity would have had the same effect.

FIXING FADED COLORS WITH A SINGLE CLICK

Just as tonal fading is common for old black-and-white photos, color shifts are common for old color photos. It's really the same problem; it's just that the different colors are fading at different rates, causing some to become more predominant. The range of what's recoverable varies with the amount of color fading.

Figure 9-6 shows a color photo from the 1960s. This photo has a magenta/red colorcast. Though this looks like a serious problem, it's possible to recover much of the color with a single click.

If you recall the discussion about the Levels and Curves Gray Point Eyedropper back in Chapter 2, you'll remember that it's used to neutralize colorcasts. The tool does a pretty decent job as long as something in the image is supposed to be neutral in color, where RGB values are all the same (128, 128, 128, for example). That's because the Gray Point Eyedropper forces all color channels to the same value wherever it's used.

Here's how I use it to fix the color of this old photo with a single click:

1. Open a Levels adjustment layer and make the usual tonal adjustments.

2. Click the Gray Point Eyedropper to activate it. Now it's simply a matter of finding something neutral to click on. The blade of the saw that the boy's holding is a good candidate because it should be silver or gray. In this case, when I check the Info panel I see that it's Red, Green, and Blue values are 95, 35, 60 — which confirms the red, magenta hues.

3. Click on the saw blade to neutralize it and the values become 50, 50, 50. Figure 9-7 shows the remarkable results obtained with a single click with the Levels Gray Point Eyedropper.

9-6

9-7

191

For good measure, I try clicking in a few other spots on the saw, giving me a little color variation, but for the most part, all parts of the saw give me similar results.

It's always good to try more than one spot just to see what kinds of variations you can get; one might look a little better than another.

Figure 9-8 shows a more extreme example of this one-click technique. This image is older than the image in Figure 9-6, and it's obviously more severely damaged. In this case, I clicked the turntable of the phonograph in the foreground. The result is still pretty amazing.

PRO TIP

After using the Gray Point eyedropper, it's always a good idea to visit the Color Balance and/or Hue/Saturation commands for final color adjustment.

BASIC SPOTTING AND TEXTURE CONTROL

Almost every scan needs some level of dust spotting to remove dust captured during the scan. Sometimes the spotting encompasses flaws in the original, such as surface damage. When large tonal adjustments are made, they often make these dust spots and damage more obvious.

Figure 9-9 shows a photo after a strong Levels adjustment. The tonal changes to this 100-year-old photo really help, but they also exaggerate many of the image's imperfections, including the texture of the paper.

When dealing with this many spots, it's a good idea to zoom in to 100 percent (⌘/Ctrl+0) and work on the image section by section. Begin in a top corner of the image.

When the first section (everything you see on your screen) has been spotted, move sideways one screen to the second section.

9-8

When the top row is complete, drop down to the next row and begin working your way across again. It's kind of like mowing the lawn: You go back and forth until the entire image has been spotted.

PRO TIP

Zooming in and checking for spotting is a good idea even if you don't notice any dust at first. After you're zoomed in to 100 percent, the dust will reveal itself if it's there. Doing this early prevents surprises later.

Figure 9-10 shows what the first section of this image looks like. The best strategy is to fix the larger problems with retouching tools and then come back with a filter and a mask to tone down the countless tiny white spots and the general texture of the paper.

My goal with this example is to discuss the main points of the workflow. I've included the photo Old_Photo.tif file with the online sample files (www. wiley.com/go/phoprestorationandretouching) in case you want to explore some of the techniques discussed in the following steps.

1. I duplicate the Background layer and name it Retouching so that all of the retouching is isolated to this layer.

2. I go over the image with the Spot Healing Brush using the Content-Aware option, which is perfectly suited to this task. When I come to larger areas of damage, I switch to the Patch tool to work with them. When I work on or near the man's face, I work a bit more deliberately because any flaws here will be more noticeable. (In this exercise I don't address the stain on his collar and tie.)

   Figure 9-11 shows what the image looks like now. Everything is good, except that the texture of the paper is a little strong in the background around the man.

9-9

9-10

9-11

3. I duplicate the Retouching layer so that I can use a filter on it to soften the texture of the paper and then mask out anything I don't want softened. I name this layer Dust & Scratches. I now have four layers in the Layers panel: the original Background layer, the Retouching layer, the Dust & Scratches layer, and a Levels adjustment layer.

PRO TIP

When you start creating several layers that look alike, it's a good idea to name them so you know which one is which.

4. I choose Filters⇨Noise⇨Dust & Scratches to minimize the tiny white specks of dust and the texture of the paper. When the Dust & Scratches dialog box opens, I type 5 for a Radius value and 7 for a Threshold value, as shown in Figure 9-12, and click OK.

The Threshold value controls the range of dissimilar pixels that are affected. The higher the number, the greater the affected range. The Radius value controls the size of the area that's evaluated when searching for dissimilar pixels. The greater the value, the stronger the blurring effect. It's best to keep this value fairly low.

5. The filter blurs the entire layer, so I create a mask that can be used to hide any of the filter's effects on the man. I paint his face with black and then lower the Opacity of my brush to 50 percent as I work my way down his suit. This allows me to partially tone down the speckles without blurring his clothes too much. Figure 9-13 shows the finished project.

PRO TIP

When you use a technique like this with the Dust & Scratches layer it's okay to overdo the effect a bit because you can always reduce the layer's opacity to fine-tune the overall look.

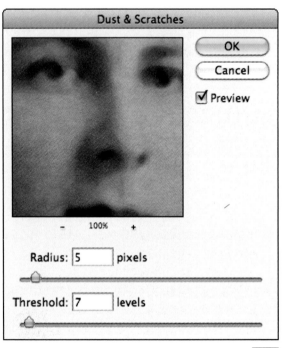

9-12

9-13

As you can see from this demonstration, the Dust & Scratches filter is useful for dealing with many kinds of *noise,* from dust to light paper texture.

Just remember that there's a trade-off to using this filter. It blurs detail in the image; that's how it works, after all. Use a mask to contain this filter so that its effects are selectively limited to areas with little important detail.

REPAIRING PHYSICAL DAMAGE

Photographs are very fragile items that can be easily damaged, especially old ones. In this section, I cover the kinds of problems I see most often and the ways I typically deal with them. Keep in mind that these techniques can be used to solve a variety of problems.

RIPS, TEARS, AND FOLDS

Figure 9-14 shows one of the antique photos you saw at the beginning of this chapter. This photo is in remarkable condition, considering its age: It's easily over 100 years old.

The main problems with this image are the rip in the side, the folds in the print emulsion at the top, and the fold that runs through her face and down into the couch. You can also see several mold spots to the left of the girl.

I want to keep the old border around the image, so it has to be retouched, too. The good news is that much of the damage is in areas that contain *neutral detail:* They don't contain lots of important information.

Here's the way I handle this one:

1. The first thing I do is duplicate the Background layer so that all my restoration work is on this duplicate layer.

2. I begin with the easiest big problems first, the two emulsion folds at the top, by using the Patch tool to quickly repair them. I draw a selection around each of them and drag it to the clean area between them to sample it. I'm careful to try not to pick up many of the dark spots so I'm not creating more work for myself later.

Figure 9-15 shows these first two moves. Notice in both of them I'm very careful to move the selection straight to the side so that the lines on the border will match up when the sample is taken. For this same reason, I have to break the second fold into two separate applications of the Patch tool. I patch the upper section, then patch the

9-14

lower section. This is necessary because it's not possible to find a suitable sample for the entire fold. I also have to be careful around the white outer border. If I get too close to this with my selection, I'll pick up the dreaded smudging that the Patch tool is known for.

NOTE

The Patch tool can be a tricky tool to work with in a situation like this. It does a good job with literal copies as long as the boundaries of the sampled and targeted areas are well defined and similar.

3. I finish the second part of the second fold and then move to the left side of the image. When I get to the big tear halfway down, I again have to address it in two pieces. If I try to do it all in one move, the details on the border in the background won't line up at the same time, as shown in Figure 9-16.

With only five moves with the Patch tool, most of the severe damage is gone. Now it's time to work on the hardest part of this image — the tear that goes from behind the girl's head, down through her body and the couch, and into her dress. There's no way this will be handled as easily as the other repairs.

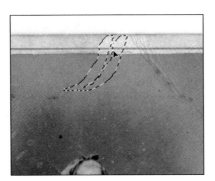
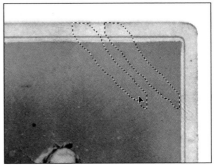

9-15

4. The only way I can continue using the Patch tool is to start breaking my moves into smaller pieces. Figure 9-17 shows one of the small selections necessary to use when working with this kind of detail. The arm of the couch takes 15 to 20 separate moves with the Patch tool. Within a few minutes, I'm ready to move on to the spots in the background.

9-16

NOTE

It's necessary to be careful with the Patch tool when doing this kind of restoration work. Because it tends to blend sampled information with the targeted information, you can end up with smeared, blurry retouching. This can be a blessing when working on portraits, but the goal here is to preserve reality.

5. After using the Patch tool to quickly take care of the big spots, I switch to the Spot Healing Brush. I work in a grid pattern, starting at the top left and moving across and down. Because this original is only 2×3.75 inches, the dust is really apparent when zoomed in. I don't plan to make a big print, so I keep that in mind as I retouch.

PRO TIP

Keep the end use of the image in mind as you work. Even though you can zoom in and see every flaw, you don't need to fix them if they won't show in the final print. Having this awareness can be a huge timesaver.

6. After the biggest offenders have been removed, I use the Dust & Scratches technique from the last example to blur everything and then mask the important detail back in. I choose to leave the curtains a little blurry so that the girl stands out more.

Figure 9-18 shows the finished restoration job.

9-17

9-18

Most of the heavy lifting on this project was done with the Patch tool. Other retouching tools, such as the Clone Stamp and the Healing Brush, could have been used in some cases, but the process would have taken much longer.

The key to working with the Patch tool in this kind of environment is to be sure that the edges and detail you're sampling line up with edges and details in areas where the sample will be placed.

MINIMIZING STAINS

Stains are usually translucent areas on a print where the emulsion came into contact with some kind of moisture. Because detail can often be seen through a stain, they're handled a little differently than a spot that completely hides image detail.

Sometimes, you can remove stains with the usual retouching techniques, but when lots of detail is involved, that approach is extremely complicated.

The photo in Figure 9-19 is a photo from a previous exercise. It still has a dark stain right on the man's throat where his collar and tie come together. Even though it's not too dark, I want to remove it because it's distracting.

This is a tough area to retouch because of all the detail. Fortunately, I know a much better way to deal with a stain like this one. I use a technique involving adjustment layers and masking:

1. I first create a Levels adjustment layer at the top of the layer stack. (I want it to be on top so it won't be affected by any of the existing adjustment layers.) I don't make any adjustments with the Levels settings. I'll come back to it in a moment.

2. Then I choose the Brush tool from the Tools panel and set it up to paint with black at 100 percent opacity, using a soft brush. I want to paint a mask on the new Levels adjustment layer that covers the stain.

Because the Levels adjustment layer isn't affecting the image yet, this is hard to do; I won't see any change to the image as I paint, so I won't know if I am adequately covering the stain. The solution to this dilemma is to press the \ key to change the viewing mode to Quick Mask. Now all painting is indicated by a reddish color, enabling me to see exactly where my brush strokes are.

3. I paint the area covered by the stain. Figure 9-20 shows what this looks like in Quick Mask mode. When the stain is adequately covered, I press the \ key again to go back to Normal view. Because I'm working with a mask, I can always come back later and tweak it if I need to.

Even though I can't see it yet, there's a problem with the mask that I just created. It's the opposite of what I need. Everything but the spot I masked is being affected by the Levels adjustment layer (Black on the Levels layer mask hides any levels adjustment, and white reveals the adjustment.) There's an easy solution to this.

4. I go to the Masks panel and click the Invert button. This inverts the mask so that black becomes white, and white becomes black.

5. After I have the mask in place, I open the Levels adjustment layer and move the gray slider to the left to lighten the stained area. Because I know that this Levels adjustment will have an effect on the color, I change the adjustment layer's blending mode to Luminosity.

The stain is beginning to look really good, but I can still see a slight color mismatch. The colors inside the masked area look a little duller. It's barely perceptible, but I know it will show in a print. To resolve it, I need to add a tiny bit of warmth back into the masked area. This is easily accomplished with a Hue/Saturation adjustment layer.

6. I ⌘/Ctrl+click +click the Levels adjustment layer mask to load it as a selection. This way, when the new adjustment layer is created, it uses the selected area to create a mask on the fly.

7. I create the Hue/Saturation layer and change the Master channel's Saturation to +7. This stain completely disappears.

Figure 9-21 shows the final image and its layer stack in the Layers panel.

9-19

9-20

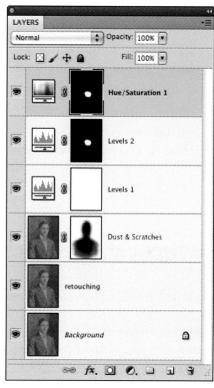

9-21

Sometimes, an adjustment layer affects another adjustment layer that's below it. For example, a strong Levels or Curves adjustment affects a Color Balance layer below it. For this reason, it's best to make sure that any color adjustment layers, such as Color Balance or Hue/ Saturation, are above tonal adjustment layers such as Levels and Curves.

Examine this figure, and make sure that you understand how each of these layers affects the overall image. Taking the time to do so will serve you well when you get to Part IV of this book.

Sometimes, a stain like this has a dark ring around the outside where sediment accumulated as the stain dried. When this happens, retouching must take place around the edges of the stain before the preceding process is undertaken.

Notice that everything that's been done to this image has been done on an individual layer. I can't stress the importance of this enough. If I notice any problems with the steps I performed on this image, I can go back and adjust individual layers to address those problems.

Extreme Damage Control: Replacing Missing Information

The image in Figure 9-22 is one of the most difficult restoration cases I have ever attempted. The print suffered severe water damage during a fire. Its emulsion had been stuck to the glass for so long that removing the pieces of glass would have completely destroyed the print.

You can see where some of the glass was removed from the top of the print, taking the print's emulsion layer with it and leaving the paper base behind.

As I mentioned at the beginning of this chapter, I scanned this print glass and all. Because I knew this job was going to require some extreme measures, I scanned it as a 16-bit file to give myself more to work with.

I also scanned it at 600ppi resolution because the original print is quite small — 2.5×3 inches. This allowed me to double the size of the new print by converting the resolution to 300ppi with the Image Size command with Resampling turned off (see Chapter 8).

9-22

> ## PRO TIP
>
> Though it can be tempting, be careful when increasing the size of a small original print. Sometimes, small prints have so little information that they don't really look very good when enlarged. Carefully evaluate the image before going more than twice the original size.

This was a big job, so I can't take you through the entire project. Instead, I show you what my thought process is like on this kind of project and how I use Photoshop's retouching tools in that process:

1. Because I know that I'll be copying existing detail, like the boards on the wall to create new boards where the emulsion is missing, I begin by retouching some of the damaged boards to prepare them for use.

The big scratch on the lower right is a good place to start. (Naturally, I duplicated the Background layer before doing any retouching.) This first round of retouching must be as literal as possible so I use the Clone Stamp.

2. After the lower boards have been cleaned up, I begin using them to reconstruct the right side of the image. I start sampling the lower boards and painting them on top of the damaged and missing upper boards. The most important thing to be aware of when using the Clone Stamp for something like this is to be sure that the sample point and the application point are perfectly aligned with each other.

The best way to do this is to sample and then paint at corresponding points, as shown in the first image in Figure 9-23.

9-23

After that relationship's in place, I am able to work my way up the wall, copying boards from lower in the photo. The second image in Figure 9-23 shows how the two cursors stay aligned as I move upward. The new boards may not be falling into the exact location of the old damaged and missing boards, but no one will know when I'm finished — except for you, of course.

3. I continue using this strategy (sampling clean boards to reconstruct damaged ones) as I work my way around the outside of the boy. I continually

sample and paint in alignment; I sample a straight line and begin painting in a spot where I expect to see a line just like it.

I also take care of any spotting before sampling a section so my samples stay clean. I want to avoid cloning spots that need to be removed later.

The hardest part of this is matching the tones of the boards. I am careful, but I don't want to get too caught up in this right now.

Seeing all the boards fall into place is a big confidence booster. I don't want to get sidetracked. I can address those tonal variations later with additional retouching or burning and dodging. (I cover burning and dodging in Chapter 11.)

Figure 9-24 shows the progress so far. The wall behind the boy looks great. It needs some more work, but it's much better than it looked when I began.

Now the hard work begins. I was able to get away with some inconsistencies as I reconstructed the wall, but as I begin retouching the boy, I must be more careful.

4. I begin by attacking all the cracked emulsion in the dark pants and shoes. I don't get carried away with the small white dots because they add some texture to the dark area. I use a combination of the Healing Brush and the Patch tools to work on this area.

5. After the pants are taken care of, I tackle the jacket. Here I'll have to be more careful about smudging, so I continue to use the Clone Stamp. I increase its Hardness value to 60 percent to facilitate working around the edges of the boy. (I don't want to make the brush too hard just yet because there aren't many hard edges in this image.) Again, I work on small sections until I build up larger, cleaned areas to be used for sampling.

The first image in Figure 9-25 shows me sampling one of these clean areas as I reconstruct the main line down the center of his coat.

After that relationship is established, I continue to use it as I move across the coat on the right side, as shown in the second image in Figure 9-25. This keeps all of the details in perfect relationship.

If you look closely, you can see that I am picking up a repetitive pattern, seen as short, white diagonal lines. That's because the relationship of the sample

9-24

and target areas stayed the same as I moved across the coat. (I kept recopying the pattern every time I moved the brush to the side.) This isn't a problem as long as I remember to come back and do a little cleanup later.

The hardest parts of the jacket are the arms. There's barely enough good detail to use for samples. I have to slow down here and work deliberately.

6. After I'm happy with the jacket, I move to the most difficult part of this project: the face. When I was retouching the wall, and even the clothing, I could get away with some inconsistencies. With someone's face, you can't fake it. The only thing working in my favor is that the quality is so low on the small original that you can hardly tell what the boy looks like.

I'm forced to clone the eye on the right to create the eye on the left. (You look closer at working with eyes in Chapters 13 and 14 — no pun intended.)

Solving Typical Repair Problems

I also have some trouble working with his cheek. Here I have to raise the hardness of the Clone Stamp's brush to 90 percent so that I get a harder edge along the outside of his face.

Figure 9-26 shows the efforts of about two hours of work on this project. The image can still use some more work to fine-tune it — mostly spotting — but it's much better than it was. Compare it to Figure 9-22 to see if you agree.

This project is about as extreme as it gets. The whole process is exacerbated by the fact that the original is so small. When you first begin restoring old photos, try to stay away from projects that are this complicated. Cut your teeth on the easier stuff before biting off a project this complex.

9-26

Q & A

While following you through the projects in this chapter, I was surprised to see how much you use the Patch tool. Because of the Patch tool's smudging issue when working near an edge, I thought that it would be easier to work with the Clone Stamp tool for some of these tasks. Can you explain why you used the Patch tool instead?

My goal when working on a restoration or retouching job is to work as quickly as possible. The Patch really facilitates this because large areas can be repaired in a single use of the tool. Yes, the tool does have issues when used near an edge, but when the sample area and the patch area are both near the same edge, it often works quite well. I always try to use this tool whenever I think it will speed things up. If the tool doesn't work for a specific task, I back up and switch to a more accurate and more time intensive tool.

You mentioned that the final project took two hours to complete. That seems like a lot of time to spend on a single photo. When you do restoration professionally, are people actually willing to pay for that much time?

The photos shown in this chapter are interesting to us because of the problems they pose. However, for the people who own these photos they are cherished heirlooms. The photo of the little boy in the final project was the only photo this man's mother had of him as a child. After he passed away, it became one of her most important links to memories of his childhood. She was extraordinarily grateful that I was able to restore it to the point that I did.

When you work on restoration projects of your own family photos, it's easy to spend countless hours perfecting individual images. When you do the work for a client, it can be harder to feel the emotional connection to the job. Naturally, you need to consider how important the image is to your client before beginning to work on it. Quite often you'll be surprised by how much someone is willing to pay for your work because you may be the only person who can recover an important part of his or her history.

I know that you do this kind of work professionally, but I'm more interested in using my restoration skills to help my community. Do you have any tips on how I can do that?

One of my favorite photo-related nonprofits is Operation Photo Rescue (www.operationphotorescue.org). This organization was founded by two photojournalists after the devastation of hurricane Katrina. The mission of the group is to repair photos damaged by unforeseen circumstances, such as natural disasters and house fires. Operation Photo Rescue consists of a global network of volunteers who donate their time to help people put their lives back together by restoring some of their most prized possessions. The organization is always on the lookout for skilled Photoshop users, as well as tax-deductible contributions.

Chapter 10

FINISHING THE IMAGE

In the preceding chapter, you learned about various methods for repairing damaged photos. The results of those types of processes are often beyond amazing. However, repair techniques represent only half of the restoration process. The second half of the process involves finishing the image so it looks its best and is ready to be shared with others. This chapter explores the second part of this two-stage process.

WORKING WITH BLACK-AND-WHITE PHOTOS

Many photos being scanned and restored today began their lives as black-and-white prints. Some of these originals have faded over the years, turning a yellowish color. This color is generally referred to as sepia, though isn't a true sepia-toned print, as you learn in this chapter. When you restore an old photo you should be aware of this because you may want the restored version to be black and white so that it resembles what the image originally looked like.

PRO TIP

I scan black-and-white prints as color files and convert them to black and white in Photoshop. I do this because my scanner does a better job of capturing information in the full-color mode. Also, if the old photo has a faded color tone, I can record it in the scan in case I want to try to preserve it.

There are a number of methods you can use in Photoshop for converting color files to black and white. A couple of years ago, I researched the subject and found people using at least a dozen different processes. Some of those are better than others. This section focuses on three methods, ranging from the least flexible to the most flexible.

CONVERTING TO GRAYSCALE MODE

One of the easiest ways to change an image from color to black and white is to convert the image's mode to grayscale. You do this by choosing Image⇨Mode⇨Grayscale. An image's mode describes how the tones and colors in the image are being interpreted by Photoshop.

This is very similar to the idea of color spaces discussed in Chapter 3. Changing an image's mode permanently changes the values of the colors. Colors are mapped to the closest color within the gamut of that mode. In the case of the Grayscale mode, there is only one color channel — Gray — so grayscale images can't contain any color. Because of that, all colors are mapped to a tone of gray.

PRO TIP

It's best to do all of your retouching to an image before converting it to grayscale. That way you can save it in its original color mode in case you change your mind later.

When you use the Mode command to convert to grayscale, a couple of dialog boxes appear. Figure 10-1 shows the dialog box you get if the image you're converting has layers. This warning appears because Grayscale mode doesn't support some adjustment layers that work with color, such as Color Balance and Hue/Saturation.

When you see this first warning dialog box, you have the option of flattening the layers so that their adjustments are applied before the conversion. If you don't

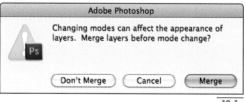

10-1

flatten before clicking OK, the unsupported adjustment layers are deleted, along with their effects on the image.

The second warning, shown in Figure 10-2, reminds you that all color information will be discarded. It also suggests that you use the Black & White command before using the Mode command to control how colors are mapped to grayscale.

Something to keep in mind about converting to the Grayscale mode is that the effects of this change are permanent. After the color has been removed, it's gone forever. Yes, the image can be switched back to RGB Color mode by choosing Image⇨Mode, but it will still look black and white.

Another thing to consider when using the Mode command is that it isn't very discriminating. It handles all colors the same as it converts them to grayscale. When working with faded originals, this isn't much of an issue because they are monotone to begin with. However, when colors are present, the way they're mapped to grayscale becomes important.

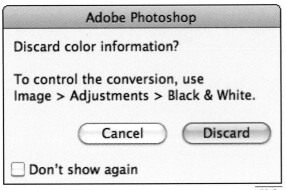

10-2

DESATURATING COLOR

In Chapter 3, you learned that the Hue/Saturation command can be used to desaturate all the colors in an image by dragging the Saturation slider to -100. You can accomplish the same thing by choosing Image⇨ Adjustments⇨Desaturate.

This is like converting to Grayscale and then converting back to RGB Color. The image becomes black and white, but it's still in the color mode. Another difference is that not all colors are mapped the same when using this method as they are when converting to Grayscale mode. When using the Desaturate command, all colors are assigned the same Red, Green, and Blue values.

If you want to see the difference between these techniques, try this:

1. Convert a color photo with a wide range of colors in it to Grayscale.

2. Save a copy of the Grayscale image.

3. Return to the original and desaturate it.

4. Save a copy of the desaturated original.

5. Open both copies and compare them.

Figure 10-3 shows the results of a photo I used for this experiment. The first black-and-white rendition was created by converting to Grayscale mode and the second by using the Desaturate command. Notice that the skin tones look fairly similar, but the sweater is much darker in the second image. The lipstick on the lips is also lighter in the second image.

As you can see, both of these methods leave something to be desired when converting a color image to black and white. The biggest issue with both of them is that they provide limited control over the conversion process. That's why the Black & White command is the preferred method for converting color to black and white.

USING THE BLACK & WHITE COMMAND

You may recall from Chapter 3 that RGB Color images are composed of three different grayscale channels — one for each color (Red, Green, and Blue). These channels can be seen by clicking on each of them in the Channels menu. Figure 10-4 shows the three color channels of the color photo in Figure 10-3.

Each of these individual channels in Figure 10-4 is its own version of a grayscale interpretation of this color image. The channels look different because each is accenting different parts of the color spectrum.

For example, the skin tones are light in the Red channel because reds are always light in the Red channel, just as greens are light in the Green channel and blues are light in the Blue channel. The cyan/green sweater is dark in the Red channel because those colors are on the opposite end of the spectral scale from red.

Figure 10-5 shows the Black & White command's dialog box that appears when you choose Image⇨ Adjustments⇨Black & White (Alt+Shift+⌘/Ctrl+B). It

Red   Green   Blue

10-4

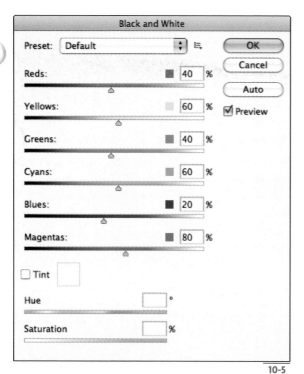

10-5

Follow these steps to use a Black & White adjustment layer to create custom black-and-white conversion:

1. Open the Bike_Racing.tif practice file from the downloadable practice files on the Web site (www. wiley.com/go/phoprestorationandretouching).

2. Go to the Adjustments panel and click on the Black & White adjustment layer button, fourth from the left on the second row. The image turns black and white when the layer is created. The Adjustments panel loads the Black & White settings at their default values, as shown in Figure 10-6.

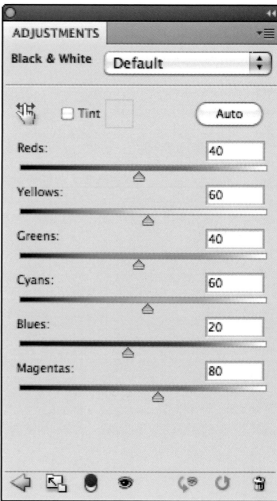

10-6

has six sliders, one for each of our six main colors: Reds, Yellows, Greens, Cyans, Blues, and Magentas.

These sliders are used to lighten and darken specific colors. This is indicated by the color ramps below each color. Moving a slider to the right lightens the color's tones and moving to the left darkens it.

PRO TIP

The Black & White command has one of the dreaded four-finger keyboard shortcuts. If you use it often, you may want to change its keyboard shortcut to something a little easier. To do so, choose Edit⇒Keyboard Shortcuts.

3. Click Auto to let the command make its own adjustment. For the most part, I'm not a big fan of auto adjustments in Photoshop. However, this one often does a decent job of getting you into the ballpark by maximizing the distribution of gray values in the image. Because of this, it almost always gets you closer than the dialog box's default settings.

4. Slide the Red slider to 80 percent, and watch how the reds in the rider's jerseys become much lighter.

5. Slide the Cyan slider to -25 percent, and watch the cyan colors of the jersey sleeve on the second rider get darker. I imagine you're getting the point. You can use these six sliders to customize the way each color is converted to black and white. If you want a certain tone to be lighter, raise the value. If you want it to be darker, lower the value.

6. Slide the Green slider to the right and left and notice that nothing in the photo changes. That's because there are no greens in the photo.

7. Click the Reset button at the bottom of the panel to reset the sliders to their default values. The button looks like a curved arrow.

   Sometimes, it's hard to tell exactly which slider to use for a particular color. For example, in Step 5 I told you to use the Cyan slider to change the tone of the second rider's jersey. If the color looked more green to you because your monitor isn't calibrated or you suffer from a bit of color blindness, you may have been tempted to use the Green slider.

Fortunately the Black & White adjustment layer has a built-in feature that enables you to intuitively modify the tone of a color range without actually knowing which color it is.

8. Click on the Targeted Adjustment tool, which looks like a hand with one finger pointing upward. This tool works the same as the Targeted Adjustment tool in the Hue/Saturation panel that was discussed in Chapter 3. Move to the image and click and drag on a specific color to change it. Click and drag to the right to lighten it and click and drag to the left to darken it. Just be aware that all similar colors in the image are affected.

9. Experiment with other areas of the image, clicking and dragging until you like the tonality of the black and white. Figure 10-7 shows a section of my conversion on the left, compared to a straight grayscale change with the Mode command on the right.

A good example of the difference is the color of the first rider's blue bike.

10-7

There's one more cool thing about the Black & White command: It allows you to use and save presets. Figure 10-8 shows the Preset pop-up menu at the top of the Adjustments panel. As you can see, the command comes with several canned presets.

If you find a black-and-white formula that you really like, you can save it by clicking the Panel Options button and choosing Save Black & White Preset. If you're using the standard Black & White command, click the Preset Options button just to the right of the menu.

When working with old, faded black-and-white originals it's okay to use the Mode➪Grayscale method for quickly converting to black and white. That's because these photos don't have any real color in them so the Black & White command won't have much of an effect. Just remember to convert the image back to RGB Color mode afterward. This makes life easier because some things in Photoshop don't work with grayscale.

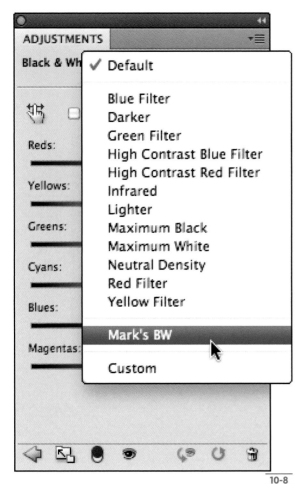

10-8

Figure 10-9 shows two of the old photos you saw in Chapter 9. The one on the left is a true sepia-toned print, and the one on the right is a faded black and white. Notice the difference in the tones. The color of the sepia-toned print is more of a chocolate brown, while the faded print on the right leans more toward yellow.

When restoring an old photo, you can reinvigorate the old sepia tone or add a sepia tone to an image that was never sepia in the first place. Also, keep in mind that this technique isn't limited to restoring old photos. Sepia toning, or *browntone* as it's often called, is still a very popular portrait finishing technique today.

Like converting it to black and white, you can digitally tone a print using a few different methods. In this section, I show two methods: the Hue/Saturation command, which has been the most popular method for many years, and a newer method using the Black & White command.

USING THE HUE/SATURATION COMMAND TO TONE AN IMAGE

When I first discussed the Hue/Saturation command way back in Chapter 2, I mentioned that the dialog box has a check box called Colorize.

Figure 10-10 shows the Hue/Saturation dialog box with this check box selected. Notice that the color bar at the bottom of the dialog box is a solid color. This color is modified using the Hue, Saturation, and Lightness sliders. As those values are changed, the color of the bar changes as well as the tone of the image.

I prefer chocolatey browns, so the settings I use the most are Hue = 30 and Saturation = 22. (I always leave the Lightness value at 0 when doing this.)

APPLYING SEPIA TONES

I've mentioned sepia toning a few times in this book, but I've never stopped to precisely define the term. Sepia toning is a chemical process that photographers have been using in the black-and-white darkroom since the early days of photography.

The process involves soaking a black-and-white print in bleach to remove all traces of silver. Then the print is soaked in a toning solution, giving it warm brown tones throughout. Though the effect can look very nice, this wet-darkroom chemical process is time consuming and stinky.

When old photos fade, they tend to look sepia toned, even though they may have started out black and white.

NOTE

Remember that the Hue/Saturation command also is available as an adjustment layer.

10-9

If the foreground color (the top swatch at the bottom of the Tools panel) is set to either black or white, then the default tone is red (Hue = 0). If the foreground color is any other color, then the hue used for toning is the same as that color.

PRO TIP

A handy way to select a hue for toning that matches an existing image is to use the Color Sampler tool to sample the existing image. This sets the foreground color to that sample color. Now, when you use the Colorize option, the hue is the same as the sampled image.

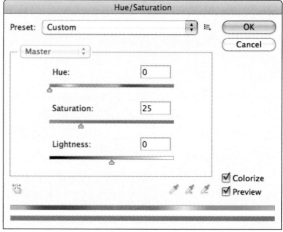

10-10

You need to be aware of an important issue when using the Colorize feature on the Hue/Saturation command to create a sepia tone. Because this command adjusts color, it has a different effect on an image that's been converted to grayscale and back to color than on one that still has a color tint. Figure 10-11 shows one of the photos from Figure 10-9.

The version on the left was colorized with the Hue/Saturation command without converting it to grayscale first. The version on the right was converted to grayscale with the Mode command and then converted back to RGB Color before the Hue/Saturation command was used. As you can see, the color of the tone in the outcomes is different.

If I were using Hue/Saturation to tone several old images, each with slightly different original tones, I'd want to convert them to grayscale and back to color before toning so that they would all have the same sepia color when I was through with them.

Just remember that if you use the Mode command to convert to grayscale, you have to use it again to bring the image back into RGB Color mode before using the Hue/Saturation command. Otherwise, if the image is grayscale, the Hue/Saturation command won't be available because it can't be used in true Grayscale mode.

10-11

USING THE BLACK & WHITE
COMMAND FOR TONING

Earlier, you probably noticed that the Black & White command has a Tint option. You can see it in Figures 10-5 and 10-6. When this option is selected, a tint is added to the effects of the black-and-white conversion. When it's used with the standard Black & White command, Hue and Saturation sliders can be used to choose the color, much like when using the Hue/Saturation command.

When using the Tint feature on a Black & White adjustment layer, it's necessary to click the small color swatch, next to the Tint check box, to open the Color Picker dialog box shown in Figure 10-12. You then use the Color Picker to choose a color by typing specific values, using the color ramp, or by clicking on an image.

The main advantage here is that the sepia toning is handled during the black-and-white conversion process. This saves time by combining both of these adjustments in the same place. It's also handy that when adjustment layers are used, both adjustments are on the same layer.

Either of the options discussed here works fine for creating sepia-toned images. Both of these techniques also are useful for creating other types of toned prints, like blue tones, which are also popular.

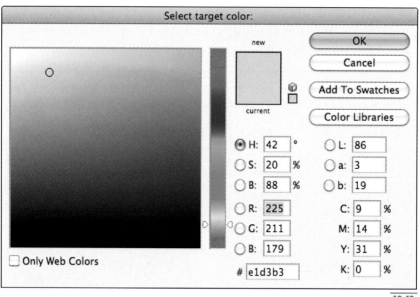

10-12

ADDING COLOR TO A BLACK-AND-WHITE PHOTO

I've spent some time talking about the best ways to convert a color image to black and white, so it only seems appropriate that I discuss how to add color to a black-and-white photo. I am often asked to use this technique on old photos to give them a different kind of antique look.

Back in the days before color film was available, hand-coloring black-and-white photos was very popular. Tinted oils were used to add various color washes to different parts of the image. The effects were sometimes uneven, but at the time some color was perceived as better than none. This hand-tinting effect was used so much that it has an antique feel to it when we see it now. Figure 10-13 shows an old photo before and after hand tinting in Photoshop.

Creating this kind of effect is a two-part process, though those parts can be combined. The first part is to use layers to isolate individual colors as they're applied. The second is to use the correct layer blending mode when creating those layers. Follow these

10-13

steps to learn how I created the hand-colored effect in Figure 10-13:

1. I create an empty layer above the Background layer and name it **couch**. I'll use this layer to paint the couch. Before I begin applying color, I change the layer's blending mode on the Layers panel to Color.

2. I click the foreground color swatch on the Tools panel to open the Color Picker dialog box. I choose a deep red and click OK. I then carefully paint the couch with this color.

3. When the couch is fully painted, I repeat the process on a new layer with a bright green for the girl's dress. I name this layer **dress** and make sure to change the layer's blending mode to Color. Figure 10-14 shows the difference between the Normal blending mode and the Color blending mode with the painting I've done so far. In the first image, both of the new layers with paint in them are using the Normal blending mode. In the second image, the blending modes are set to the Color blending mode.

4. I create another new, empty layer and set its blending mode Color. I name this layer **skin**. I then select a color for the girl's skin tone and begin painting all of her skin. One of the challenges to using this technique is that colors don't look the same when you paint them as they do in the Color Picker dialog box. That's because the Color blending mode allows the color to only affect hue and saturation.

The luminance (brightness) of the color is supplied by the underlying layer. This is one of the reasons I use different layers for different colors. If a particular color isn't exactly what I want after I apply it, I can tweak it using the Levels or Hue/Saturation commands.

Another advantage to using separate layers is that I can easily use the Eraser tool if I accidentally paint "outside the lines." Because each main color is on its own layer, I can erase bits of it without affecting the other neighboring colors.

5. After creating and painting all the layers for the girl and the couch, I turn my attention to the background. I create a new layer with the Color blending mode below the girl and couch layers. Then I use the Paint Bucket tool to fill it with a gray-blue. If I were willing to spend more time on this project, I'd paint each of the background details — curtains, floor, wall — a slightly different color.

10-14

▶

PRO TIP

With each of these colors on its own layer, I can control the detail edges by giving the layer a slight blur with the Gaussian Blur filter to soften transitions from one color to another.

6. I create a mask on the layer with the gray-blue color so that I can mask out the border of the image to preserve its original look. I also mask out the girl's legs and shoes because I don't want them to be blue, either.

The legs and shoes are still a little too yellow, even though they're back to their original color. So I need to use a Hue/Saturation adjustment layer to adjust them.

7. I create a Hue/Saturation adjustment layer just above the Background layer so it won't affect anything else. I lower the Master channel's Saturation value to -100. This removes all color from the image. I then use the Paint Bucket tool to fill the layer with black to hide the effect.

After that's done, I paint the shoes with white to reveal the Hue/Saturation adjustment only on

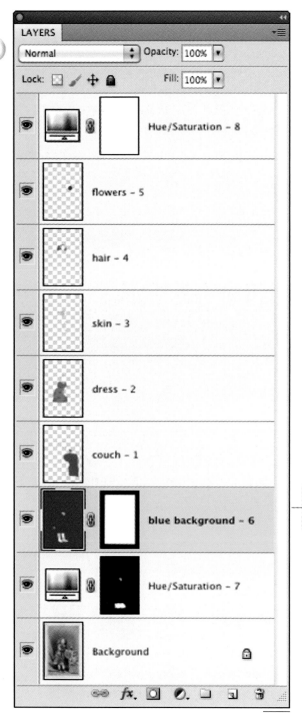

them. This removes all of the original yellowish color from them. I also use this mask to whiten the small amount of the girl's face by masking it back in.

I'm almost done. All the colors are in place, and all masking is done. The only thing I don't like is the overall intensity of the colors. The hand-tinted effect isn't quite convincing because the colors are too rich.

8. I go to the top of the layer stack and add another Hue/Saturation adjustment layer to control the overall color of the image. I lower the Master Saturation to -30, and I'm done. Figure 10-15 shows the layers in my Layers panel. They're numbered in the order in which they were created to help you follow my workflow.

Review the preceding steps as you inspect the layer stack in Figure 10-15 and the final result in Figure 10-13.

This overview is somewhat general, but it should give you lots of insight into creating this effect for yourself. I have used this technique in many different ways over the years to solve a variety of problems.

FINAL CROPPING AND SIZING

After all the restoration work is done, it's time to start thinking about preparing the image for its final use. When preparing a file for final output, whether it's for printing or Web, some cropping and sizing invariably needs to be done to get the file to its final size.

However, before you make permanent changes, such as cropping and sizing, it's best to make sure that you save a master file with all of its layers intact. That way you can return to this master file if you need to tweak it after seeing a print or if you want to prepare it for a different output option. These output files are saved separately as flattened TIFF or JPEG files.

10-15

Additionally, each of these files should be saved in separate folders, as discussed in Chapter 1.

There are two ways to change the size of an image in Photoshop. The first is the Image Size command, which you learned about in Chapter 8. The second method is to use the Crop tool. Because you already know about the Image Size command, the focus here is on using the Crop tool

USING THE CROP TOOL

There are two ways to use the Crop tool. It can be used to crop to a predetermined size (such as 5×7), or it can be used to create a custom crop to suit special needs. Follow these steps to learn the best practices for using this tool:

1. Open the practice file called Antique_Girl.tif from the downloadable practice files on the Web site (www. wiley.com/go/phoprestorationandretouching).

2. Choose Image⇨Image Size (Alt+⌘/Ctrl+I) to open the Image Size dialog box, as shown in

Figure 10-16. It shows that the image measures 5.75×8.6 inches at 300ppi, white border and all. (I scanned this original at 600ppi and converted it to 300ppi using the method described in Chapter 8. It now measures twice the size of the original print.) Click Cancel to close the dialog box.

This tells you that you can crop this image to 5×7 without having to enlarge the file much more. If you decide to make an 8×10 from the image, then it will have to be enlarged substantially through upsampling. Doing so would make the already marginal quality of the image more noticeable, so it might not be a good idea with this image.

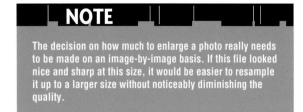

NOTE

The decision on how much to enlarge a photo really needs to be made on an image-by-image basis. If this file looked nice and sharp at this size, it would be easier to resample it up to a larger size without noticeably diminishing the quality.

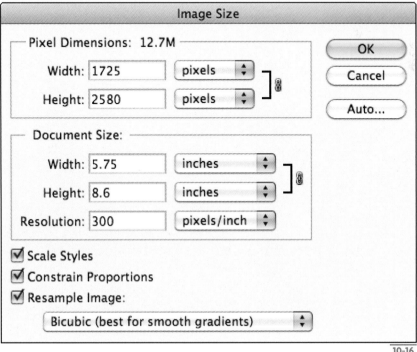

10-16

3. Select the Crop tool (C) from the Tools panel; it's fifth from the top on the single-column Tools panel. Go to the options bar at the top, and click the Clear button to clear any settings from the Crop tool's options in case any were previously used. When all settings are cleared, the tool is ready to handle any aspect ratio of custom cropping. No resampling occurs when the tool is used in this way.

4. Click at the top-left corner and drag down to the bottom-right corner, as shown in Figure 10-17 to even out the white border so that the top, bottom, and sides have the same amount of white.

10-17

If the cropping marquee isn't exactly where you want it, there are a couple of ways to adjust it after it's drawn instead of redrawing it:

> If the crop box is off by just a bit, you can nudge it right, left, up, or down with the cursor keys on your keyboard.

> If it needs to be dragged farther, click and drag inside the selection to move it.

> You can use any of the boxes that are at the corners and sides of the selection to adjust that corner or side.

> If you want to bail and start all over, press Esc (or right-click and select Cancel).

PRO TIP

If a setting called *Snap* is turned on, you may be having trouble with the cropping selection trying to jump to the image boundary instead of where you want it. Snap allows the cursor to move in smart ways so that it lines up with other things in the image. Sometimes, though, it's not smart enough. To solve this problem, choose View and click Snap to deselect it. (This is one of the few commands you can access while the cropping selection is active.)

When your cropping marquee looks like Figure 10-17, press Enter (or right-click and select Crop). Now the white boundary is about the same all around.

NOTE

A third way to accept or decline a cropping marquee is to click the Commit or Cancel buttons that appear on the Crop tool's options bar after a cropping marquee has been drawn.

In the last exercise, you cropped the image to an undefined aspect ratio. Quite often it's necessary to crop to a specific size. Follow these steps to use the Crop tool to create a 5×7:

1. Open the Antique_Girl.tif file from the downloadable practice files on the Web site (www.wiley.com/go/phoprestorationandretouching). If the file is still open from the preceding exercise, return it to its opening state using the History panel.

2. Select the Crop tool and go to the options bar and type 5 in for Width and 7 in for Height. Type 300 in the Resolution box. It's important to set the Resolution value even when it's the same as the resolution of the photo. If you don't specify a resolution, Photoshop has a tendency to come up with some pretty crazy values. This isn't a good surprise to find later.

PRO TIP

If the reading beside the numbers says something other than *in* (inches), then your ruler preferences are set to something other than inches. This is easy to fix. If the ruler isn't currently visible, choose View⊹ Ruler (⌘/Ctrl+R), right-click the ruler, and select Inches.

3. Click at the top of the image area, inside the original border area, and drag down to the right, stopping just before the border on the right, as shown in the first image in Figure 10-18.

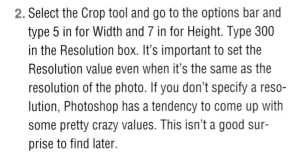

10-18

It doesn't take long to see that this original image isn't proportional to the aspect ratio of a 5-×-7-inch print. The aspect ratio is the mathematical relationship between the image's height and width dimensions. For example, a 16×20 and an 8×10 are both a 4×5 aspect ratio. The dimensions of the 16×20 are exactly four times as big as the 4×5, while the 8×10 is twice as big.

4. One solution to this is to reposition the cropping marquee lower by clicking inside it and dragging it downward, as shown in the second image in Figure 10-18. This enables you to get the entire girl inside the crop, but you lose most all of the area above her. When you press Enter or right-click and choose Crop, you get a cropped photo that looks like Figure 10-19.

This solution worked, but sometimes you either can't or don't want to crop any of the original image. This problem can be solved by cropping and sizing the entire image to a custom size and floating it onto a 5-×-7-inch canvas.

WORKING WITH THE CANVAS SIZE COMMAND

The Canvas Size command is used to add empty space around an image. In this exercise, you work with the same image to crop and float it so that the entire image fits on a 5-×-7-inch piece of photo paper:

10-19

1. Open the Antique_Girl.tif file from the download-able practice files on the Web site (www.wiley.com/go/phoprestorationandretouching). If the file is still open from the preceding exercise, return it to its opening state using the History panel.

2. Select the Crop tool (C) and click the Clear button on the options bar to clear all size and resolution values.

3. Click and drag from the top-left corner all the way down to the lower-right corner, just inside of the original border, as shown in Figure 10-20. Adjust the marquee if necessary and then press Enter to commit the crop.

4. Choose Image⇨Image Size (Alt+⌘/Ctrl+I) to check the size of the cropped image. You should see that the size is approximately 4.25×7.56 inches. The height is a bit too big to fit on a 5×7 piece of paper, so you need to adjust it.

5. Make sure that the Resample check box is selected and choose Bicubic Sharper for the resampling method. Then change the Height value to **6.5** inches, and click OK. This gives you a bit of room at the top and bottom of the photo when floating it on a larger canvas.

   Now you should have an image that measures approximately 3.66×6.5 inches. All you need to do is increase the canvas size around the image to 5×7.

6. Be sure you're on the Background layer, and choose Image⇨Canvas Size (Alt+⌘/Ctrl+C). When the Canvas Size dialog box opens, change the Width setting to **5** and the Height setting to **7**, as shown in figure 10-21.

10-20

Make sure that Black is selected in the Canvas extension color pop-up menu. (If you plan to print on an inkjet printer, you may want to choose white instead of black so you don't consume too much black ink.) Click OK to add the new canvas. Keep this file open so you can use it in the next exercise

The Anchor arrows in the Canvas Size dialog box enable you to select where the new canvas is added. By default the arrows all point away from the center of the image. This means that new canvas is added on all sides of the image.

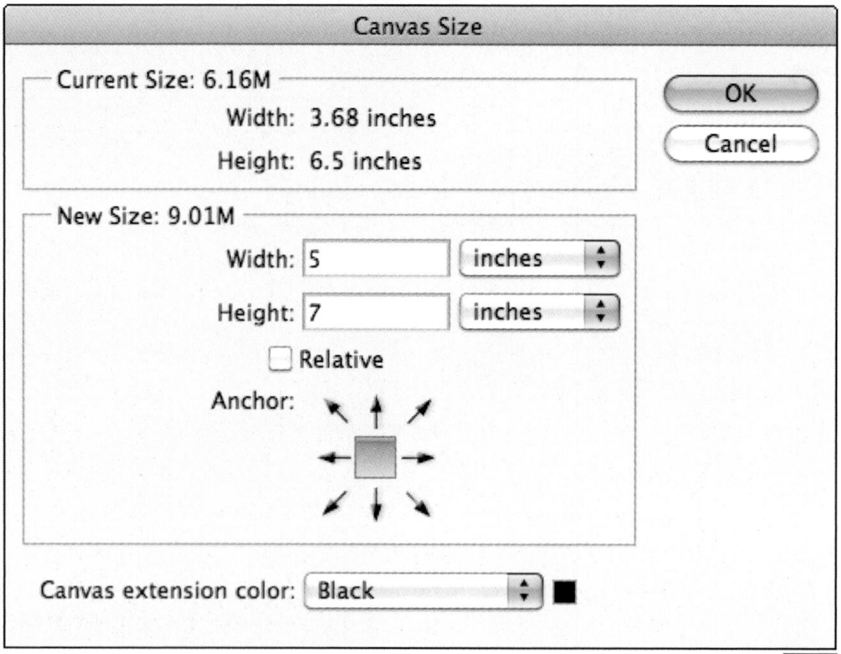

Canvas Size

Current Size: 6.16M
Width: 3.68 inches
Height: 6.5 inches

New Size: 9.01M
Width: 5 inches
Height: 7 inches
☐ Relative

Anchor:

Canvas extension color: Black

OK
Cancel

10-21

If you don't want to add the new canvas to the top of the image, click the top arrow. When you do this, the top arrow disappears and the remaining arrows point to the sides and the bottom.

Your finished photo should now look something like Figure 10-22. If you wanted to preserve the original decorative border around the image, you would do everything the same, except that you would include the border in the original crop.

It would also be best to use white for the new canvas color because it would work better with the existing white background from the scanner lid that shows around the outer edges of the image.

As you can see, there are some options when cropping an image for print. If the original's aspect ratio is different from the intended print size, you can crop part of the original or float the entire image on a larger canvas size. Now that you know how to handle both scenarios, the decision is up to you as you deal with your own images in the future.

All of the previous also applies to images destined for the Web or screen preview. The main difference is that you have much more freedom over aspect ratio when working with a screen presentation. You aren't limited to 5×7 or 8×10 sizes. The only thing you're limited to is the number of pixels that will fit on someone's screen.

10-22

When sizing a file for Web or e-mail, use the Pixel Dimensions section of the Image Size dialog box to size the photo. For example, if your Web designer tells you that images should be no larger than 450 pixels wide, change the Pixel Width value to 450.

Because you're specifying actual pixel dimensions, it isn't necessary to change the resolution. No matter what, the resolution of the image will still be 450 pixels wide.

SHARPENING SCANNED FILES

Now that the Antique_Girl image is sized and cropped, there's one last thing that must be done before printing or uploading it to a Web site. It needs to be sharpened. The reason output sharpening is the last thing you do is because the amount of sharpening is dependent on the size of the image. It can't be applied accurately until the image is at its final size.

Photoshop has a very powerful sharpening filter named Smart Sharpen. However, when working with scanned files, especially when the original paper texture is an issue, it's necessary to use a different sharpening technique that works with a filter named High Pass. This filter is designed to find edge detail where sharp transitions occur, and suppress the rest of the detail in the photo.

X-REF

Sharpening and the Smart Sharpen filter are discussed in detail in Chapter 14.

Because people use a variety of screen resolutions, it's best to make sure the resized image will fit at the lowest resolutions. Today, the lowest common denominator for screen resolution is 1024×768 pixels. If you're sending a file to someone make certain it fits his or her screen by sizing it smaller than this. If you're preparing a file for a Web site, use the Web site's format to determine your final size.

Follow these steps to sharpen the image used in the last exercise:

1. Return to Step 6 from the previous exercise.

2. Duplicate the Background layer (Layer⇨Duplicate Layer) so that you can run the filter on this layer and then blend it back into the Background layer. Name it **Sharpen**.

3. Zoom to a magnification of 50 percent.

4. Choose Filter⇨Other⇨High Pass. When the High Pass dialog box opens, adjust the Radius slider until just the edges are visible in the image, as shown in Figure 10-23. I chose a value of 2.7. If you see the texture in the background behind the girl being picked up by the filter, reduce the Radius value until it isn't as obvious. Click OK.

5. Go to the Layers panel and change the blending mode of the Sharpen layer to Overlay. This blends the Sharpen layer with the Background layer so that only the dark lines in the Sharpen layer are intensified causing them to look sharper. Conversely, it has little effect on the paper texture in the background behind the girl because the High Pass filter didn't enhance it.

Because all sharpening is on its own layer, you can lower the opacity of the layer to fine-tune the sharpening. In fact, I often use a stronger value with the High Pass filter and then lower the opacity of the layer to dial it in.

Another advantage of the sharpening being confined to its own layer is that you can use a layer mask to locally tone down or remove the sharpening from any areas where it's not needed.

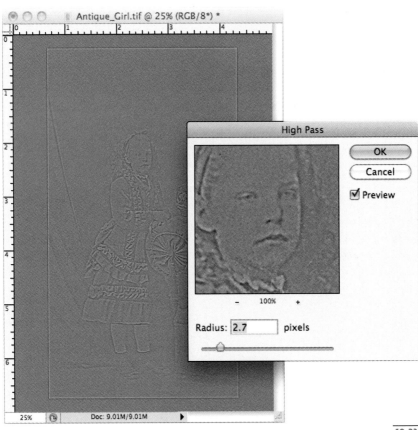

10-23

Q & A

I've often heard that Photoshop's Channel Mixer is the best way to convert a color image to black and white. How come you didn't mention it here?

For many years the Channel Mixer (Image⇨Adjustments⇨Channel Mixer) was the preferred method for making this conversion. In fact, I used to teach this method. The reason it was considered one of the best ways to create black and whites is because it enabled you to mix the Red, Green, and Blue channels as you converted to black and white so that you could control the tones of the colors as they were converted.

This channel mixing strategy may sound familiar because it's similar to the method used with the Black & White command. In fact the Black & White command, which was introduced with Photoshop CS3, was modeled on the Channel Mixer method. Because the Black & White command is more intuitive to use and it allows you to work individually with all six colors, it has replaced the Channel Mixer as the preferred method for doing black-and-white conversions.

You mentioned that using the High Pass filter is a good way to sharpen scans, but you also said that you plan to show a different way to sharpen other photos in Chapter 14. How come the High Pass method isn't used for everything?

Many people use the High Pass sharpening method for all of their sharpening needs. Most of them began using this sharpening strategy when Photoshop's sharpening filter arsenal was more limited than it is today. At that time the primary sharpening filter was the Unsharp Mask. The downside of this filter is that it applies the same sharpening to everything in the image, no matter how much detail is in it.

When Photoshop CS2 was released, a new sharpening filter named Smart Sharpen was added to the filter lineup. This filter is designed to sharpen areas of the photo with detail more than areas that are detail free. In theory, its objective is similar to the High Pass sharpening method. The reason I demonstrated the High Pass method here is that it's still superior when working with scanned prints that have a heavy paper texture of film scans that have lots of film grain in them. Another reason I demonstrated it in this chapter is because it is still a popular sharpening solution, so I want you to be aware of it.

If image size is upsampled or downsampled by the Crop tool, what resampling method is used?

By default, the Crop tool uses the Bicubic resampling method. This is a general method, though it's not as exact as using Bicubic Smoother or Bicubic Sharper methods available in the Image Size dialog box. If you know that an image's size will be changed a lot when the Crop tool is used, it's best to use the Image Size command to get it close to final size and then use the Crop tool to apply final cropping.

Chapter 11

HANDS-ON RESTORATION PROJECT:
THE COMPLETE WORKFLOW

Every restoration project is like a jigsaw puzzle. Some are simple, and others seem impossible. Each is different in its own way. If I wanted to teach you how to assemble jigsaw puzzles, I wouldn't show you how to put together a puzzle and say, "Do this every time." Instead, I'd teach you about puzzle-solving strategies so that you'd be prepared for a variety of jigsaw puzzles. That's what I want to do here as we move through this project together.

My goal is to take you through my thought process as I solve this restoration puzzle so that you walk away from the project with an overall concept rather than just a bunch of cool techniques. As you work through this project, you'll encounter many of the concepts you learned about in earlier chapters. Be sure to revisit those chapters if you need to review some of those concepts.

UNDERSTANDING WORKFLOW

Before digital — when everyone was shooting film — most photographers didn't give much serious thought to the flow of their process. That's because most of their complicated post-production was being done by sophisticated photo labs with well-trained production employees. A photographer just took the picture and told the lab how to process and print it.

Now, everything has changed. Photoshop's powerful image-editing tools are available to anyone who wants to use them. However, people who aren't used to thinking in terms of workflow have trouble figuring out which tools to use and when to use them.

That's why developing a consistent workflow is so important. It spells out the order in which each step is to be carried out. This codification saves time by removing much of the decision making from the process. However, it must also have flexibility built in to it to allow for abnormal or unexpected issues.

Here's an analogy. Imagine that I live in the suburbs and work downtown. I have to be at my job by 8:00 a.m. every day. Instead of looking at a map, I decide to use the streets that I already know to see if I can find my way to work. Depending on traffic and road construction, I sometimes get there on time, and other times I'm late.

This is the way lots of people approach their Photoshop workflow. They don't really have a plan; they just know they'll get there eventually. It's understandable because Photoshop is a complex piece of software. If you dig through the menu commands in Photoshop and explore every submenu, you'll find more than 400 commands and subcommands. This is compounded by the fact that often there are multiple acceptable methods to solving a particular problem.

If I instead choose, when driving to work, to use a map to find the quickest route, I can use this route every time. Over time, I can perfect that route and learn everything about it. If the road is blocked by a crash or construction, I know the best way to get around it. Eventually my commute will become automatic so I can sit back and enjoy it instead of wondering when I'll get where I want to go.

A digital *workflow* is very similar to this. It's a system of mapping out the best route for handling digital projects so that similar situations are handled in similar ways. It's a system of guaranteeing consistent results in the least amount of time, yet it leaves room for handling special circumstances when they show up. Be sure to notice the workflow as you move through the following sample project.

EVALUATING THE PROJECT

Figure 11-1 shows the image you'll be working on in this chapter. It's called Antique_Man.tif and can be downloaded from the practice files on the Web site (www.wiley.com/go/phoprestorationandretouching). If you've already downloaded it, open it now.

This original photo is in pretty decent shape, especially considering that it's almost 100 years old. The original photo measures about 2.25×3.75 inches, which is smaller than a modern snapshot.

I scanned the original at 600 ppi. I then used the Image Size command to convert it to 300 ppi with Resample Image deselected. The image now measures 4.66×7.36 inches at 300 ppi. (If you don't remember how this works, review the resolution section of Chapter 8.)

Here's what I see when I look at this image:

> Because this original is small to begin with, it won't be fruitful to make any final prints larger than 5×7. This is good to know up front because it affects the amount of work that needs to be done. A larger final print requires more attention to detail than a small one.

> The image looks flat. The brightness and contrast need to be adjusted.

> It suffers from many of the usual problems such as spots, streaks, and smudges, but overall it's in pretty good shape.

> The man's beard has a major scratch, and he has smudges on his cheek.

> His eyes are a tad too dark, and part of his hair is a bit too light.

> The scanner caused a *moiré effect* where the pattern of his tie meets his vest. A moiré is a digital artifact created by digital capture devices, such as scanners and cameras. It's caused by two different patterns coming together. This sawtooth effect isn't in the original photo.

11-1

> The texture of the paper shows through onto the man's skin. If the final print was going to be larger than 5×7, then some additional retouching would be necessary to smooth the effect.

> This faded tone of the original doesn't have much snap. It will look better as a sepia tone.

> The oval shape is pleasing, but the border outside it is quite beat up. It would be better to replace it with a clean border, which in this case, requires less work in the long run.

The evaluation list is quite standard. Fundamentals like brightness and contrast must be addressed, light damage must be repaired, and certain creative decisions need to be made. It shouldn't take more than about an hour to complete this project.

PRO TIP

There are two ways to try to avoid moiré when scanning. If the scanner software has a descreening filter, give it a try. If that doesn't work, try scanning the original at an odd angle and then rotating it back into alignment in Photoshop. (I tried both of these techniques with this original, but neither worked because the effect is so strong.)

PUTTING THE PIECES TOGETHER

Now that you see the big picture, it's time to divide the project into manageable parts. After each part is addressed, the restored image will be ready for printing.

FINE-TUNING TONALITY

Begin by addressing the tonality of this image. After the brightness and contrast are corrected, you'll get a better look at what else needs to be done. Follow these steps to begin the project:

1. If you haven't already opened the practice file Antique_Man.tif, open it now.

2. Create a Levels adjustment layer using the Adjustments panel. Use the black Input slider to adjust shadow clipping. Use the white Input slider to adjust the highlight clipping. Remember to hold down the Alt key to display the clipping preview as you adjust these sliders (as discussed in Chapter 2). After the shadows and highlights are adjusted, use the gray Input slider to adjust the overall brightness of the image. When you're happy, click OK. My final values are 18, 1.10, 220.

SPOTTING

Now that the image's tones are looking better, it's time to get into the meat of this project and begin the repair process. Pick up where you left off after Step 2, and follow these steps:

3. Duplicate the Background layer so that all work with the retouching tools is isolated to this layer. Rename the layer **Restoration**. Begin your retouching with the splotchy background area around the man's head, just above his shoulder on the left. The strategy is to clean up a good-sized area so it can be used for sampling when repairing other areas. There's so much going on here that the Spot Healing Brush won't perform well because of smudging.

4. Choose the Clone Stamp tool (S) and change its blending mode on the options bar to Darken. Make sure you're working with a soft brush at 100 percent opacity. Also make sure that Sample is set to Current Layer. Start off with a small brush size of about 25px.

NOTE

A tool's blending mode is similar to a layer blending mode, except that it affects each individual stroke with the tool, rather than the entire layer. Choosing Darken causes the tool to affect only areas that are lighter than the sampled area. Conversely, the Lighten mode causes the tool to only affect areas that are darker.

5. Zoom in and begin retouching the background, changing your sample point often. After you get a good-sized area clean, you can increase the brush size and sample the larger area and begin painting on the other side, as shown in Figure 11-2. When you need to work close to the man, increase the Hardness setting and decrease the size of the Clone Stamp's brush. Don't worry if some of the retouching spills onto the light border surrounding the oval.

TIP

You should zoom in while you work, but don't go over 100 percent. Zooming in to more than 100 percent can be counterproductive because it causes you to work on small things that will never be seen in reality.

6. Continue working with the Clone Stamp tool until all of the dark background around the man is spotted. Keep using the area you cleaned up first as a sample point to keep the tones consistent. Use your best judgment in places where it's hard to tell where his hair begins and the dust stops.

7. After the background around the man is under control, turn off the visibility of the Restoration layer. Notice how much better this image looks already, and give yourself a quick pat on the back. When you finish patting, turn the visibility back on.

8. Use the Clone Stamp tool to begin retouching the scratches and scuffs on the man's right shoulder. Continue working with the Darken blending mode to eliminate the lighter spots and streaks. When necessary, reduce the size of the brush, and begin sampling close to the area being removed to reduce the possibility of tonal shifts.

    In Figure 11-3, you can see how I sampled and cloned in line so that areas of detail, like the edge of his coat, line up. Use this technique when removing long scratches, too.

9. When you're ready to work on the left side of his clothing, switch to the Spot Healing Brush (J) with the Content-Aware options selected. Use it to remove any remaining light or dark spots. Just remember to keep the brush as small as possible so that it doesn't leave any smearing behind. (I set it to 20px.) Also, keep the brush's Hardness setting low.

    This tool works well on small areas. It's especially useful here because you're working around lots of details (see Figure 11-4). If you have problems with this tool smudging, especially around the boundary of the oval, switch the sample type to Create Texture or Proximity Match on the options bar. Spot as much of the left side with the Spot Healing Brush as you can.

    Figure 11-4 shows what my version of the image looks like at this point. The background behind the man and his coat are looking pretty good. There's still some damage on the suit, and his head and tie still need to be addressed. Even so, this is a huge improvement in a short time. Turn the visibility of the Restoration layer off and on a few times to check your work.

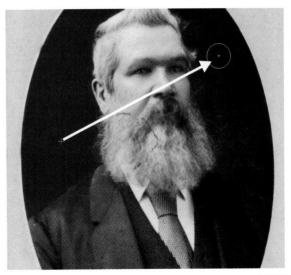

11-2

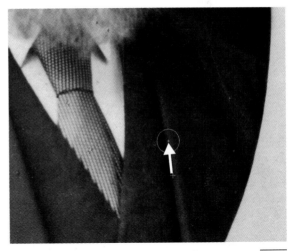

11-3

10. Choose the Patch tool (J) so you can use it to retouch groups of the white spots on the lower part of the coat. Draw a selection similar to the selection in the first image on Figure 11-5 that encompasses a clean area. Be sure to keep detail in the coat aligned as you drag the selection upward, as shown in the second image. This way, everything lines up when you release the mouse button and remove the spots.

You are able to use the Patch tool here because you've already cleaned up the man's coat, giving you large areas to use for sampling. This is one of the tricks to restoration and retouching. Use one tool to clean up an area that can be used for sampling by another, more powerful tool.

Continue spotting any other damage to the man's coat and vest. Use any of the tools you've used so far to repair them. For the moment, stay away from the area where the tie and vest meet.

REPAIRING DAMAGE

At this point, everything should look good except for the man's tie and head. Begin working on the tie by picking up where you left off after Step 10 and follow these steps:

11. Use the Patch tool to repair the three damage spots on the tie. Keep the pattern lined up in the target and sample areas, as shown in Figure 11-6.

Now you can use some of the area of the tie you just cleaned up to repair the jagged moiré pattern where the tie and the vest meet. You can fix this with one of my favorite techniques. You copy part of the tie and paste it on top of the jagged lines. This technique is fast and effective.

12. Choose the Polygonal Lasso tool (L), which is stacked with the Lasso tool on the Tools panel. (You may recall from Chapter 5 that this tool is used for drawing selections with straight lines between two points.) Click to the top right of where the tie and vest meet. Release the mouse button, move the cursor down to the "V" at the bottom of the vest where the two sides of it meet, and click a second time. When you do, a selection line is drawn between the two clicks.

Move up just a bit and click a third time, then move up and to the left and click a fourth time, and then move back down to the first click to complete the selection. Make the selection just large enough to enclose the jagged edges. It should look like Figure 11-7.

11-4

11-5

11-6

11-7

PRO TIP

After clicking, if you don't like the placement of the selection anchor, undo it by pressing the Delete key and click again where you want the point to be positioned.

13. Choose Select⇨Modify⇨Feather, and feather the selection 1 pixel to soften the edge just a bit so the edge won't be obvious when you copy the selected area. When feathering only one pixel the preview capability of Refine Edge isn't helpful. Additionally, other unnoticed settings may affect the selection in unexpected ways. This is a much faster and surer way to apply a simple one-pixel feather.

14. Move your cursor inside the selection, and drag it upward to reposition it, as shown in the first Figure 11-8. The idea is to find an area where the pattern matches the pattern inside of the original selection.

PRO TIP

Use the arrow keys on your keyboard to nudge the selection 1 pixel at a time for fine positioning. These keys can also be used for positioning in other circumstances, such as when using the Move tool.

15. Choose Layer⇨New⇨Layer via Copy (⌘/Ctrl+J) to copy the area inside it to a new layer. Notice that the selection disappears as the new layer is created.

16. Use the Move tool (V) to drag the new layer into place to cover the jagged lines, as shown in the second image in Figure 11-8. Then merge it back down to the Restoration layer by choosing Layer⇨Merge Down (⌘/Ctrl+E).

This process may seem familiar because it's almost exactly the same thing that the Patch tool does. The only difference is that the Patch tool is automated and attempts to blend the duplicated pixels as they're automatically merged, which wouldn't have worked here. If you had tried to use the Patch tool to fix this problem, the area around it would be smeared.

Everything looks great now, except for the face and beard. Continue with these steps to clean them up:

17. Use the Patch tool to remove the main dark scratch on the beard. Break it down into three or four sections, being careful to match the beard's texture when sampling. When the main scratch is gone, use any tool you want to remove the rest of the spots and blemishes on the beard.

11-8

18. After you finish with the beard, continue retouching the spots and damage on his face. Notice that the rough texture on his skin is caused by the texture of the original print's paper. In this case, we're going to leave it, because it helps to define his face on a small print like a 5×7. If you want to tone it down with one of the tools we've used so far, go ahead.

When you finish, zoom to 100 percent and make one more pass over the entire image, section-by-section, to see if you missed anything. When all the repair work is done, your version of Antique_ Man.tif should look similar to Figure 11-9.

Hands-on Restoration Project: The Complete Workflow

11-9

on the paper become. When an area of a print needs to be darker than the rest of the print, the printer makes a second exposure onto the paper.

During that second exposure, he holds a sheet of cardboard with a small hole between the enlarger and the printing paper, allowing the light to hit only the area to be darkened. This process is called burning or burning-in.

Dodging is the opposite. If something needs to be lighter than the rest of the print, the printer blocks some of the light passing from the enlarger to the printing paper during the initial exposure. By doing this, he holds back some of the light from hitting the sensitive paper, making those tones lighter.

In the days of the traditional darkroom, burning and dodging was hit and miss. You never really knew how well you did until the photo paper was developed. Fortunately, the process is much easier and more controllable in the world of digital imaging and Photoshop.

BURNING AND DODGING WITHOUT THE BURN AND DODGE TOOLS

Since its earliest days, Photoshop has had a Burn tool and a Dodge tool. However, I don't discuss them here because I rarely use them myself. In fact, I don't know many serious Photoshop users who do. There are two reasons these tools aren't always preferred: The first is that they can be difficult to control, especially for someone new to photo manipulation. I know a couple of people who have spent time mastering the tools, but I don't think it's worth the time because of the second problem: They're destructive to the image.

When Photoshop's Burn and Dodge tools are used, they permanently change pixels. If you change your mind tomorrow, you can't undo their effects. The only way to isolate the effects of these tools is to duplicate a layer and use them exclusively on that duplicate. This is one of the least flexible ways of isolating burning and dodging to an independent layer because it

ADJUSTING TONES LOCALLY WITH BURNING AND DODGING

Global tonal adjustments are mandatory when restoring old photos. However, local tonal adjustments are also quite effective when particular areas of the original photo are too light or too dark.

WHAT ARE BURNING AND DODGING?

The terms *burning* and *dodging* refer to techniques that have been used in chemical darkrooms since the earliest days of photography. When using an enlarger to print a negative onto a piece of light-sensitive paper, the longer the light hits the paper, the darker the tones still isn't easy to make modifications if you change your mind later. Also, duplicating a full image layer adds to the size of a file.

Let's go back to the project file so you can learn a more flexible method for burning and dodging. Pick up where you left off after Step 18, and follow these steps:

19. Click the Levels 1 layer in the Layers panel to make it active. It should be at the top of the layer stack. The goal is to create a new layer for burning and dodging that is above this layer so the Levels adjustment layer does not affect its tones.

20. Add a new layer by choosing Layer⇨New⇨Layer (or click the New Layer icon on the bottom of the Layers panel.) Name the new layer **Burn & Dodge**.

21. Change the Layer blending mode of the Burn & Dodge layer to Soft Light. Remember that this blending mode is selected from the menu on the Layers panel.

22. Select the Brush tool (B) from the Tools panel. Lower the Hardness value to 0 percent, set the Opacity to 15 percent, and make sure Flow is 100 percent. You're going to be painting with black to darken areas and white to lighten, so make sure the color swatches on the Tools panel are set to their defaults of black over white by pressing D on your keyboard. Press X to swap the colors so that white is the foreground color.

23. Adjust the size of the brush to about 30px so it's small enough to work on the eyes. Now use white paint to lighten each eye. Be sure to also lighten the eye socket area between the eye and the eyebrow. The effect should be barely noticeable. Use a couple of strokes to get the lightness to where you like it. This is the reason for beginning with such a low opacity on the Brush tool. It's much better to reach the desired tonality by building up a couple of strokes than it is to try to nail it with one stroke at a special opacity. If you find that you

still can't get the desired tonal change, increase the Opacity value incrementally. Occasionally turn the Burn & Dodge layer's visibility off and on to check your work.

24. When you like the eyes, move down to the mouth and lighten the right side of his moustache with a couple of light strokes. You may want to work with a larger brush here.

25. When that's done, switch the foreground color to black (X) and paint the top part of his hair where it's a little light to bring some darker tones back into it. Continue using black to darken some of the light areas on his face, like his cheek, but be careful about magnifying the paper texture on his face.

26. One last thing while you're working with black paint: Lower the size of the brush, and go back to the eyes. Darken only the pupils, which were lightened during the eye-lightening step.

The first image in Figure 11-10 shows the man's face after burning and dodging. The effects are subtle because the goal here is modest. The second image of Figure 11-10 shows what the Burn & Dodge layer looks like when its blending mode is set to Normal. This shows you why the Soft Light blending mode is important and what will happen if you forget to set the layer's blending mode to Soft Light.

When working with burning and dodging, be aware that if the detail is gone from a blown-out highlight, no amount of burning will bring it back. The same goes for detail lost to a shadow. If you try to recover it, you'll end up with a ghostly gray area.

Because all of the burning and dodging is on its own layer, you have lots of control over it. You add black or white paint to the layer, use the Eraser tool to remove paint, or lower the layer's opacity if you want to tone down the overall effect. And, of course, you can delete the layer and begin again, all without permanently changing the underlying image.

Before you move on, here's a quick review of this easy, nondestructive burning and dodging technique:

> Create an empty layer.

> Change its blending mode to Soft Light.

> Use the Brush tool at a low opacity (I usually begin with 15 percent) to paint with black to darken and white to lighten.

PRO TIP

If you know how to make a Photoshop action, build one that creates the layer, changes its blending mode, and renames it. You can also have it select the Brush tool and set the colors to their defaults.

ADDING THE FINISHING TOUCHES

All of the hard work on this image is complete. Now you can make some creative decisions before you make final preparations for printing.

TONING

One of the creative decisions is to decide if you want the image to be black and white or tinted with a sepia tone. You could have made this decision early in the process because the change will be on an adjustment layer. I chose to leave it until now because the issue didn't need to be addressed earlier. Pick up where you left off after Step 26 for burning and dodging:

27. Make sure the Burn & Dodge layer at the top of the layer stack is active and then create a Black & White adjustment layer using the Adjustments panel. When the dialog box opens, click the Auto button to let it make its own adjustment to the image tones. Because you're dealing with a mono-toned original, you don't need to do much tweaking here. If you want to make any changes to the auto adjustments, do it now.

The image looks okay in black and white, but I prefer the sepia look for an old image like this one. Click the Tint box on the Black & White adjustment layer, in the Adjustments panel to tone the image. If you want to choose a different color for the tone, click the color swatch to the right of the Tint check box to open the Color Picker.

This image is looking really great. Now it's time to get rid of the old, light-colored border area that surrounds the oval-shaped photo.

REPLACING THE BACKGROUND

Because this image will be printed on rectangular paper, it must remain in a rectangular aspect ratio. The oval has to be surrounded by something. As I mentioned earlier, I'm not wild about this beat-up, light-colored border outside the oval. Continue where you left off, and follow these steps to replace it:

28. Click the Burn & Dodge layer to make it active. Create a new, empty Layer just like you did in Step 20. Name the layer **New Background**. This layer will become the new light-colored field that surrounds the oval area.

    Here comes the tricky part. You need to use the Elliptical Marquee tool to draw an oval-shaped selection around the photo. This is tricky because the Elliptical Marquee takes a little getting used to.

29. Select the Elliptical Marquee tool (M), which is stacked with the Rectangular Marquee tool, and make sure that Feather is set to 0px and Anti-alias is selected.

30. Start your selection at the top-left corner, and drag down to the lower-right corner, as shown in Figure 11-11. Don't worry if the selection isn't perfectly centered over the image. Just try to get the shape right. When it looks good, drag it into final position by clicking inside it and dragging. (This whole procedure is complicated by the fact that this oval isn't a perfect oval.) Be willing to try this several times before getting the hang of it.

31. After the Elliptical Marquee selection is in place, choose Select⇨Inverse to invert it. Now the area outside the oval is selected.

32. Select the Paint Bucket tool (G). Choose a color that is similar to the existing color by Alt+clicking the background. Do it a couple of times while watching the foreground color swatch at the bottom of the Tools panel. When you like the color, click the image to fill the selected area with the new color. The image should look something like Figure 11-12.

11-11

FINAL CROPPING AND SIZING

So far, you've been working as nondestructively as possible with this image. Now you're about to begin making changes that are permanent once the file is closed. Before you proceed, this layered master file must be saved.

33. Choose File➪Save As. When the Save As dialog box opens, click the New Folder button and create a subfolder named Master. Use this folder to save edited versions of all master, layered files. Name the file Antique_Man_Edited.psd.

PRO TIP

You should intermittently save a file as you work on it in case your computer crashes unexpectedly.

If you recall, this image measures 4.66×7.36 inches, which isn't proportional to a 5×7 print. Cropping it as is would require cropping to the top and bottom edges of the oval shape, eliminating the background outside it. To solve this problem, the entire image needs to float on a 5×7 canvas.

34. Choose Image⇨Image Size. When the dialog box opens, make sure that Resample is selected and that Bicubic Sharper is selected as the resampling method. Under Document Size, change the Height value to **7** and click OK. The image's new size is 4.43×7.

35. Choose Image⇨Canvas Size. When the Canvas Size dialog box opens, type a value of **5** in the Width field and click OK to extend the width of the image. It should look like Figure 11-13.

Even though this section is called "Cropping and sizing," notice that you didn't use the Crop tool. That's because you were able to control the process by using the Image Size and Canvas Size commands.

11-12

11-13

APPLYING OUTPUT SHARPENING

ow that the image is at its final size for printing, it's time for the last part of the restoration workflow: output sharpening. As discussed in Chapter 10, scanned files sometimes need a special sharpening treatment that utilizes the High Pass filter.

Pick up where you left off after Step 35 and follow these steps to complete the restoration process:

36. Zoom to 50 percent for this procedure. (The significance of this is discussed in more detail in Chapter 14.)

37. Click the Retouching layer in the Layers panel to make it active. Duplicate the layer by choosing Layer⇨Duplicate Layer, and rename it **Sharpen**.

PRO TIP

You can also duplicate a layer by copying it. To do it with a shortcut, make the layer active and press ⌘/Ctrl+J to invoke the Layer⇨New⇨Layer Via Copy command.

38. Choose Filter⇨Other⇨High Pass. When the dialog box opens, set the Radius to **5** and click OK. Your image now looks like Figure 11-14.

39. Change the layer blending mode of the Sharpen layer to Overlay to get the image to look normal again. When you do, the Sharpen layer is blended with the Restoration layer, enhancing only the edges that the High Pass filter found. Because the new background area you created is on its own layer, the edge that transitions from the oval image area to the background is not affected.

In Chapter 10, when you explored this sharpening method, the outer edge of the image was sharpened, which detracted from the image a bit (refer to Figure 10-22).

11-14

You can dial the sharpening down a bit by reducing the opacity of the Sharpen layer. You also can click and drag the Sharpen layer upward in the Layers panel to move it above the Levels 1 layer. Doing this ensures that the Levels adjustment isn't affecting it.

PRO TIP

You also can try the Soft Light and Hard Light blending modes to vary the strength of the sharpening effect.

Now that the image is sharper, any remaining dust becomes more obvious. This is quite common, especially with restoration projects that involve scanning old photos. If you notice any dust, drop down to the Restoration layer and clean it up. Then discard the Sharpen layer and then recreate it without the dust. Figure 11-15 shows the final image along with the layers it's composed of.

Now the image is ready for printing. Because it's being printed by an inkjet priner, it isn't necessary to flatten the file. Save it as antique_man_5x7.psd. If it were being printed at a photo lab, a flattened version would need to be saved.

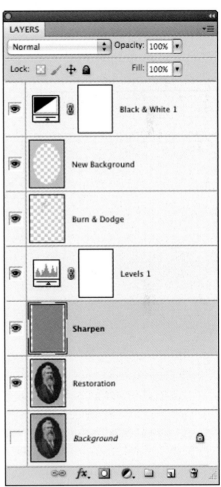

11-15

PRINTING WITH AN INKJET PRINTER

Inkjet printing has come a long way since its early days. The output from modern printers rivals traditional photographic printing in quality and longevity.

Additionally, the variety of printing papers is way beyond the limited range of traditional photographic printing papers. However, inkjet printing isn't for everyone. The downsides are the cost per print and the amount of time involved, especially when the color doesn't match like it's supposed to.

However, for many people, these issues are outweighed by the convenience and control of using an inkjet printer.

UNDERSTANDING THE SETTINGS

When someone asks me to help solve an inkjet color-matching issue, I usually find that the problem is an incorrect Print dialog box or printer driver setting. That's because three important settings have to be correct for Photoshop and the printer to have an intelligent conversation.

If any one of these is set incorrectly, the chances of a good color match become slim. I point these settings out as you proceed through this section.

Figure 11-16 shows Photoshop's Print dialog box that opens when you choose File⇨Print (⌘/Ctrl+P). Some of these settings, listed from left to right, are as follows:

> **The Preview window:** Allows you to see how the image is positioned on the paper. This preview is very useful because it alerts you to sizing errors. There are three settings below the image preview that are used to change the view of the preview.

> **Match Print Colors:** Allows you to simulate the color of the printed image. Changes made in the color management settings on the right affect this preview.

> **Gamut Warning:** If any of the colors in the image are outside of the printable gamut of the printer, they are highlighted with gray.

> **Show Paper White:** Simulates the color of the paper in the preview. This is helpful because the white of paper isn't as bright as the white on a computer display.

> **Middle of the dialog box:** Mostly self-explanatory, this section includes options for number of copies, adjusting the page setup, changing the position of the image on the page, and scaling the print size. Additionally, you can add a bounding box, which applies a black outline to the image. The corners of the box can be used to resize the image.

I prefer to not allow the Print command to do any resampling of the image. It's better to take care of all sizing before opening the Print dialog box. This also ensures that output sharpening is accurately applied.

> **Color Management:** This section on the right is where the important settings are. If you don't see a heading that says Color Management at the top right of your Print dialog box, click beside Output to open the pop-up menu and select Color Management. When you do, these are your choices:

PRO TIP

Notice that as you hover the cursor over different sections of the Color Management area, a contextual description appears at the bottom of the screen. Use this to learn more about the options here.

> **Document:** Selecting this option informs Photoshop of the starting color profile for the document. In this case, it's Adobe RGB (1998). Be sure this radio button is selected instead of Proof.

> **Proof:** This is used to make one output device simulate another output device; for example, to make an inkjet print that looks like it was printed on a particular offset press. This is

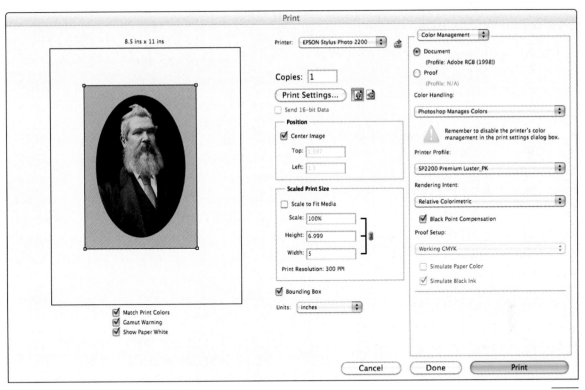

Print

Printer: EPSON Stylus Photo 2200

8.5 ins x 11 ins

Copies: 1

Print Settings...

☐ Send 16-bit Data

Position

☑ Center Image

Top: 3.597

Left: 1.5

Scaled Print Size

☐ Scale to Fit Media

Scale: 100%

Height: 6.999

Width: 5

Print Resolution: 300 PPI

☑ Bounding Box

Units: inches

☑ Match Print Colors
☑ Gamut Warning
☑ Show Paper White

Color Management

⦿ Document
(Profile: Adobe RGB (1998))
○ Proof
(Profile: N/A)

Color Handling:

Photoshop Manages Colors

⚠ Remember to disable the printer's color management in the print settings dialog box.

Printer Profile:

SP2200 Premium Luster_PK

Rendering Intent:

Relative Colorimetric

☑ Black Point Compensation

Proof Setup:

Working CMYK

☐ Simulate Paper Color
☑ Simulate Black Ink

Cancel   Done   Print

11-16

useful when you want to know what an offset print will look like without going through the expense of offset printing a single proof print. Only use this option when working with that type of proofing scenario.

> **Color Handling:** This tells Photoshop whether you want it to handle color management or if the printer is taking care of color. It's usually best to let Photoshop manage the color. This setting is one of the big three that people often get wrong.

> **Printer Profile:** This is the second important setting that can cause color matching problems if it isn't set correctly. By default, this is set to the color space that the image is currently in — in this case, Adobe RGB (1998). For the most part, that's useless information.

What Photoshop needs to know is something about the way a specific printer reproduces color. This information is contained in a printer profile that describes the printer, the paper, and the ink used to make the print. When you install a printer onto your system, its profiles are usually added to this menu.

> **Rendering Intent:** This tells Photoshop what system to use for mapping colors from the computer to the printer. It helps to compensate for differences between the color space of

Photoshop and the printer's color space. Photographers tend to work with Relative Colorimetric and Perceptual.

Perceptual rendering tries to preserve the visual relationship between colors. Colors that are in-gamut may change as out-of-gamut colors are shifted to reproducible colors. Perceptual rendering is a good choice when your image has many out-of gamut colors.

Relative Colorimetric rendering preserves all in-gamut colors and shifts out-of gamut colors to the closest reproducible color. The Relative option preserves more of the original color and is a good choice when you have few out-of-gamut colors.

Changing the rendering intent sometimes affects colors, and sometimes it doesn't. It really depends on the image and the printing environment. If the Match Print Colors option is selected, any changes in Rendering Intent are reflected in the preview.

> **Black Point Compensation:** Selecting this option helps to map the black from the image in Photoshop to the black that the printer is capable of printing, instead of clipping out-of-gamut blacks. It's usually best to leave this selected so that your printer uses the full range of your image's tones.

> **Proof Setup:** This section is grayed out unless Proof is selected in the Color Management area at the top. These settings affect how the proofing simulation is handled.

The two key settings so far are Color Handling and Printer Profile. These settings enable Photoshop to manage the color, and provide it useful information describing the intended printing environment.

The third key setting has to do with the printer's settings. This dialog box is opened by clicking the Print Settings button. It enables you to choose which paper and printing options to set for your particular printing needs.

For the purposes of color management, there is one option that's very important. It is the one that tells the printer to not manage the color. Instead, it accepts the color-managed file from Photoshop and prints it exactly the way it is. This avoids the problem of having the printer try to override color decisions that you make in Photoshop.

Printer dialog boxes vary from printer to printer, as well as between the Mac and Windows platforms. Because of that, it isn't possible for me to show you every scenario. Figure 11-17 shows the dialog box for my printer on a Mac. With this dialog box, it was necessary for me to find the Color Management area of the software in order to select No Color Adjustment.

Figure 11-18 shows the advanced section of the Windows version of this printer's dialog box. In order to disable printer color management, it was necessary to first disable ICM. When I did, the No Color Adjustment option became visible.

As you can see, there's quite a difference between the dialog boxes shown in Figure 11-17 and Figure 11-18. The main point is to find the right place to disable color management by the printer's software.

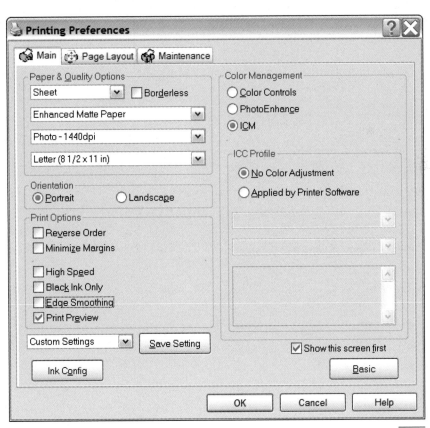

11-17

11-18

Okay, now that you know what's going on with the Print dialog box, here's how to use it to make a 5×7 print of the project photo, floated on an 8.5×11 sheet of paper. Pick up where you left off after Step 39, and follow these steps:

40. Open the Print dialog box by choosing File⇨Print (⌘/Ctrl+P). When The Print dialog box opens (see Figure 11-16), choose your printer from the Printer Profile pop-up menu. Select Photoshop Manages Colors from the Color Handling section, and use the Printer Profile menu to choose the appropriate profile for the combination of paper and ink that you're using.

In Figure 11-16 you can see that I choose Epson's Premium Luster with the Photo Black (PK) ink.

NOTE

Unfortunately, some printer manufactures use profile names that don't make any intuitive sense. If you can't figure out which one to use, contact the manufacturer or visit its Web site to learn about the profile names.

41. After the Print dialog box is filled out correctly, click Print Settings. This opens the printer's dialog box. Select the type of paper you're using, and choose a printing resolution. As discussed in Chapter 8, I use1440 dpi as the printer's resolution unless I'm printing on absorbent paper, such as watercolor or fine-art paper.

Though most inkjet printers have a higher dpi setting of 2880 dpi, often called SuperPhoto, I never use it. This higher setting uses twice as much ink with negligible improvements to overall quality.

NOTE

Some printer software doesn't show the actual dpi numbers. It uses names such as Draft, Photo, and SuperPhoto to indicate 720 dpi, 1440 dpi, and 2880 dpi, respectively.

42. Use Figure 11-18 as a guide for entering the rest of the appropriate information. Be sure to leave High Speed unselected. This causes the print head to print in both directions, but on some printers it seriously degrades the overall quality of the print. Select Print Preveiw if it's an option. Then when you click Print on the Photoshop Print dialog box, a preview dialog box opens before printing.

This final dialog box enables you to make one final check of the print layout before a print is made.

PRO TIP

When all of the printer settings are the way you like them for a particular setup, it's a good idea to save the setup as a preset in the printer software. On a Mac, you do this using the Presets menu. On a Windows machine, you do it by clicking the Save Settings button. The next time you want to print, you simply choose the appropriate preset to fill out all of the boxes with the necessary settings.

Now you're ready to make an inkjet print. Here's a recap of the three important settings when using the Print dialog box. Getting these setting correct is the first step to getting reliable color from your inkjet printer:

> **Color Handling:** Set to Photoshop Manages Colors.

> **Printer Profile:** Use a printer profile for your exact printer and paper/ink combination.

> **Printer Color Management:** Be sure it's turned off in the printer software.

EVALUATING THE PRINT

The goal with printing — whether it's done on an inkjet printer or by a lab — is to match the way the image displays on the monitor as closely as possible. Naturally, if the monitor isn't calibrated and profiled, it is hard to determine whether the print is a match to the screen. I have seen cases where a photographer's color-matching problems disappeared when she calibrated her monitor.

PRO TIP

Be sure to give inkjet prints time to completely dry before making a critical analysis of their color. Absorbent paper, like fine-art paper, dries faster than less-absorbent paper, such as glossy paper.

The other key to determining if the print is a match to the display is to be sure that the print is being viewed under a daylight-balanced light source. If the viewing light being used is normal household light (incandescent), it appears warmer than it really is. If it's being viewed under florescent light, it appears cooler. If you aren't using daylight-balanced light, you can't evaluate the print's color in relation to the monitor because you won't be able to see it correctly.

There are a number of lighting solutions you can turn to when you need a daylight-balanced light source. On the high end are custom viewing booths that can cost upward of $2,000. A more affordable solution for someone just starting out are the daylight-balanced lights made by Solux (www.solux.net). These lights are endorsed by the Nikon School of Photography and the Epson Print Academy.

There it is: a restoration workflow from start to finish — including inkjet printing. Remember that everything doesn't always need to be done in the exact order described here, unless specified. For example, it would have been fine to work on the spots on the face before working on the clothing.

But it isn't okay to do output sharpening until the image is at its final size. The main thing to get about this workflow is that it represents a series of repeatable steps. This saves time and helps to guarantee consistent results.

The other thing to get about this workflow is that it's built on the premise of creating flexibility by incorporating layers whenever possible. If you look back at the layer stack in Figure 11-15, you can see that everything you did to this image can be undone on some level. That way, if you want to redo only the retouching, you don't have to start all over again.

Are there any other issues that need to be considered when restoring a photo that is full color?

For the most part, no. Naturally, you need to add a Color Balance adjustment layer and possibly a Hue/Saturation layer to manage color. You may also find that you need to occasionally use an adjustment layer with a mask to modify color locally. But when it comes to using the tools and techniques in this chapter, the process is the same. In fact, when printing a full-color image small color shifts aren't as noticeable as they are when printing a toned image.

In the section on printing, you mentioned that printer profiles for a printer are installed on the system when an inkjet printer is installed. What if I'm using a paper and ink combination that isn't covered by the manufacturer's profiles? Is there any way to create my own custom profiles?

Yes. You can create your own printer profiles. You can create them for unusual printer/ink combinations, and you can create your own profiles for standard printing scenarios. These are sometimes better than the manufacturer's canned profiles. There are two typical ways to get your own custom profiles: You can have a profiling service create one for you, or you can purchase a device and create your own.

There are a number of companies that can create profiles for you. You can find them online and you can probably find a few locally. These companies usually provide you with a special color chart file that you print on your printer with your paper and ink. Then you send the print to them and they measure the actual colors on the print and compare the values to what they should be. Then they generate a printer profile that compensates for any deviations from standard measurements of their control print. If you use only a couple of print/paper combinations, this can be an affordable solution for acquiring high quality custom printer profiles.

If you use lots of paper/ink combinations, or more than one printer, it's more economical to purchase your own profiling system. These consist of a device that's used to measure color charts printed from a special file that's included with the device. This way you can quickly make profiles whenever you need them. My favorite printer-profiling device is the ColorMunki by x-rite (www.colormunki.com) because it can also be used to profile a display and a digital projector.

RETOUCHING: TAKING YOUR IMAGES TO THE NEXT LEVEL

Chapter 12

USING STRATEGIES FOR SUCCESS

Photo by Mark Fitzgerald

When it comes to retouching a photo in Photoshop, just about anything is possible. When faced with unlimited options and possibilities, even a seasoned retoucher may struggle to find the most efficient path to finishing the project. That's why it's important to step back and consider the retouching process before exploring the tools and techniques that make it possible.

What Is Retouching?

When most people hear the word *retouching,* they usually think about portrait retouching. It's no wonder. In the days before digital, when photographers were shooting film, the things that could be done in post-production were quite limited. A film workflow had two basic types of retouching: film retouching (mostly negatives) and print retouching.

Film retouching was done with dyes applied to the negative, and print retouching was done with pencils, dyes, and sprays applied to the print.

Print retouching was often necessary after film retouching because of the limited abilities of the film retouching. Any other limited tonal and color manipulation took place in the darkroom and was considered enhancement or correction, not retouching.

Today, the term *retouching* has taken on a whole new meaning because so many things are possible using only a handful of tools. A wrinkle can be smoothed out, or a complete head can be swapped between images. Now retouching is defined as image enhancements that go beyond basic tonal and color adjustments, yet typically occur before final cropping and sizing.

Retouching is a process used to improve an image beyond what was possible at the time the image was captured by the camera. In many cases, the process involves fixing problems and mistakes. But in its purest form, retouching is about taking an image to the next level of quality and creativity.

Adding Value with Retouching

Photographers who understand the retouching process know that their job is only half done when they click the shutter, because so much value can be added to an image during the post-production process.

Figure 12-1 shows a portrait I shot of some good friends. The original photo in the first image is a nice photo of this couple and their dog. Many people would be happy to have a photo of themselves like this. However, after a little more than an hour of retouching I transformed the photo into the second image in Figure 12-1.

This second photo is more of what I envisioned as the finished product when I clicked the shutter.

After adjusting global tonality and color, I did several things to increase the value of this image through retouching:

> I removed a number of distractions from the background and foreground, including dead flowers in the bushes and on the ground. Also I removed and toned down bright, distracting plants and leaves because they tend to pull the viewer's eye away from the subjects.

> I did some facial retouching on both of the people to tone down wrinkles and smooth skin. (I didn't have to touch the dog!)

> I burned and dodged to balance out tonal discrepancies on the subjects and the background.

> I blurred the background to add separation between it and the main subjects, causing them to stand out better.

> I darkened all the corners to keep the viewer's eye focused on the center of the image, rather than its edges.

12-1

Individually, the modifications in this list are subtle. Some of them may be hard to see here. But when combined, they add a polish to the portrait, making it feel complete. For a professional photographer, the extra hour spent with an image like this means more money. It also means that the final image is beyond what the average photographer produces. It has become a true creative expression. If you're a professional photographer, this ability to take images to the next level is one of the best ways to set yourself apart. You become an artist with a unique vision.

Whether or not you're a professional photographer, these skills are essential for another reason. They allow you to completely explore your creative vision because you'll know that the click of the shutter is the beginning of a whole process. When you fully understand that process, it changes the way you shoot because you know what's possible in post-production.

COMPARING SOFT-EDGE RETOUCHING AND HARD-EDGE RETOUCHING

Retouching adds value to all kinds of images. Figure 12-2 shows before and after versions of another photo.

The primary changes to notice in this example are:

> All of the distracting electrical and traffic congestion, as well as signs and parked cars are gone. It's almost as though a layer of junk was peeled off the image.

> Geometric distortion caused by the angle of the camera and lens is adjusted, giving the building more apparent character and stature.

> Though the before and after images are strikingly different, the underlying integrity of the subject remains the same.

X-REF

The photo in Figure 12-2 is the project photo for the hands-on retouching project in Chapter 15.

The images in Figures 12-1 and 12-2 each underwent extensive retouching. Many of the same Photoshop tools were used on both projects, but much of the process was different. The goal with the portrait in Figure 12-1 was to tone down distractions and give the image a more romantic feeling.

Because many of the things that needed to be removed were in the background foliage, I had lots of flexibility when retouching. No one would notice if I replaced one dead leaf with a live one from an adjacent branch. When someone looks at this image, she doesn't care what the bushes look like or whether this is a depiction of reality.

The main subjects are what they're most interested in seeing. I even had some flexibility when retouching the people. How will someone know if I patch a blemished section of skin with a clean section.

The goal of the photographer of the building image in Figure 12-2 was to get a good photo of this hotel. He did an excellent job. I've stayed at this hotel is in downtown Seattle many times. I can tell you that this photo was taken from the one place where the hotel wasn't surrounded by other buildings. And the photographer was able to shoot this on a day with a beautiful sky, which can be quite a feat in Seattle!

As a retoucher, my objective when working on this building image was similar to the portrait Figure 12-1. I wanted to make a nice image even better by removing distractions. However, the process of doing this was very different from my process for the portrait in Figure 12-1.

12-2
Photo by Seattle Photography, Inc

With this project, not altering the underlying qualities of the building and its surrounding area was supremely important; the interpretation had to be very literal. In a sense, it's more like a photo restoration project with fewer creative options.

Figures 12-1 and 12-2 are examples of two retouching styles I call *soft-edge retouching* and *hard-edge retouching*.

In Figure 12-1, most of the retouching has a soft edge to it, causing it to blend more easily with the surrounding pixels.

In Figure 12-2, much of the retouching has a hard edge to it. Blending had to be minimized because it would smear important details. All retouching had to be faithful to the original scene. If a light post is removed, it needs to be replaced with windows that look like they belong in that location. With the portrait in Figure 12-1, the original was a jumping-off point.

So the terms *soft-edge* and *hard-edge* not only refer to the types of edge detail that's being manipulated in the image, but also to the tools and techniques used with that style. Here's a quick-and-dirty explanation of the differences:

> **Soft-edge retouching** deals mostly with edge detail that's soft. The retouching tools used with this style are tools that have soft edges or blending capabilities. This style is flexible because you don't need to strictly adhere to the underlying detail. Soft-edge retouching lends itself to creative interpretation.

> **Hard-edge retouching** is a style of retouching that deals mostly with hard-edged transitions. Retouching is done with tools and techniques that preserve those hard edges. With this style, it's important to honor the details in the image. Because of that, hard-edge retouching doesn't leave much room for creative interpretation.

In some cases, a project may require both soft-edge and hard-edged retouching. For example, if the building in Figure 12-2 was in a natural setting with lots of trees and foliage behind it, I would have lots of flexibility while working with them, but not with the building.

In Figure 12-1, if I decided to remove some of the folds in the man's shirt, I would be stepping into the realm of hard-edged retouching because I would have to be careful to preserve the underlying structure of the shirt, especially if it had a dominant pattern.

The reason I'm making this distinction between soft-edge and hard-edge retouching is because both of these retouching styles have slightly different thought processes. You explore the differences in these two thought processes in the hands-on projects in Chapters 14 and 15.

For the time being, focus on the commonalities these two retouching styles share, as you explore the retouching workflow.

MANAGING THE RETOUCHING WORKFLOW

Even though every retouching project has its own idiosyncrasies, they all share a general methodology for approaching the process. When that methodology is refined and documented it becomes a roadmap that can be trusted to provide repeatable results every time — a workflow.

PLANNING AHEAD

With any retouching project, you should take some time to evaluate the project and formulate a mental plan of the actions you need to take. Think about where the image is and where you want to take it. Visualize the outcome. After you have that picture in your mind, ask yourself these questions:

> Does that timeframe fit into the time you're willing to allot for the project? How long will it take to move the image from where it is to where you want it to be?

> Does the project fit your skill set? Will you be able to accomplish what needs to be done with what you currently know? Don't be afraid to take on a challenge or two, but be careful about getting in over your head and making commitments that are hard to fulfill.

> Will you need to learn something new in order to accomplish the project? If so, take the time to seek the resources you need in order to make the project a success. Every time you learn to use a new tool or technique, you can add it to your retouching toolbox.

> What are the intended uses of the image? Will it be an inkjet or photographic print? If so, what size? The retouching process for an image being printed as a 30×40 is much more demanding than the process for an 8×10 because every flaw will be seen at 30×40. If the image is for commercial use, will it be used in a magazine or a Web site? Again, how big will it be?

Knowing the answers to some of these questions will help you to know how you want to handle the project. After that plan's put together, it's time to do the work.

THE FOUR-PHASE WORKFLOW

Most retouching projects differ in many ways, but they all share this basic overall workflow:

> **Phase 1 — Adjusting image fundamentals.** This is where the foundation for a successful project begins. Brightness, contrast, and color are adjusted to their optimal settings. Even if these settings were adjusted previously, they're reevaluated at this time. Other things that might fall into Phase 1 are preliminary cropping and size adjustment, geometric correction, and spotting.

> **Phase 2 — Fixing distractions.** This phase is the core of the retouching process. It's where all the hard work is done. As you can see in Figures 12-1 and 12-2, those things can run the gamut from toning down wrinkles to removing telephone poles.

> **Phase 3 — Finishing the Image.** After all the hard work is finished, creative techniques are used to create the type of visual experience you want the viewer to have. Some of the techniques used here are nonstandard cropping, selective sharpening and blurring, and burning and dodging.

> **Phase 4 — Output and archiving.** Prints can be output with a variety of printers and media. Output files are sized and sharpened accordingly. The master retouched file is archived appropriately so that you can quickly find it later if necessary.

NOTE

The different phases in this workflow aren't so much about the order in which specific tools are used. They're about a systemized approach to looking at a project from different points of view.

Each of these four phases must be considered during the process. For example, when I adjust the brightness and contrast of an image in Phase 1, knowing that it will be cropped to a horizontal panorama in Phase 3 is helpful. That way, if I have difficulty with tones at the top of the image, I can ignore them because they'll be cropped out later.

Another thing to remember is that sometimes more than one phase is being addressed at the same time. When I removed the bright plants above and to the right of the woman in Figure 12-1, I was removing something unwanted in the image as well as controlling the viewer's experience by removing something bright that would take the eye away from the subjects.

Some images require different mixtures of these three phases. The portrait in Figure 12-1 mostly requires Phase 2, with a healthy amount of Phase 3. The building in Figure 12-2 needs plenty of Phase 1 before all the work in Phase 2 can begin. Very little of Phase 3 is needed.

Knowing when to stop

Knowing when to stop working on an image is just as important as knowing how to begin. I've consulted with and trained lots of professional photographers and digital assistants. Quite often, they bring me in because they've lost control of their retouching workflow.

When we begin to deconstruct their workflow, they quickly see that they tend to spend too much time on things no one will see.

12-3

Don't get me wrong — I'm all about perfecting an image. However, if its final use is going to be an 8×10 inkjet print and you're zoomed in to 200 percent, as shown in Figure 12-3, retouching every pore in someone's skin is probably wasting your time. (You may even be wasting your time if the image is going to be a 30×40 photographic print that will be mounted on canvas hung high where people can't get close to it.)

I know this is a difficult pill for some people to swallow. They take comfort in knowing that every detail is managed. I understand this. If you're working on a labor of love, then by all means go for it. But if you're a professional, or if you have other important images you want to work on, you have to learn to use your time efficiently.

One of the things at play here is that with film we were never able to see the image larger than it would be printed. The things we saw were the film and the print itself. It was impossible — or at least prohibitively expensive — to micromanage a retouching project at the level some people do today. Remember that as you work. Zoom in when you need to, but avoid the temptation to do unnecessary work.

Using Strategies for Success

Q & A

I photographed a high school student for her senior photos. Her mother ordered several different poses, which is great. However, the girl's skin needs retouching. Several of the poses are similar, so can I retouch them all at once, or can I automate the retouching so that after I do it on one image, I can easily apply it to the others?

It's possible in Adobe Camera Raw to use simplified versions of the Clone Stamp and the Healing Brush tools on one RAW file and then synchronize those same changes to other similar files. Though it sounds good in theory, each of the images would have to be identical for this to work. About the only time this feature is useful is when you're dealing with sensor dust that falls in exactly the same place on consecutive images. Even then, the surrounding image content needs to be consistent for this shortcut to work on every image. The best example is a bunch of product shots with a white background.

Another method is to automate retouching with Photoshop Actions, which allow you to record editing steps. But again, the retouching would be happening in exactly the same places. Any variations in image content would have a serious effect on the retouching of different images.

So what it boils down to is this: If you're faced with a scenario like the high school senior shoot, you'll have to retouch each of the images individually. When you work on a project like this, keeping three key things in mind can make the process flow more efficiently:

> Take notes as you retouch the first image, especially if you plan to work on other photos from the project in different sittings. I can tell you from experience that it's frustrating to not remember what you did to the first image when it comes time to work on the next one.

> Try to limit the amount of work you do, especially when working on the first image. If you set a high standard, be prepared to stick to it with the rest of the images. As long as you're ready to follow through, it's okay. (Limiting your work makes the recommended note-taking process much easier.)

> Use adjustment layers to share adjustment settings. After an adjustment layer (such as a Color Balance layer) is created, it can be dragged onto another image directly from the Layers panel. Even if the second image's color needs are a little different, you already have a starting place that's consistent with the first image.

If you keep these three tips in mind, the process of retouching multiple images of the same subject will go more smoothly.

Chapter 13

SOLVING SPECIAL PORTRAIT RETOUCHING PROBLEMS

Photo by Brannon McBroom

Even though the kinds of problems solved by retouching run the gamut, much of the focus in the retouching world today is in portrait retouching. In the next chapter, we work together retouching a standard business portrait.

During that project, you go through the entire portrait retouching workflow. However, you won't encounter several special issues while working on that project, such as swapping heads, replacing missing eyes, and smoothing wrinkled clothing.

Photographers and retouchers often ask me about how to handle these special kinds of challenges, so I'm devoting this chapter to solving some of the most common portrait retouching challenges.

SWAPPING HEADS

Back in the olden days of film, the option of switching someone's head from one image to another was a daunting task. Because of this, it was rarely an option for most photographers.

With digital photography and Photoshop, the ease of performing head-swaps has changed modern portraiture. It's no longer necessary to make sure everyone in a group is perfect in a single exposure.

The photographer simply needs to be sure she gets plenty of exposures with at least one good picture of each person in the pose. This is especially beneficial when photographing groups with children or pets.

Though this technique is most often used to combine individual expressions for group portraits, it's not limited to them.

Figure 13-1 shows two images of a young man. He liked the way his hands are positioned in the image on the left, but he wanted a more serious face like the one in the image on the right. With Photoshop, that's no problem.

NOTE

Swapping heads — and even entire bodies — is a very common technique today. I worked on one family portrait where I completely changed three people's bodies and the heads of two other people.

This procedure is very straightforward. Simply copy the head in the second image to its own layer and then drag it into the first image.

The whole process with this particular pair of images is facilitated by the fact that his body position and the background are very consistent. The only wrinkle is that the head is larger in the second image.

Follow these steps to see how I accomplish this head swap:

1. If the two images are tabbed together, I click and drag the second image out of the tab so that both images are visible at the same time.

2. I Use the Lasso tool to draw a loose selection around his head in the second image. I always prefer to keep a selection like this fairly loose so I can fine-tune the copied material with a mask after it's in the main image.

   This means I don't need to feather the selection at this point because I'll be removing its edges later with a soft brush. After the selection is in place, I copy the information inside it to its own layer, as shown in the first frame of Figure 13-2, by pressing ⌘/Ctrl+J.

PRO TIP

If the young man's head was in exactly the same position on both of these images, I would only copy his face from the second image, instead of his entire head.

13-1

Photo by Denyce Weiler

13-2

3. After the head is on its own layer (Layer 1), I grab its thumbnail in the Layers panel and drag it into the main image, positioning it over the original head. Then I lower the new layer's opacity to help position it over the head below. As you can see in the second frame of Figure 13-2, it's a bit too big.

4. I Choose Edit⇨Transform⇨Scale. An adjustment box appears around the edges of Layer 1. I scale the layer by clicking and dragging any of the boxes at the corners or the sides of this box. As I do so, I hold down the Shift key while adjusting to lock the aspect ratio of the layer as it's scaled.

5. As I scale, I reposition the layer a couple of times to realign the eyes. I use them as a registration point because I know that when the eyes on Layer 1 line up with the eyes on the Background layer, the scale will be correct, as shown in the first frame of Figure 13-3.

6. After the scaling is correct, I press Enter to accept it and complete the Transform command. I then turn the visibility of Layer 1 off and on a couple of times to check my work.

13-3

The new head looks good, but it's sitting a bit too low. The eyes on the layer were aligned with the old head, which was positioned looking downward. When you have this problem, it can be solved in two ways. Mask out everything below the chin on Layer 1, or reposition the new layer a little higher. The second solution is better here because it positions his eyes in the right place. It's also faster.

7. I use the Move tool (V) to drag the layer upward until the collar of his jacket matches on both sides.

8. I add a layer mask to Layer 1 and use a soft brush around the edges of the replacement to blend the edges of the new layer with the layer below it. Figure 13-4 shows the Layers panel with the mask on Layer 1.

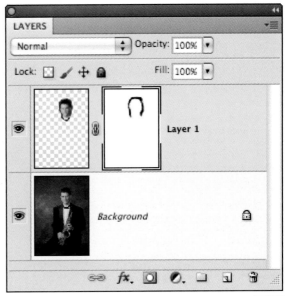

13-4

PRO TIP

In this example, these two exposures were identical. If there had been a tonal or color discrepancy, for example if the new layer was a little darker and greener, I would adjust Layer 1 before flattening.

If I hadn't stopped to record my steps, this head swap would have taken about two or three minutes to complete. Even if it took a little longer, it would still have been worth it because it's what made the client happy.

REPLACING MISSING EYES

Human eyes are one of the most complicated things to retouch. They're not only rich with intricate detail, they also are one of the first things people look at when they view a well-designed portrait. Because eyes are so important to the viewer, you must always make sure that a portrait subject's eyes look their best. In Chapter 14, we look at ways to enhance the eyes in a portrait. For now, we explore a couple of extreme eye problems and solutions.

CLOSED EYES: REPLACING MISSING EYES WITH DONOR EYES

One of the hardest things a retoucher can be asked to do is to replace a missing eye. Eyes go missing for a variety of reasons: Sometimes people blink right when the exposure is being made, and sometimes light reflects off their glasses, causing glares.

When you're faced with having to replace missing eyes, the best-case scenario is to have another set of eyes that can be used as donors. Naturally, it's best if those eyes actually belong to the subject and were photographed similarly with the same kind of lighting and exposure. The direction the head is facing also makes all the difference here because of the way it affects the shape of the eye.

Figure 13-5 shows two different photos of the same young woman. For the moment, let's imagine that these two photos are the only ones the photographer shot during the session. Because the woman has such a pretty smile, the only way to salvage this job is to combine the eyes from the unsmiling face with the smiling face.

On the surface, this job looks straightforward. Most things between the two photos are consistent. Both have the same lighting, and the angle of the head is very similar.

The only real difference is that the head is a bit larger in the second image. The procedure is much like the head swap I detailed in the preceding section: you copy the eyes from the donor image and drag them into the target image.

Here's the lowdown on how I approach this project:

1. Make a loose selection around both eyes in the second image.

2. Copy both eyes in the second image to a new layer, and drag that new layer into the first image.

3. Lower the opacity of the new set of eyes so I can see the underlying layer. I use the eyebrows as a reference point to align both layers.

4. Because the new eyes are bigger, I use the Transform command to scale them down to the correct size.

13-5

Photos by Denyce Weiler

5. The new eyes are a little dark because the image they came from was a bit darker, so I use Levels to lighten them a tad.

6. I finish by using a layer mask to mask out everything I don't need on the new eye layer, leaving only the eyes and some of the skin around them. You can see what this looks like in the first frame of Figure 13-6.

Something still doesn't look right in the new image. The eyes are too wide open for someone who's smiling so much. I included the second image in Figure 13-6 to show you what this woman's eyes really look like when she's smiling. It isn't possible to make the first image in Figure 13-6 look like the second one, but it can be improved.

I use the Transform command to scale the new layer containing the eyes. I drag downward, as shown in the first image in Figure 13-7, compressing the height dimension of the eyes.

When I'm finished, they look more realistic. (Some might argue that they look better in this portrait than the squinting, natural eyes in the second image in Figure 13-6.)

13-6
Photos by Denyce Weiler

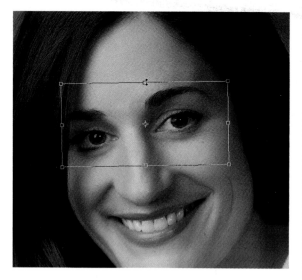

13-7
Photos by Denyce Weiler

This project looked like a no-brainer on the surface because the two images are so similar. But after the new eyes were placed into the image, something looked funny.

The thing to walk away with here is that eyes are very tricky to work with. When you're doing a project like this, try to find donor eyes that match the expression of the main image. Follow your gut instinct when you see them in the context of the new image. If something doesn't look right, try to figure out why.

GLASS-GLARES: REBUILDING WITHOUT DONORS

Glass-glares are the bane of retouchers everywhere. They represent one of the most common difficult retouching problems that a portrait retoucher is likely to run into. Glass-glares are caused by light reflecting off the portrait subject's glasses. When they're severe, they completely obliterate the eye, as well as anything else behind the glass like eyebrows and skin.

I've seen glass-glares in studio portraits where the whole surface of the glasses was a blown-out reflection of the photographer's umbrella or softbox. This shouldn't be happening in the digital world.

If you're photographing someone with glasses in the studio, check your exposures often. If you see that the glasses are reflecting light you can use an old studio trick to eliminate them. Tilt glasses downward ever so slightly so that the glass isn't parallel to the camera lens and lights. Be careful, though, because if you tilt too far, it becomes obvious.

Sometimes, tilting won't do the trick. This is especially the case when you're shooting outside with natural light. If you can't control glass-glares when you're shooting, you can cover yourself by having the subject remove her glasses for a couple of frames every time you change poses. That way, you'll have a set of donor images to use if you need to borrow some eyes.

Working with donor eyes like this is about the cleanest way of retouching glass-glares.

With that said, severe glass-glares still happen, and they have to be dealt with. Figure 13-8 shows a section of a portrait of a high school senior with some serious glass-glares. The way I'd normally handle a retouching problem like this would be to look at all the other photos from the session to see if I could find an eye or two to act as donors.

For this example, imagine that this is the only photo I have to work with. Before I even begin a job like this, I want to know something about how the image will be used. In this case, the client wants a 5×7 print with minimal cropping. This means that her head — from the top of her hair to the bottom of her chin — will only be 1.5 inches in height on paper; the eye itself will be only .05 inches.

That small size makes this project doable. If it were going to be printed larger, or if it were being cropped closer, it would be much harder to reconstruct these eyes convincingly.

This glass-glare removal procedure is complex and detailed. I'll break it down into general steps so you can follow my thinking as I work on this image:

1. First, I need to reconstruct one eye so I can use it to rebuild the other eye. The eye on the left is in the best shape, so I begin with it. I use the Clone Stamp tool to sample areas of skin that are similar to what I think the skin underneath the glare should look like.

   I don't worry if I'm off in tone a little in this first pass because I'll come back and fine-tune if I need to. The objective is to get some detail into the glare areas. I use parts of the eye on the lower left to rebuild the upper-right area of the eye, as shown in the first frame of Figure 13-9. I work with the image zoomed in close, using short brush strokes with the Clone Stamp.

13-8
Photo by Ted Miller Jr.

13-9

2. I look for opportunities to extend lines like the upper and lower eyelids. If some of these details were showing in the right eye, I'd try to sample them from there. I also pay attention to catch lights. It's hard to tell where they should be, so I have to improvise. After I get most of the area filled in, I do some fine-tuning.

3. Now that the tones are similar, I use the Patch tool to blend them together better. I also use the Clone Stamp at 50 percent opacity to do some blending around the edges. I then clone the shadow along her nose because there should be one inside the glasses, as shown in the second frame of Figure 13-9.

4. With the left eye looking good, I can copy it and use the copy for the right eye. I draw a loose selection around it and then copy it to a new layer. Before I can move it into place on the right side, I have to flip it horizontally so that it's oriented correctly. To do that, I choose Edit⇨Transform⇨Flip Horizontal. Then I use the Move tool to drag it into place on the right side, as shown in the first frame of Figure 13-10.

5. After the new eye is in position, I use a mask to remove everything around it that I don't want, trying to salvage as much as possible from the

underlying eye. I use a soft brush with its opacity set to 50 percent to get better blending of my strokes.

When you look at the first image in Figure 13-10, you probably notice something strange. The girl looks cross-eyed because the right eye is backward; the catch light is on the wrong side. If her pupils were more visible, it would look even weirder.

6. Here's how I solve this problem. Now that the right eye is mostly reconstructed, I go back to the left eye and sample it with the Clone Stamp. (I make sure that Current and Below is chosen next to Sample on the Options bar so that I can sample from the Left Eye layer and paint on the Right Eye layer.) Then I clone the iris area from the left eye onto the right eye, as shown in the second frame of Figure 13-10.

Now the eye is looking in the right direction. Essentially, I unflipped the orientation of just the central part of the eye.

7. The eyes are starting to look pretty good, but the lack of dark pupils bothers me. To solve this, I create a new layer above the new eye layer and name it Pupils. Then I use the Brush tool to paint a small black pupil in the center of each eye.

Because these two paint spots are on their own layer, I have lots of control over them. I take advantage of this control by changing the layer blending mode to Soft Light. That way, any light-colored catch lights that are below the paint will show through it.

I use the same technique on another new layer with Normal blending mode to use white paint to add a couple of very light catch lights. Because catch lights aren't always in the same position in both eyes, I'm sure to vary them a bit. I then lower the opacity of the layer so they're very translucent. I also use the Gaussian Blur filter (Filter⇨Blur⇨ Gaussian Blur) to smear them a just bit.

8. Next I add a burn and dodge layer (see Chapter 11) and use it to add some contour to the eye sockets and to darken areas where I think the glasses frame would cast a shadow.

9. I then use the Clone Stamp to tone down some of the reflections on the frames of the glasses. Sometimes these can be as bad as the glass-glares themselves.

NOTE

Sometimes, the glare on the frame is worse than the glare on the glass. It doesn't always have to be completely removed, but it does have to be toned down.

10. Now it's a matter of fine-tuning. This step can take as long as all the previous steps combined because this is where everything comes together. I repeatedly turn off all new layers so I can compare the new and old images.

This is a good way to spot anything that doesn't look right. Because I'm working on this project at 100 percent zoom, I occasionally zoom out to 50 percent to see the image closer to its actual size. This always puts things into perspective.

Don't be afraid to back up and try again at this point. Sometimes, you need to work though a complicated project like this a couple of times to get it right. Just save your layers from the first attempt so you can compare both attempts. You may even find that you can combine parts of your first attempt with parts of your second attempt to get it right.

13-10

Figure 13-11 shows the final portrait and the layer stack in its Layers panel. Notice that I used a Curves adjustment layer with a mask on the top layer to darken the edges of the image.

Use this technique only as a last resort. If you do attempt it, be sure to give yourself plenty of time to work on it. Also, don't be afraid to fail as you search for the best path to making the image work.

PRO TIP

The most important step in a project like this is to walk away from it and do something else for a while. When you come back, you can see the project from a fresh perspective and know immediately if it isn't working.

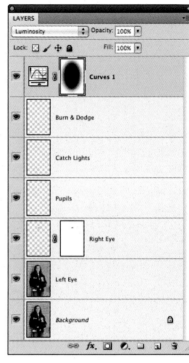

13-11

REMOVING BRACES

When it comes to a portrait, teeth are almost as important as eyes. Retouchers are often asked to repair broken and missing teeth. (They're often asked to lighten and whiten them as well, which is covered in Chapter 14.)

One of the hardest things a retoucher can be asked to do is remove braces. At least with eyes, it's possible to find donor eyes in another image. With teeth, that's rarely an option. It's left to the retoucher to determine what the teeth should look like without braces.

The young woman in the portrait in Figure 13-12 has a pretty smile that's being obscured by her braces.

My job as a retoucher is to use as much of the existing teeth as possible to rebuild the missing teeth. This is a tall order here because some of her teeth are completely hidden.

The good news is that the two front teeth are completely free of braces, which gives me plenty of material to sample.

The process for this project is very similar to the process that I detailed in the preceding example, so I'll only hit a couple of high points.

First, I fix the easy problems, like the teeth next to the clean front teeth, by using the Clone Stamp tool to clone parts of the two front teeth, as shown in Figure 13-13. I work with a soft brush unless I'm near the edge of a tooth. When I am near an edge, I raise the Hardness value closer to 60 percent.

After I have some teeth reconstructed, I begin using them to reconstruct other teeth. This takes a while because several teeth have to be created from scratch using this process. When everything starts coming together, I make another pass to fine-tune any problem areas.

The first frame in Figure 13-14 shows what the teeth look like when they're mostly reconstructed.

They're getting close, but they still look too flat. To remedy this, I add a burn and dodge layer and use a small, soft brush with the Brush tool to shape the teeth by darkening the shadow sides with black paint and lightening the highlight sides with white paint. This helps to make them look more believable, as shown in the second frame of Figure 13-14.

Figure 13-15 shows the finished portrait. Like the project with the glass-glares, this one requires lots of time and patience.

When you do a project like this, be sure to step away from it once in a while to give yourself a chance to see it from a different perspective. Don't be afraid to try again if you don't like what you get the first time.

When you get drawn into a complicated project like this, it's easy to lose your point of view and go past the point of what's needed. Keep the final use of the image in mind as you work. If you bite off more than you can chew and find it's beyond your current ability, be willing to chalk it up to the learning process and move on.

13-12
Photo by Emily Andrews

13-13

FIXING WRINKLED CLOTHING

So far, the focus has been on facial retouching. But a complete retouching job covers the entire image. Sometimes, the clothes in a portrait require more attention than the face. The portrait in Figure 13-16 looks great, except that the woman's shoulder looks funny because of the wrinkle in her jacket.

Fortunately, this is easy to fix. All I need to do is copy a piece of jacket, drop it into the shoulder area, and then blend it all together.

1. I draw a selection outlining where the sleeve needs to be extended, as shown in the first frame of Figure 13-17. The selection boundary from her shoulder to her collar has to approximate where the shoulder line should be. The inner part of the selection doesn't have to be as exact. Because the real shoulder line is a bit soft, the selection needs to be feathered 1px after drawing it.

2. I drag the completed selection to a fairly clean part of the jacket, as shown in the second frame of Figure 13-17. I look for an area that doesn't have lots of detail like seams or shadows. When the selection is in place, it's copied to a new layer (⌘/Ctrl+J).

3. I Use the Move tool to drag the new layer into position so it's covering the space that needs to be filled, as shown in the first frame of Figure 13-18. I must be careful to line it up because I'll be merging it down to the Background layer in the next step.

4. After the new layer is positioned, I merge it back into the background layer (⌘/Ctrl+E). Now I just need to use the Patch tool to clean up any seams that are left, as shown in the second frame of Figure 13-18.

The finished image looks like Figure 13-19.

This simple fix took only a few minutes, yet it adds so much to the image. If a pattern on the clothing had been involved, the process would have been more complicated, but still very doable. It would have just taken a little more time and patience when choosing and aligning the pattern.

13-16
Photo by Dan Christopher

13-17

SMOOTHING SKIN

When discussing retouching with a portrait photographer, a common question that comes up is, "What's the best way to smooth skin?"

One thing about modern digital cameras is that they see everything. When someone is photographed with a high-end dSLR, every pore in the skin is visible upon close examination. Sometimes, this is too much.

In the world of portrait retouching, the word porcelain has become quite popular when describing the desirable skin texture in a portrait, especially when photographing women. Lots of portrait photographers want the subjects in their portraits to have skin almost as smooth as porcelain. Naturally, this term means different things to different people. Some retouchers really pour it on, while others only introduce a hint of skin smoothing.

PRO TIP

Men and women require different levels of smoothing. You can smooth a woman's skin quite a bit, but take it easy on men's skin. If you're smoothing skin in a portrait of a man and a woman, work on them separately.

Whether you want a lot or just a little, you essentially have two ways of smoothing skin in Photoshop.

One is to use a blurring filter on a duplicate layer and then mask it so the blur shows only on the skin. The other is to use a plug-in that's specially designed to smooth skin. Let's look at both techniques.

USING THE SURFACE BLUR FILTER TO SMOOTH SKIN

Before you use this technique, or any other skin-smoothing technique, be sure to take care of basic facial retouching, such as large blemishes and bags under the eyes. That way, your retouching gets blended during the smoothing process.

The young woman in the portrait in Figure 13-20 has fairly nice skin. The photographer who shot the portrait wanted the image to have a high-fashion look. Here's how I use a filter and a mask to smooth the skin:

1. I make a duplicate of the main retouching layer — after the primary retouching has been completed — to use for blurring. I rename this layer Blur.

2. I choose the Surface Blur filter (Filter⇨Blur⇨ Surface Blur), which opens the dialog box shown in Figure 13-21.

   The Surface Blur filter is one of Photoshop's newer filters. It was introduced in version CS2. The filter is designed to protect edge detail while blurring everything else. It has two sliders: Radius and Threshold. (As is the case with most filters, the values used with these sliders depend on the size of the image file.)

   > **Radius** controls the amount of blur. It specifies the size of the area being sampled for blurring. Higher values result in more blurring.

   > **Threshold** controls the range of tonal values being considered for blurring. Lower values preserve more edge detail.

13-20

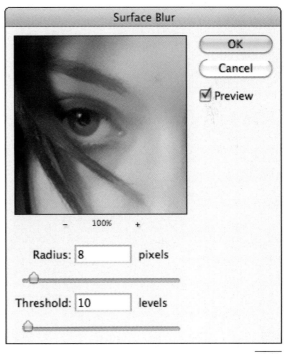

13-21

I set the Radius value to 8 and the Threshold value to 10. I know this is a little strong, but because the effect is on its own layer, I can tone it down by reducing the layer's opacity.

The blur on the skin looks better, but everything else, including the hair hanging by her eye is blurred too. I need to mask out everything except for the skin.

3. I use the Masks panel to add a Pixel Mask to the Blur layer. Because I need to mask out everything except for the skin, it's faster for me to fill the entire layer with black paint and then come back and reveal the skin using white paint.

4. I choose the Paint Bucket tool (G), select black as my foreground color, and make sure that the tool's Opacity is set to 100 percent. I click on the image to fill the mask with black and hide all of the effects of the blur.

5. I choose a medium-sized, soft brush and begin painting at 100 percent only where I see skin. This rereveals the softening done on the layer by the Surface Blur filter. I have to be sure to paint all the skin — such as hands and fingers. I also have to be careful around detail like the hair in front of her face and her necklace, as well as her eyes.

6. I reduce the layer opacity of the Blur layer to dial in the softening effect.

This technique is effective, but it's time consuming, especially when painting around hair. Experiment with it on a couple of portraits until you get a feel for the effect. After you understand the concept, you'll find many different ways to apply it for softening — or sharpening — specific areas of an image.

SMOOTHING SKIN WITH A PLUG-IN

As you may recall from Chapter 8, a plug-in is supplementary software designed to work with Photoshop. Plug-ins allow you to do all kinds of things that can't be done as easily, or at all, in Photoshop. Plug-ins work within Photoshop, so using them as part of your workflow is seamless.

My favorite skin-softening plug-in is Portraiture 2 by Imagenomic. This software does the best job of skin smoothing I've seen from a plug-in. The dialog box for Portraiture 2 is shown in Figure 13-22.

This powerful filter provides a huge amount of control over the smoothing process. For one thing, I can use the eyedropper to select the exact color of the skin. This is important because the filter affects only the range of skin colors I define. That's why its smoothing effect doesn't affect things like eyes and teeth.

However, if I don't feel like fiddling with the dials, I can use one of the presets in the pop-up menu at the top left, which is what I'll do now.

For the portrait, I selected the Smoothing Medium preset from the Preset menu at the top left. I then used Portraiture's eyedropper to click on the skin to identify the exact color of the skin. The final effect is shown in Figure 13-23.

Because this filter only affects colors similar to the color I identified, it isn't necessary to go back and do any masking on the hair. However, this plug-in filter works on all similar colors. So any color that's similar to the selected skin tone is affected.

13-22

You may not be able to see it in this book, but the flesh-colored stripes on the woman's blouse have been blurred along with the skin. That isn't a problem here because I ran the filter on its own layer, so I can go back and do some quick masking to hide the effect on the clothing.

This is intended only as an introduction to this powerful filter. I wanted to mention it here because it's one of the most useful portrait retouching plug-ins I've tried. If you want to know more, visit the Imagenomic Web site at www.imagenomic.com.

13-23

When using the Surface Blur filter to smooth the woman's skin, you created a mask and then filled it with black paint to hide everything on the layer. Is there a way to fill a mask with black when you create it?

Photoshop enables you to create two kinds of masks: a reveal all mask and a hide all mask. This means that the mask doesn't hide anything on the layer. A hide all mask is a mask that's filled with black when it's created. The masks created so far in this book were all reveal all masks. They were created in one of two ways. In some cases they were created using the Select the pixel mask button on the Masks panel. In the other cases they were automatically created when a new adjustment layer was created.

Like most things in Photoshop, there is more than one way to create a mask. For example, if you want to add a hide all mask to a layer, choose Layers⇨Layer Mask⇨Hide All. You'll also notice that you can create a reveal all mask using this method. If you're used to using the Masks panel to create your masks, you can also use it to create a hide all mask by holding down the Alt key when you click the Select the pixel mask button.

What if I shoot a photo of a large group of people, and I notice a glass-glare on someone later. How do I repair the glass-glare without a donor photo of the person with the glare?

When photographing a large group of people it's difficult to be able to manage individual glass-glares. Sometimes it's all a photographer can do to get everyone into position and all smiling at the same time. When you do get a glare off a person's glasses in this situation, your options are more limited. I've been known to borrow someone else's eyes to fix missing eyes caused by glass-glare in a photo of a large group of people. You can get away with this only when the heads are so small that seeing detail in the eyes is difficult. Even so, try to match the eye color if you know it because sometimes it's the only detail that can be seen when the head is so small.

13

Solving Special Portrait Retouching Problems

Chapter 14

HANDS-ON PORTRAIT RETOUCHING PROJECT: THE COMPLETE WORKFLOW

Photo by David Hitchcock

It's time to put theory into practice by completing a retouching project from start to finish. You'll get to see how all of the pieces come together and experience a complete portrait retouching workflow.

Along the way, I'll share the thought process I use when working on a project like this one, giving you insight into the problem-solving process. By the end of this chapter you'll be ready to take on most portrait retouching jobs with confidence.

EVALUATING THE PROJECT

Figure 14-1 shows the portrait for this chapter's project. It's a standard business portrait of an attractive professional woman. This is a nice business portrait, and it won't take much to make it into a very nice business portrait.

I chose this image because it has most of the standard portrait retouching issues like wrinkles and skin that needs smoothing, eyes and teeth that need attention, and flyaway hair that needs to be toned down.

Here's the scenario: The client wants a print of this portrait to hang in the lobby of her office, next to portraits of other professionals she works with. That means she needs an 8×10 finished print. A project like this one requires soft-edge retouching to create an overall refinement and smoothing of the details.

This image will be cropped closer than shown in Figure 14-1. That means you won't need to worry about anything outside of the intended crop zone like some of the wrinkles in her clothing in the lower-right portion of the image.

Even though you know about the intended close cropping, it's best to hold off on cropping until you get to the end of the workflow. That way, if anyone decides changes about cropping need to be made you can back up to an uncropped master file that's been fully retouched.

The photographer also asked to limit retouching time on this project to no more than 30 minutes because

that's all he budgets for a business portrait. An experienced retoucher can do this job in that amount of time. It will take you longer as you work through it the first time. Give yourself plenty of time to explore what you're learning as you move through the project.

PHASE 1 WORKFLOW: ADJUSTING IMAGE FUNDAMENTALS

Before you begin retouching this image, you need to address fundamentals like brightness and contrast, color, and any rough cropping that needs to be done. Follow these steps:

1. Open the practice file titled Biz_Portrait.tif from the downloadable practice files on the Web site (www.wiley.com/go/phoprestorationandretouching). Press Ctrl/⌘+0 to fit the image onto your screen.

PRO TIP

Pressing ⌘/Ctrl+0 is the same as choosing View⇔Fit on Screen. Pressing ⌘/Ctrl+Alt+0 zooms the image to 100 percent, which is the same as choosing View⇔Actual Pixels.

2. Create a Levels adjustment layer by clicking the Levels button on the Adjustments panel. The overall contrast of this image is quite flat. This can be seen in the histogram because most of the data is clumped in the middle of the graph. Hold down the Alt key and adjust the black and white input sliders one at a time. Push both sliders until they almost clip shadows or highlights, as discussed in Chapter 2.

   Figure 14-2 shows the values I use. It's okay to see a small amount clipping on the teeth here because you'll be toning down the brightest highlights later on. But be careful about clipping too much highlight detail in the teeth.

NOTE

If you feel comfortable with Curves, then use a Curves adjustment layer instead.

3. After the two end sliders are adjusted, check the gray (middle) slider to see if you want to adjust the overall brightness of the image. The Levels adjustment layer works wonders on this image. Now, it's easier to get a better look at the color. This image has few reference points for color. The hair looks really close to the right color, but the highlights in the skin are a little yellow. The teeth look a little yellow too, but they might look like that in real life so you can't use them as a guide.

4. Create a Color Balance adjustment layer using the Adjustments panel. Click the Highlights button so that the color adjustment mostly affects the lighter tones of the image. Change the Blue value to **5** to add a touch of blue to the highlights. If you want to do any additional color balancing, go ahead and do so.

X-REF

See Chapter 3 if you need a refresher on color balancing.

Now that the global tone and color of this image has been fine-tuned, it's time to move into Phase 2 of the retouching workflow.

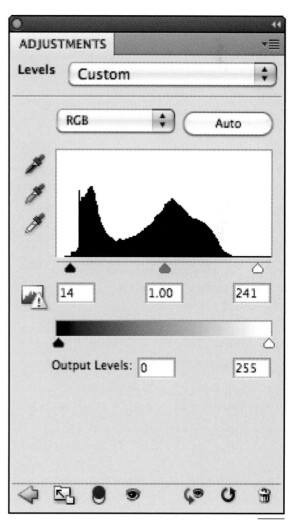

14-2

PHASE 2 WORKFLOW: FIXING DISTRACTIONS

There are several things in this portrait that need to be addressed. Here's a list of the primary issues that need to be addressed during Phase 2 of this project:

> Remove blemishes and soften wrinkles.

> Do some preliminary smoothing on the skin on the forehead and chest area.

> Tone down the shine on the lips.

> Enhance the eyes by cleaning the whites, brightening the irises, and removing one of the catch lights.

> Lighten and whiten the teeth. Also tone down or remove bright reflections on the teeth.

> Remove all the flyaway hair around the outer edges of the head.

> Do final skin smoothing.

With the exception of final skin smoothing, these steps don't necessarily need to be carried out in this exact order. I tend to take care of some of the bigger issues and then move around the image, focusing on the lesser problems. After those are handled, I turn my attention to smaller distractions.

Working this way allows me to solve the big problems and set the tone for the rest of the process for the image. It also allows me to see how I'm doing with my time budget after the bigger issues have been managed. If I need to make any adjustments to my schedule of expectations for the image, I can do so then.

Keep in mind that the goal of all portrait retouching is to make the portrait subjects look the way they think they look. Very few people come to a photographer to get a portrait of themselves exactly the way a professional dSLR camera sees them. When they look in the mirror, they don't see every pore the same way a camera does, nor do most people want to.

At the same time, the typical middle-aged portrait subject doesn't want to look 21 again, either (at least not just in a portrait).

As retouchers, we have to find the balance in the middle where portrait subjects look as good as they feel, but not so unrealistic that the retouching becomes noticeable and distracting. This is where working in layers truly becomes handy.

In addition to creating flexibility, they allow you to reduce the opacity of a retouched layer to blend it back into an unretouched layer until you find the perfect balance. That's why this type of retouching is considered soft-edge retouching.

PRO TIP

Remember that when working with layers, if something isn't working the way you think it should be, there's a strong chance that you're on the wrong layer.

To begin Phase 2, pick up where you left off after Step 4 and follow this step:

5. Duplicate the Background layer by choosing Layer⇨Duplicate Layer, and rename it **Retouching**. This is the layer on which most of the retouching will be done. The Background layer will remain untouched throughout the entire process. In fact, you can click the eyeball next to it to hide it as a reminder you won't be using it. Your Layers panel should look like Figure 14-3 with four layers.

SOFTENING WRINKLES AND BLEMISHES

Begin by toning down some of the main wrinkles, starting with the deeper ones around the eyes. Continue the project by following these steps:

6. Zoom to 50 percent, and use the Hand tool to center the eye on your screen.

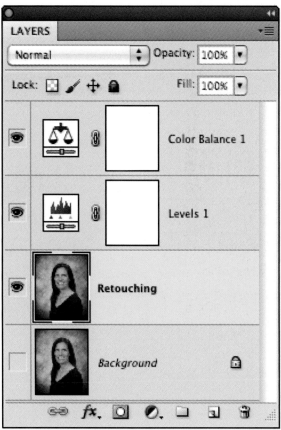

14-3

skin on the cheek, as shown in Figure 14-4, and release the mouse button. Before you do anything else, choose Edit➪Fade Patch Selection. When the Fade dialog box opens, lower the value to 50 percent, and click OK. Without the fading step, the Patch tool's effect would be way too strong and affect the shape of the eye socket by removing too much detail.

PRO TIP

Remember that the Fade command must be the very next thing you do after using a tool or making an adjustment.

8. Do the same thing with the dark lines below and to the right of the eye that extend down onto the cheek.

9. Use the Patch tool to completely remove the small dark spots just below the eye, this time without fading.

Now you can take care of the deeper wrinkles to the right of the eye. Because you can't remove all of them with one selection without making a mess because the area is too big, you'll need to break the area down into smaller groups.

10. Use the Patch tool to draw a selection around the upper set of wrinkles, as shown in Figure 14-5. Drag the selection to the same clean area of skin on the cheek to sample it again. Use the Fade command to fade the Patch tool to 50 percent.

11. Use the same technique with the rest of the wrinkles to the right of the eye. Be careful not to get too close to the dark areas by the corner of the eye. Also be sure to fade the effect about 50 percent after each use of the tool.

PRO TIP

Remember that you can use ⌘/Ctrl ++ (plus) to zoom in and ⌘/Ctrl +- (minus) to zoom out to standard zoom settings that include 50 percent, 66.6 percent, and 100 percent.

7. Choose the Patch tool, and make sure the Patch option on the options bar is set to Source. The cheeks in this image have the cleanest skin — especially the cheek on the right — so use it as your starting sample point. Draw a selection around the dark line under the eye on the right. Click and drag the selection down to the smooth

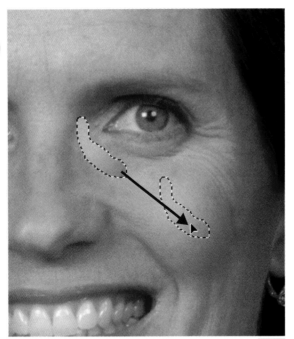

14-4

PRO TIP

This is a good time for a reality check. Turn on the visibility of the Background layer and then hide the visibility of the Retouching layer. This gives you a reminder of what the image looked like before you began. Do this often throughout this process to help keep your retouching in perspective. Just remember to be on the Retouching layer (or whichever layer is appropriate at the time) before beginning again.

12. Repeat the process on the lines and wrinkles of the left eye. Remember to keep your selections loose and to fade most applications of the Patch tool. When you get to the horizontal lines that run from the corner of the eye to the hair, be careful to sample an area that has a similar dark shadow at the left edge, as shown in Figure 14-6.

Doing this ensures that the dark edge of the hair blends easily with the similar dark edge of the sample area. Fade this application of the Patch tool to 60 percent so the blending effect is a bit stronger, removing more of the line.

The wrinkles around the eyes should be looking pretty good at this point. Now you can focus on the forehead area.

13. Use the Patch tool to begin removing the blemishes over the eye on the left. Don't fade it because you want the blemishes to completely disappear. Work your way across the brow area to the other eye, removing any blemishes or rough skin above the eyes. Keep using the cheek on the right for sampling. When you finish, look for and remove any other blemished areas on the forehead. Leave the longer lines for now. You take care of them in the next step.

Now that the forehead is cleaned up, we can use the clean areas we created to tone down the lines on the forehead.

14-5

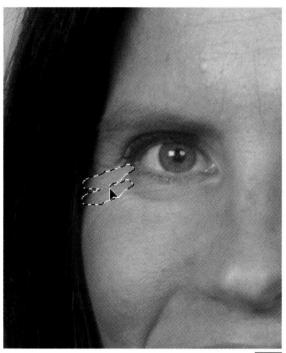

14-6

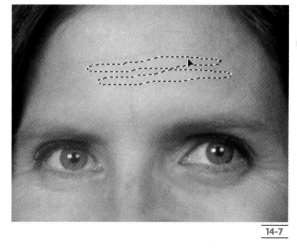

14-7

14. Use the Patch tool to draw a selection around the lower horizontal line on the forehead, and use the area just above it for sampling, as shown in Figure 14-7. Use the Fade command if you want to fade the effect a bit. Do the same thing to the other horizontal lines.

When you get to the vertical line between the eyes, fade it to 40 percent so that more of the original line remains — providing some important contours that describe this woman's facial structure.

NOTE

Because you used the cheek to get the forehead in good shape, you could potentially use it for sampling larger areas.

15. Make one more pass over the forehead with the Patch tool, looking for any other blemishes. Also be on the lookout for evidence of your retouching that needs to be blended in. Remember that you'll be smoothing the skin later, so you don't need to get carried away. Just knock off the rough spots right now. When you finish, turn off the Retouching layer's visibility for a reality check.

16. Move down to the nose, and use the Patch tool to remove the spots on the bridge and right side. Be careful when working on the nose with the Patch tool because you can easily remove too many details, which tends to flatten the nose, changing the character of the subject.

The shine on the left side of the nose is a little too strong. You don't want to completely remove it, but it should be toned down. Use the Patch tool on it and fade it to about 25 percent to let most of the shine show through the retouching.

17. Now move down to the cheeks and remove any major blemishes you see. If it's a wrinkle, fade it back to about 50 percent.

18. Move to the area around the mouth. This woman has very nice smile lines, but they're a little too strong because of the lighting. Use the Patch tool on them one at a time, fading after each use. Use your judgment on the amount to fade them. I used 30 percent on the left and 20 percent on the right. Do the same thing with the little wrinkle near the right nostril.

PRO TIP

This would be a good time to save your master file if you haven't already. Name it Biz_Portrait-edited.psd.

19. Use the same technique to tone down the rest of the smile lines on the woman's face. Remember, you don't want to completely remove the lines because the shape of her face won't make sense without them. Begin with the line to the left of the mouth, as shown in Figure 14-8. Use the smooth skin on the cheek for sampling.

Fade each area appropriately, usually somewhere between 20 percent and 40 percent.

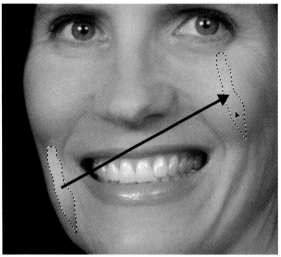

14-8

20. When you get to the large area on the cheek shown in Figure 14-9, select it all as one. Because of the size of this selection, you can't use the cheek for sampling. Drag it to the shoulder and sample the area with the cleanest skin. Fade the effect to about 50 percent to blend the original line back in.

21. Tone down any remaining smile lines as well as the spot of shine on the chin. Make one final pass over the face before moving to the neck.

22. Use the same technique to address the three sets of lines near the back of the neck. You don't need to completely remove them, but you do need to tone them down. Because the skin on the face is in pretty good shape, try to use it for a sample. Also remove any other lines you see just below the chin.

Now the face and neck are looking good. You just need to do some blending on the skin on the chest area to tone down blemishes and wrinkles.

23. Use the Spot Healing Brush tool with a diameter of about 30px to remove any obvious blemishes. Work with a soft brush and be careful not to remove any spots that look like moles. After all the smaller blemishes are eliminated, you can address the splotchy tones on the skin.

NOTE

When you retouch someone's photo, you have to be careful to honor the "imperfections" that are part of the person's normal appearance. For example, a mole or a scar on someone's face is always there. If you remove it, the person will look different than he usually looks.

24. Increase the size of the Spot Healing Brush to 50px, and begin working on the dark and light splotches, blending them with the background. This step is the last step to get the skin ready for final smoothing. This blending takes a few minutes but will be worth it later.

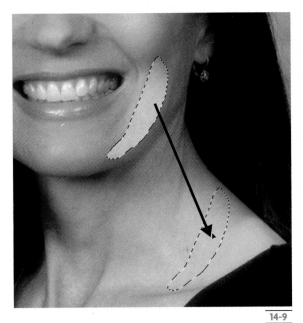

14-9

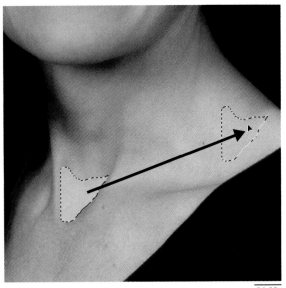

14-10

25. Use the Patch tool to select the area on the throat, as shown in Figure 14-10. Drag the selection to the same shoulder area you used in the last step. Then fade the effect to 50 percent. The fading is what makes this technique work without changing the contours too much. Use this technique along the collarbone region and anywhere else you need it.

By now, the skin should be looking good. You come back and do final softening in a bit. First, spend a few minutes improving some other key features.

ENHANCING EYES

This portrait is already looking much better than it did a short while ago. Some attention to the eyes would make it look even better. The first step is to remove one of the catch lights from each eye. Most serious portrait photographers don't like to see multiple eye catch lights in a studio portrait, so it's standard procedure for a retoucher to remove all but one.

Pick up where you left off after Step 25, and follow these steps:

26. Zoom to 100 percent, and use the Clone Stamp with a small, soft brush set to Normal blending mode to remove the smaller catch light on the left of each eye. If you have All Layers selected in the Sample options, be sure to select the Ignore Adjustment Layers option, just to the right of the Sample menu. Sample the iris or the pupil when needed, as shown in Figure 14-11.

Now's a good time to remove the redness in the eyes.

27. Use the Adjustments panel to create a Hue/Saturation adjustment layer above the Retouching layer. Double-click on its name and rename it **Red Eye**. Lower the saturation value of the Red channel to **-100**, and click OK.

You only need to desaturate the whites of the eye, but the whole image is being affected. That means that you need to fill this layer's mask with black, and then come back and mask the whites of the eyes back in using the Brush tool with white paint.

X-REF

Masking is covered in detail in Chapter 6.

28. Go to the Masks panel and select Invert to invert the reveal all mask that automatically came with the Hue/Saturation adjustment layer into a hide all mask. Now the adjustment layer's effect is completely hidden by the black mask.

29. Select the Brush tool, and paint the whites of the eyes with white to mask the Hue/Saturation adjustment layer's effects back in. When you finish, zoom back to 50 percent and look at the eyes. If the desaturation is a little too strong, causing the whites to look gray, lower the Red Eye layer's opacity to about 50 percent to allow a touch of red to show through.

30. Zoom to 100 percent. Click the Retouching layer to make it active. Use the Patch tool to remove some of the blood vessels on the left side of the eye on the right, as shown in Figure 14-12. Try to find a very smooth piece of skin to sample so that you don't add any texture to the eye.

While you're there, take a moment to do any other retouching around the eyes — such as toning down the reflections at the inner corners.

31. Create a burn and dodge layer at the top of your layer stack. (Create an empty layer, and change its blending mode to Soft Light, as discussed in Chapter 11.) Rename it **Burn & Dodge**. You need to do one more thing with the eyes before you move on. You need to darken the pupils a bit.

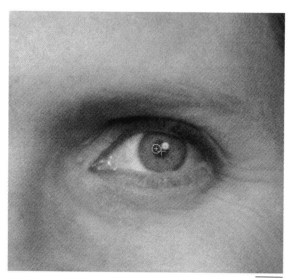

14-11

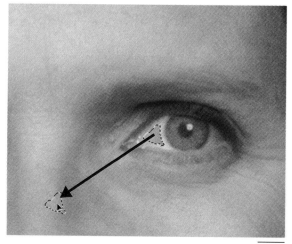

14-12

32. Choose the Brush tool, and lower its opacity to 15 percent. Use a small, soft brush to paint each pupil with black paint on the Burn & Dodge layer, darkening as you paint. If the iris in either eye was darker, I would switch to white paint and use the brush to lighten it and give it a little more of a glow. In this case, it's not necessary.

The eyes are looking great. In fact, they look so good that they really make the yellow tint in the teeth stand out.

ENHANCING TEETH

This woman has really great teeth. It isn't necessary to do any reconstruction on them. All you have to do is remove the bright reflections, and then brighten and lighten all the teeth. Pick up where you left off after Step 32, and follow these steps:

33. Make sure the Retouching layer is the active layer. Use the Patch tool to remove each of the reflections by sampling other teeth, as shown in Figure 14-13. If you want a little reflection to show through, fade the Patch tool. After the teeth have been retouched, quickly use the Patch tool to remove or tone down the shine on the lower lip using the same technique. Work with small areas, so you can sample other parts of the lip to preserve the unique texture that lips have.

Now that the teeth are retouched, it's time to take care of the yellow tint. You've probably already figured this out, but you can use the same technique you used for removing the red from the eyes.

34. Create a new Hue/Saturation adjustment layer above the retouching layer, and name it **Teeth**. Select Yellows from the channel menu and use the eyedropper to click one of the teeth. This targets the exact yellows that need to be modified. Lower the Saturation value to -50, and click OK. Now the teeth look much better, but the skin doesn't because it's also being affected.

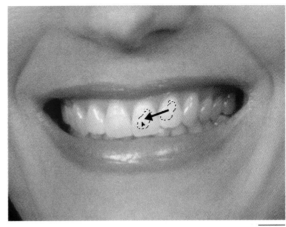

14-13

35. Select Invert from the Masks panel to invert the mask to a hide all mask. Select the Brush tool and use a small, soft brush to paint the teeth back in with white at 100 percent opacity.

Because you used an adjustment layer to alter the color saturation of the teeth, you can come back later and reevaluate the saturation after you've lived with it for a bit.

> **NOTE**
>
> If the teeth were also too dark, you could repeat the procedure with a Levels adjustment layer to lighten the teeth after whitening, which is a common procedure.

This image is looking great. Figure 14-14 shows before and after the progress so far. Take this opportunity to compare your own before and after by momentarily turning off the visibility of the Retouching, Red Eye, Teeth, and Burn & Dodge layers.

14-14

TAMING STRAY HAIR

The only problem area now is the hair. The woman in this portrait has lots of flyaway hair. If the photographer had been a little more careful when shooting the portrait, this step would be easier.

The Patch tool and the Healing Brush work well on hair that's far from the head. But those smart tools tend to cause smearing when used on a background area right next to the head, which is where most of this problem hair is. That's why it's best to use the more literal Clone Stamp to tame this flyaway hair.

Keep in mind as you work that this image will not be printed any larger than 8×10. The goal with the hair is to quickly clean up the edges without getting too crazy. Start with the hair at the top of the head and continue where you left off after Step 35 by following these steps:

36. Choose the Clone Stamp from the Tools panel, and set the brush diameter to 30px. Also make sure the brush's Hardness value is set to 0. (If you need to raise the Hardness value when working close to the head, that's okay. Just remember to lower it again later.) Make sure that the Sample option in the tool options is set to Current Layer and the Retouching layer is active.

Because the hair is darker than the background, you can make the Clone Stamp work more intelligently by changing its blending mode to Lighten. To change a tool's blending mode, use the Mode menu on the options bar.

Now the tool affects only pixels that are darker than the sampled area. In this case, that means when you sample and paint, the hair will be affected, but not the surrounding background area. This helps to reduce stroke marks around the hair. (If this were light hair against a dark background, you'd want to use the Darken blending mode.)

NOTE

A brush-based tool's blending mode is similar to a layer's blending mode. The difference is that a layer blending mode affects the entire layer. A tool blending mode only affects brush strokes made with that blending mode in effect, no matter what layer they are applied to.

Zoom to 50 percent or 66.6 percent, and begin removing stray hairs. Sample the background area as close as possible to the hair you want to work on so that the tones match, as shown in the first frame of Figure 14-15.

Resample often, especially if you notice a strand of hair that isn't being affected by the Lighten blending mode. Frequent sampling also helps to prevent a retouching-halo pattern from forming around the head.

37. Clean up some of the strays along the shoulder on the left, as shown in the second frame of Figure 14-15 but leave most of the thicker sections of hair. If all of the ends that stick out are completely removed, it will look like the hair was clipped, which wouldn't look right.

38. Make one more pass around the head, looking for any telltale retouching strokes. Use the Clone Stamp or any other retouching tool to remove them. When everything looks good, turn off the Retouching layer's visibility to check your work. This is where you'll notice any halo pattern that may have been created around the woman's head by the retouching.

This image is looking great. You only have one step left in Phase 2 retouching — final skin smoothing. Let's get to it.

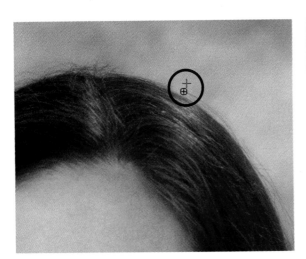 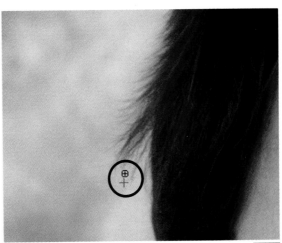

14-15

SMOOTHING SKIN

In Chapter 13, I explained two methods for smoothing skin. One of those methods used a blurring filter and a mask, and the other used special plug-in software. Because most of you may not have the plug-in I mentioned just yet, use the blur and mask system for this project. Continue the project by following these steps:

39. When you're comfortable that all retouching is completed, duplicate the Retouching layer, and name it **Skin**. Then choose Filter⇨Blur⇨Surface Blur. In the Surface Blur dialog box, set the Radius value to **8** and the Threshold value to **200**. I find that a low Radius value and a high Threshold value like this give me better blurring for skin smoothing. Feel free to experiment with different settings. When you like what you see, click OK.

40. Choose Layer⇨Layer Mask⇨Hide All to create a layer mask filled with black. This mask hides all the blurring on the Skin Layer. This is the same as using the Masks panel to create a pixel mask filled with white and then using the Masks panel's Invert option to change it to black.

41. Select the Brush tool, and set the foreground color to white. Lower the opacity of the Brush tool to 50 percent. That way, you can build up the effect where you want it by applying multiple strokes. Use a large, soft brush to paint the blurred skin back into the image.

    Try not to paint anything else, such as eyes, teeth, and hair. Remember that you can always switch the foreground color to black (X) to go back over something that shouldn't have been painted white.

    This is a good time to try using the \ key to display the rubylith masking overlay, as shown in Figure 14-16. It enables you to see exactly where your strokes are on the image. Use this preview to help you soften only the skin. If the overall softening looks too strong, don't worry. You reduce it in the next step.

14-16

42. Lower the opacity of the Skin layer to somewhere around 30 percent. Now the effect looks much better. The eyes, which were a little soft to begin with, even look a bit sharper against the smoother skin.

> **NOTE**
>
> At this point, if you notice something that needs to be cloned or patched, you'll need to do it on both the Skin layer and the Retouching layer. That's because the Skin layer is at 30 percent opacity. If you remove something from that layer, it will still show through on the Retouching layer below. Because of this, it's always best to complete retouching before smoothing skin.

43. When you're happy, save this master file as Biz_Portrait_edited.psd. Figure 14-17 shows the current layer stack with each of the layers you've created so far.

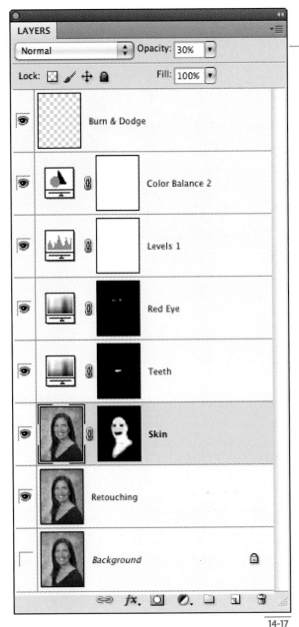

14-17

PHASE 3 WORKFLOW: SIZING AND FINISHING TOUCHES

To begin Phase 3, pick up where you left off after Step 43 and follow this step:

44. Select the Crop tool, and type a value of **8** into the Width field, a value of **10** into the Height field, and a value of **300** into the Resolution field. Make sure the measurement unit is inches, not pixels. Draw a cropping selection so that you get a crop similar to the image in Figure 14-18.

14-18

All the hard work is done. Now you can focus on finishing this image. The first thing to do is to crop and size it for printing. Because this will be a permanent change, you need to be sure that you saved the master, edited file in Step 43.

DARKENING THE CORNERS

A portrait like the one in this project will look better with some darkening on all of the corners. This vignetting effect adds a finishing touch by helping the viewer stay focused on the subject.

Continue the project by following these steps to use an adjustment layer to darken the corners:

45. Choose the Elliptical Marquee tool from the Tools panel, and draw a selection like the one shown in Figure 14-19. Choose Select⇨Inverse to invert the selection so that the corners outside the oval are now selected instead of the area inside the oval.

> ### NOTE
>
> Normally, I would have created this layer before flattening and cropping and saved it as part of the master file. However, because it was necessary to crop so much, it was hard to know exactly where to darken until the crop was done.

46. Choose Select⇨Refine Edge, and type a value of **100** into the Feather field. Leave all other settings at 0. (If you want to preview the effect, choose use on of the preview options in the View menu.) Click OK. This softens the transition of the next step.

47. Make sure you're on the top layer in the layer stack and use the Adjustments panel to create a Levels adjustment layer. Lower the gray slider's value to **.70**. As you do, notice that all of the corners are darkened and the darkening effect lightens as it gets closer to the center of the image.

If you notice a color shift at the edge of the photo caused by the adjustment layer, change the Level's layer blending mode, on the Layers panel, to Luminosity. This insures that the tonal adjustment has no effect on color.

Everything looks great except that the shoulder on the right is too dark now. Because you used an adjustment layer combined with a selection to create the vignette effect on a mask, this is easy to fix.

14-19

48. Choose the Brush tool from the Tools panel. Use a very large brush with a Hardness value of 0 and a medium Opacity value to to fine-tune the Levels layer mask that was created by the elliptical selection. Paint the inner shoulder area until you like the tonality. Let the tones fade to dark as you work near the lower corner. Figure 14-20 shows my layer mask on the Levels layer.

This portrait is almost ready for printing. It just needs one final step — output sharpening.

PROFESSIONAL SHARPENING STRATEGIES

When retouching a portrait, two kinds of sharpening can be done to the image. They are creative sharpening and output sharpening. Consider their differences:

14-20

mask to mask out everything except for the sharp eyes or the blurred background. In this case, neither is necessary.

> Output sharpening is overall sharpening that's designed to prepare an image for output, such as printing or on-screen viewing. This sharpening is applied to the entire image with the intent of getting it ready for a particular output option. It takes place after creative sharpening.

One of the things to understand here is that size matters. A file that's being prepared for printing as a 5×7 requires a completely different sharpening scenario than the same file being prepared for a 16×20. If the same settings are used for both, the 5×7 would look great, but the 16×20 would not be sharp enough.

> ### NOTE
>
> Something to avoid when possible is sharpening an image for output, changing its size, and then resharpening for a new output size. Sharpening on top of previous sharpening can adversely affect the image by introducing unwanted artifacts.

This means that any creative sharpening will be further sharpened during the output sharpening process. That's important to know because it means you want to consider it during creative sharpening. Otherwise, if it looks perfect and then you sharpen again, it will be overdone, causing details to look "crunchy" instead of smooth. The idea behind creative sharpening is to draw attention to a specific area.

USING SMART SHARPEN

The Smart Sharpen filter was introduced in Photoshop CS2. This filter is considered smart because it treats various regions of the image differently based on the image content in those regions. The Smart Sharpen filter attempts to sharpen only the areas of the image that have detail, without affecting areas that don't.

> Creative sharpening is used to fine-tune the image by selectively sharpening, or blurring, selected areas of the image. Examples of creative sharpening are blurring the background around a subject to make the subject stand out more, and selectively sharpening only the eyes in a portrait.

The main thing to understand about creative sharpening is that its effect is relative to the rest of the image. The goal isn't to make part of the image perfectly sharp. The goal is to make part of the image stand out better from its surroundings by sharpening it or blurring the detail surrounding it.

If I wanted to sharpen the eyes in this portrait or blur the background, I would have done it before cropping, To do so, I would duplicate the retouching layer, sharpen all of it using Smart Sharpen, or blur all of it using Gaussian blur, and then use a

Sharpening a digital image is all about enhancing edge contrast. The Smart Sharpen filter is really an edge contrast filter. It finds edges of tonal contrast that usually indicate the detail in an image.

After it identifies these areas, it lightens one side of the edge while darkening the other side. This causes a slight haloing effect that enhances the appearance of edge detail, tricking our eyes into thinking the image is sharper. Pretty cool, huh?

To sharpen the image, pick up where you left off after Step 48 and follow this step:

49. Make sure the Retouching layer is active and then open the Smart Sharpen filter by choosing Filters⇨Sharpen⇨Smart Sharpen. The dialog box in Figure 14-21 opens.

Let's look at the main options in this dialog box:

> **Amount:** This is just that — the amount of sharpening. Higher values equal more edge contrast, which equals more sharpening.

> **Radius:** This value determines how many surrounding pixels are considered when the Smart Sharpen filter finds an edge. Higher values expand the size of the sharpening halo. Extreme values create noticeable halos that detract from the image.

> **Remove:** This is a cool feature that adjusts the way the filter works, depending on the problem. The dropdown list has three options: Gaussian Blur, which is the same algorithm used by the Unsharp Mask; Lens Blur, which is the preferred method for sharpening most digital camera files; and Motion Blur, which attempts to compensate for blur cause by motion during the exposure.

> **Advanced:** Selecting this option gives you more control by allowing you to work with the shadows and highlights independently of the rest of the

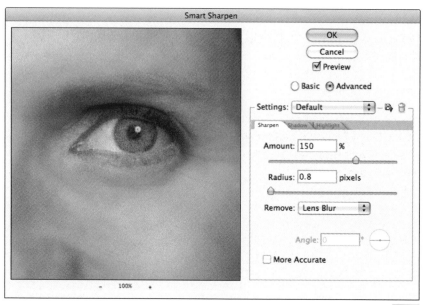

14-21

image. You can use Fade Amount to adjust the amount of sharpening and Tonal Width to restrict your adjustments to the shadows or the highlights. This is quite useful when you have lots of noise in the shadows that you don't want to sharpen.

> **More Accurate:** Selecting this option makes the filter perform a more accurate removal of blurring, but the process takes longer.

There's one more issue I need to explain before you sharpen this portrait. To accurately evaluate the sharpening effect on the image two conditions must be met. First, the image must be displayed near its print size in order to judge the effect of the Smart Sharpen filter. Additionally, it's important to know if the zoom ratio that comes closest to print size is one that displays properly on the monitor.

Some experts recommend that you zoom to 100 percent when sharpening so you can see the actual pixels. This can be helpful, but it also can be misleading.

When an image is zoomed to 100 percent for sharpening, it appears much bigger on the screen than it will be in reality — more than twice as big on my system. If you get the sharpening looking perfect at 100 percent, it will look undersharpened when you see the final print.

The optimal zoom ratio is going to vary depending on your monitor and how you have it set up. Here's how to find out which standard zoom preset is best for your particular viewing environment:

> Choose View⇨Rulers to turn on the rulers. This adds a ruler to the top of the image window and one to the left side. If your Rulers are already turned on, you don't have to do this.

> Hold a real ruler up to the screen while zooming the image using the zoom keyboard shortcuts (Ctrl/⌘++ to zoom in and Ctrl/⌘+- to zoom out.) When the file's ruler and the real ruler match up, the file is displayed at its actual size. The usual preset that comes closest is 33 percent, though you may find that 50 percent is closer.

Now that you know your optimal zoom ratio, there's one more thing to check. In versions of Photoshop prior to CS4 it was necessary to zoom to a ratio of one of the 25 percent zoom increments in order for Photoshop to accurately render the screen. This means that even if 33 percent is closest to reality for you, it would be necessary to zoom to 25 or 50 percent to be able to see an accurate rendering of a filter's effect.

When Photoshop CS4 was released a new feature implementing OpenGL was added. Open GL stands for Open Graphics Language. It consists of a standard set of video functions that can be performed by an OpenGL enabled video card.

One of these functions in Photoshop CS5 is to more accurately render the screen at any zoom ratio. What this boils down to is this: If your system supports OpenGL, you can use 33 percent as your zoom ratio and see an accurate rendering of a filter's effect. Otherwise, it's necessary to use 25 or 50 percent.

To find out if OpenGL is enabled on your system, choose Photoshop⇨Preferences⇨Performance (Mac) or Edit⇨Preferences⇨Performance (PC). When the Performance preferences dialog box opens, check the GPU Settings area, as shown in Figure 14-22. If the settings are grayed out, your video card isn't capable of working with OpenGL.

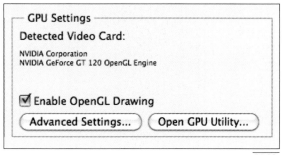

14-22

Okay, now that you know the theory behind sharpening, it's time to get this file sharpened and ready to print. To complete the project, follow these steps:

50. If the Smart Sharpen dialog box isn't still open, open it now. You can view the effects of the filter in two ways:

> Zoom your image to the appropriate zoom preset, and position the Smart Sharpen dialog box so you can see your image while you work with the dialog box (my preferred method).

> Zoom the huge preview window in the Smart Sharpen dialog box to the desired ratio by clicking the minus sign located just below the preview area.

51. Begin by selecting the More Accurate check box at the bottom of the dialog box. Then Click the Remove pop-up menu, and select Lens Blur. Change the Amount value to **100%** for a starting point. Slide the Radius slider to the right until you get to a value of about 30.

This is obviously way too high, but I want you to see the haloing effect, as shown in Figure 14-23, that the Radius amount controls. You want sharpening halos, but you don't want them to be this noticeable.

52. Decrease the Radius value to about 1, and use an Amount value of 100 percent. Use the Amount slider to increase the effect, while watching your preview. Stop when you see what you like, and click OK (I stopped at 110 percent).

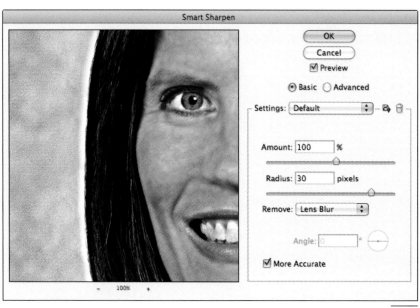

14-23

Notice that you only sharpened the Retouching layer. The skin softening on the Skin layer was untouched. Now that you see everything in place, take one last look at the Skin layer to see if it's necessary to adjust its opacity to dial in the effect with the sharpened layer below it.

PHASE 4 WORKFLOW: OUTPUT AND ARCHIVING

This image is now ready for printing as an 8×10. Printing is covered in detail in Chapter 15. Keep in mind that the final print is the bottom line. When you see it, evaluate it and compare it to what you see on-screen. Learn to see how the on-screen view is translated when it's output in a specific way.

For example, if the sharpening doesn't look as strong on the print as it does on-screen, you know that you can oversharpen a bit more than what looks good on your monitor. Be sure to evaluate sharpening with each paper type you print on and the printing processes you use so that you'll know how each responds to sharpening with the Smart Sharpen filter.

Save the file as Biz_Portrait_8x10.jpg. You can also save it as a TIFF if you prefer that for your printing purposes. At this point, you should have three different files — the original file, a fully retouched and uncropped master file with all layers intact, and a flattened and sized file ready for printing. Each should be stored in its appropriate folder.

Earlier you mentioned that zooming to 33 percent displays the photo close to its printed size. This seems odd. I thought 100 percent displays a photo at its actual size.

One would think that zooming to 100 percent would display a digital image at its actual size. However, you've probably noticed that when you zoom to 100 percent the inches on the ruler are much bigger than a real inch. The reason this happens isn't because of Photoshop. It's more related to your computer's monitor.

Most computer monitors can display only a limited range of pixels. Typically it's anywhere from 75 to 100 pixels per inch. If you're working on a file that's 300 ppi, but your display can only show 90 ppi, the inches look bigger. For example, on my Apple Cinema display, when I zoom to 100 percent and check the on-screen ruler, I see that an inch on the ruler measures 3 inches in reality. That means that my display is showing about 100 ppi — one third of the image's 300 pixels per inch. That's why a zoom ratio of 33 percent is closest to reality for me.

Okay, I understand. But what about when I sharpen photos for Web use. When I zoom to 33 percent, they look way too small?

When you size photos for online viewing, the same viewing rules don't apply. That's because the finished product is displayed in the same viewing environment as the editing environment. It doesn't matter what the resolution of a photo is, it is displayed pixel by pixel. If I have a photo that's 2×2 inches at 300 ppi, the pixel measurements of the photo are 600×600 pixels. My monitor is going to display those pixels at its resolution, which is about 100 ppi. If I change the resolution of the photo to match my monitor and make it a 6-×-6-inch photo at 100 ppi, it's still a 600-×-600-pixel image and occupies exactly the same amount of room on the display. No matter what the resolution of the photo, the monitor always displays it at the same fixed setting.

The things to remember here are: When sharpening a photo for on-screen viewing, view it at 100 percent so that you can see it as it will be shown. Also, remember that the resolution of a file for online viewing isn't really important. What matters is the overall pixel dimensions. A photo that's 400 pixels wide displays the same at 100 percent no matter what its resolution.

Photo by Seattle Photography, Inc

With the portrait retouching project in Chapter 14 you had a great deal of flexibility when deciding how much to tone down wrinkles and smooth skin.

The outcome could vary widely, depending on how much you faded tool strokes and individual layers with soft-edged retouching techniques. The goal wasn't a strict interpretation of the portrait subject. It was more concerned with making the subject look her best.

Though the goal with the project in this chapter is to make the subject, the hotel shown in Figure 15-1, look its best, some of the retouching techniques will vary. That's because it's important with this project to interpret the building as realistically as possible using more of a hard-edged retouching approach.

If you take the time to tackle this chapter, you'll learn some new tricks that are best revealed in a complex project like this one.

Evaluating the Project

As mentioned in Chapter 12, this is a nice photo of this hotel. The light on the face of the building is great, and the lighting on the left side is workable.

The photographer's client, the hotel management, wants all the power lines and streetlights removed so that the building is emphasized in the shot.

It may not seem like much at first, but consider that as each line and pole is removed, the details in the building must be retained. If there is a window behind a pole that's being removed, a window must be copied from somewhere else to replace the pole.

Because it was necessary to use a wide-angle lens to photograph this building, the vertical lines all converge as they move upward. This shift in perspective causes the building to look short and squatty. Our brains

15-1

compensate for this shift in perspective when our eyes experience it, so it really looks weird when seen in print.

This image is currently a little under 8×12 inches at 300 ppi (Image⇨Image Size). The hotel is planning to use it for a 20×24 print with some cropping on each side. This means that it will be necessary to upsample the file to the larger size at some point. It also means that the retouching needs to be as flawless as possible.

Though this project follows the same four-phase workflow used in the preceding chapter, the steps within those four phases are quite different in some cases, especially Phase 1.

PHASE 1 WORKFLOW: ADJUSTING IMAGE FUNDAMENTALS

Before you correct the distorted perspective, it's best to take care of the usual fundamentals — brightness, contrast, and color.

USING CURVES TO ADJUST MIDTONE CONTRAST

In the preceding project, you used a Levels adjustment layer to modify the tonal qualities of the portrait. In that example, you were working with an image that needed a boost in overall contrast. The building photo in this chapter is a little different.

It already has bright highlights in the clouds and dark shadows in the foreground foliage. However, the tones of the photo can be improved by adjusting the contrast in the midtones, which is a perfect job for Curves.

Follow these steps to begin:

1. Open the practice file titled Building_Remodel.tif from the downloadable practice files on the Web site (www.wiley.com/go/phoprestorationand retouching). Press ⌘/Ctrl +Alt+0 to zoom to 100 percent. Quickly scan the image quadrant by quadrant to check for any sensor dust. When you finish spotting, press ⌘/Ctrl +0 to zoom the image so it fits on the screen.

2. Use the Adjustments panel to create a Curves adjustment layer and then rename the layer to Curves 1. When you look at its histogram, you see there isn't much room for movement at either end of the tonal scale. Hold down the Alt key to display the clipping preview as you adjust the black and white input sliders.

Notice that you can't modify either of them without clipping some detail. Go ahead and leave both sliders at their default settings of 0 and 255.

3. Select the On-image adjustment tool (the hand icon) from the Curves adjustment panel. Remember that this tool is used to click and drag tones to make changes. Click on a representative highlight tone on the front of the building, as shown in the first frame of Figure 15-2.

Hold down the mouse button and drag upward to lighten the tone just a bit. Watch the Input and Output displays on the Curves adjustment panel. The Input number is the original tone and the Output number is the tone's new value after being lightened.

The second frame of Figure 15-2 shows the numbers that correspond to the first frame. As you can see, I lightened the tones in the 143 range to 151.

NOTE

The upper part of the building on the left is a little too light now. You'll take care of that later with some burning and dodging in Phase 3.

4. Click and drag downward with the On-image adjustment tool on one of the darker tones, as shown in the first frame of Figure 15-3.

Lower the value by only a few points to darken these areas, while monitoring the Input and Output boxes. The second frame of Figure 15-3 shows that I changed tone 47 to a new value of 44.

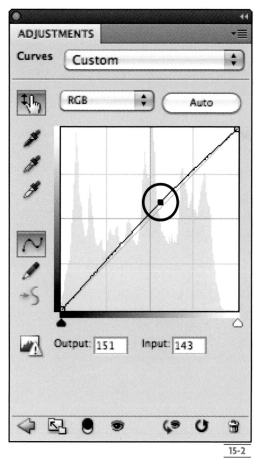

15-2

Look at the curve line in Figure 15-3. Notice that as the lighter tones are lightened and darker tones are darkened, it gently gets steeper in the middle range, which increases midtone contrast.

Click the Toggle layer visibility button (the eyeball icon) off and on to compare the image with and without the layer. Notice how much difference these subtle Curves adjustments have on the midtones.

Also notice how little of an effect they have on the highlights in the clouds and the shadows in the dark foliage. This reveals the true power of adjusting midtones with Curves.

5. Now that the contrast has a little more snap, create a Color Balance adjustment layer using the Adjustments panel. Rename the layer to Color Balance 1. Adjust the color until you like it. I changed the Cyan/Red value to **+15** and the Yellow/Blue value to **-5** to warm up the image.

Now that the brightness, contrast, and color are looking good, it's time to do something about the converging vertical lines. But before you can straighten anything, you need to know just exactly what straight is by establishing some guidelines, known as Guides.

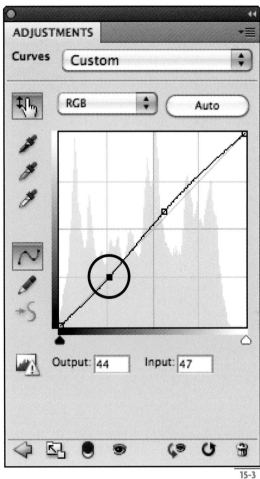

15-3

Using Guides for critical alignment

One of the coolest but least used features of Photoshop is the ability to place vertical and horizontal guide lines anywhere in the image. Continue where you left off after Step 5, and follow these steps:

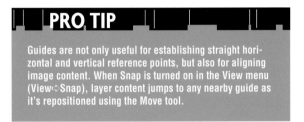

PRO TIP

Guides are not only useful for establishing straight horizontal and vertical reference points, but also for aligning image content. When Snap is turned on in the View menu (View⇨Snap), layer content jumps to any nearby guide as it's repositioned using the Move tool.

6. If the rulers aren't already showing, choose View⇨Rulers (⌘/Ctrl+R). You should now have a horizontal ruler at the top of the image and a vertical ruler on the left side of the image. To place a horizontal guide, click the horizontal ruler at the top and drag downward. To place a vertical guide, click the vertical ruler and drag inward.

7. Click the vertical ruler, and drag to the right, toward the building, until you just touch the lower-left side of it. Release the mouse button. You should now have a vertical guide.

315

15-4

Click the ruler again, and drag a second guide all the way across the image to the right side of the building. Then place a third guide somewhere near the middle of the front corner of the building, as shown in Figure 15-4.

After a guide is placed, you can easily reposition it. Simply select the Move tool, and hover the cursor over the guide. When you do, a double-sided arrow appears, circled in Figure 15-4. Just click and drag to reposition the guide.

To delete a guide, drag it back to the ruler. To delete all guides, choose View⇨Clear Guides.

PRO TIP

Sometimes, I want to temporarily hide the guides without deleting them so I can get a better look at an image. This is especially useful when making color adjustments because of the bright cyan color of the guides. To hide all guides, choose View⇨Extras (⌘/Ctrl+H). When Extras is unchecked, all guides are hidden. (This command also hides any active selection.)

When guides are added to an image, they become part of that image and every derivative file that's created from it. For example, if I save this file as a JPEG right now and then open that JPEG in Photoshop, I'll see the guides in the new JPEG file.

If I view the file outside of Photoshop (or some other Adobe design software), I won't see the guides because they're a feature of Photoshop. Still, it's best to avoid all confusion by clearing all guides before sending a file to someone else.

Another thing to be aware of with guides is that even though you see guides while viewing the image in Photoshop, they won't appear on prints. So you don't have to worry about these funny cyan lines showing up when you go to print. Now that we've got the basics out of the way, let's put Guides to use.

CORRECTING PERSPECTIVE WITH THE TRANSFORM COMMAND

The vertical lines in this image are converging toward one another at the top of the image. This convergence is caused by the fact that the top of the building is further away from the camera than the bottom is. The convergence is to be expected when photographing buildings, especially with a wide-angle lens.

However, in architectural photography, converging vertical lines are a big no-no.

NOTE

Some architectural photographers use tilt/shift lenses with their digital SLRs to compensate for shifts in perspective when shooting. Sometimes, though, additional perspective control is applied in post-production.

The easiest method for correcting the perspective in this photo is to use the Transform command. I introduced it in Chapter 8 when I discussed how to adjust the geometry of a crooked scan. In that example, I used the Distort function of the Transform command. You use it here, too.

Pick up where you left off after Step 7, and follow these steps:

8. Click the Background layer to make it active, and then duplicate it by choosing Layer⇨Duplicate Layer. Name the new layer **Straight Lines**.

9. Use ⌘/Ctrl+0 to fit the entire image onto the screen. Press the F key to go into Full Screen With Menu Bar viewing mode. (You might need to press it twice.) Now use the zoom shortcut ⌘/Ctrl +- (minus) to zoom out one increment. This is necessary to give you some room around the image to use while working with the control handles of the Transform command. If you need more room, zoom out one more increment.

PRO TIP

If you want a little more screen real estate, press the Tab key to hide all panels. Press it again to reveal them.

10. Choose Edit⇨Transform⇨Distort. You could use some of the other commands from the Transform submenu, such as Perspective and Scale, but I find that Distort is faster because corners can be addressed individually. Additionally, any scaling can be done in the usual way without going back to the Edit menu and selecting the Scale command.

    Click and drag the transformation handle at the top-left corner, circled in Figure 15-5, and drag it straight to the left. Drag until the back edge of the building is parallel to the guide next to it, as shown. It doesn't have to touch the line, it just has to be parallel with it.

PRO TIP

If you want to reposition the guide while the Transform command is active, hold down the ⌘/Ctrl key to temporarily access the Move tool. Then click the guide and drag it to its new position.

11. Do the same thing with the right side of the building by dragging the top-right corner straight to the right. This causes the left side to lean in a bit, so you need to go back to the left and readjust to compensate. Check the right again to see if it's still in alignment.

Continue this back-and-forth until both sides are parallel to their respective guides. Zoom in to check the alignment if you need to. When both sides are perfectly vertical, the front corner of the building in the middle will also be straight.

12. Click the transform handle in the middle, at the top of the image. Drag it straight up just a bit to scale the building's height, as shown in Figure 15-6. Check the vertical lines one more time to verify that they didn't shift when you were stretching the height of the building. Then press Enter to commit the transformation.

Hide the layer's visibility to compare the before and after versions. You won't need the guides anymore, so you can remove them now (View⇨Clear Guides).

NOTE

The quality of the image may look poor when you're in the middle of using the Transform command. Don't worry — it's only a preview. The quality will return to normal after the transformation is complete.

I don't know if you noticed this, but the building looks shorter than it did before this transformation. If you zoom in and look at the person crossing the street, you'll see that she too looks out of proportion.

PRO TIP

When using the Transform command, do all transformations during one application of the command. This command does some serious pixel pushing. If you combine all moves into one application of the command, the pixels are pushed around only once. If you don't like the transformation, undo it and try again, rather than performing a second transformation on top of a previous transformation.

15-6

Even though it looks like you removed some of the sky when you stretched the height of the building, it's still there; it's just hanging off the edge of the canvas. You need to increase the size of the canvas to see everything in the image. Continue with these steps:

13. Choose Image⇨Canvas Size to open the Canvas Size dialog box. Type **15** inches in the Width box and **10** inches in the Height box. Make sure that the Canvas extension color is White, and click OK. Now you can see the rest of the transformed image that was hanging off the sides and top of the canvas, as shown Figure 15-7.

15-7

14. Select the Crop tool from the Tools panel. Clear any previous values by clicking the Clear button on the options bar. Draw a cropping marquee that includes as much of the image as possible without showing any of the white canvas on the lower sides. This will make the image a rectangle again and allow you to capture all of the sky. Press Return/Enter to commit the crop.

15. Save the master file now using Save As and name it Building_Remodel-edited.psd. Continue to save the file frequently as you move through Phase 2 of the workflow.

PHASE 2 WORKFLOW: FIXING DISTRACTIONS

The work you did on the fundamentals of this image has drastically improved it. Now it's time for the main event. Here's a list of the things that you need to address during Phase 2, moving from left to right across the image. These items are highlighted in red in Figure 15-8:

> Remove all the electrical lines that come into the frame from the left edge, including the two large traffic lights that hang from them. The section against the sky will be easy. The parts in front of the building will be challenging.

> Remove the small streetlight that points away from the building's lower-left corner.

> Leave the small set of traffic lights; they belong in the scene. However, remove the top of the light pole in the foreground and the streetlight on top of it. Also remove the small, white crosswalk sign hanging to the right of the traffic lights.

> Remove the large, dark streetlight and post from the center of the image.

15-8

> Remove the large streetlight on the right that points toward the building. Leave the smaller streetlight below it because it isn't very distracting and it helps to balance the two light posts that support the traffic light that isn't being removed.

> Remove the large white area (set against black) at the bottom right of the building.

This short list represents lots of work. Some of it is fairly easy, while other parts are a little more complicated.

RETOUCHING HARD EDGES WITH THE CLONE STAMP

Begin the retouching process by quickly addressing some of the easier stuff. Pick up where you left off after Step 15, and follow these steps:

16. Duplicate the Straighten Lines layer, and rename it Retouching. This way you have a straightened layer below the Retouching layer to use as a reference for evaluating your retouching.

17. Use the Clone Stamp to remove the power lines and streetlight on the left and the streetlight on the right. Use the Lighten blending mode until you get to the top of the light on the right. You'll have to switch to the Normal (or Darken) blending mode to handle it because it's lighter than the surrounding tones in the sky.

If any part of the power line is left behind because it happens to be lighter than the sky, switch the Clone Stamp tool's blending mode back to Normal and clean them up.

Work with a soft brush when retouching against the sky. Increase the Hardness value of the brush to at least 50 percent when working close to the edge of the building; otherwise, you may have trouble getting close to the building without touching it with the brush.

18. Remove the large white rectangle at the lower right of the building. Use the Clone Stamp to clone

the upper dark area onto the lower white area. After all the white is covered with the dark gray, come back with a smaller brush and clone some of the nearby vegetation back on top of it. This helps to break up any hard edges created by your retouching.

Okay, most of the easy stuff is done. Now it's time to get down to the nitty-gritty. Begin with the large, dark streetlight in the center of the image. Continue with these steps:

19. Zoom in to 100 percent (⌘/Ctrl +Alt+0). Keep working with the Clone Stamp using a small brush with a Hardness value of between 30 percent and 50 percent. Make sure that the blending mode is set to Normal and that Opacity is 100 percent. Also make sure that the Sample option in the tool options is set to Current Layer.

20. If the Clone Source overlay isn't currently displayed, use the Clone Source panel (Window⇨Clone Source) to display it, as discussed in Chapter 7. This preview helps tremendously when aligning sample and target points while using the Clone Stamp tool.

21. Sample the vertical line in the building above the lamp. Begin painting directly below the sample point so you extend the line through the streetlight, as shown in the first frame of Figure 15-9.

If you're off in alignment at all, undo (⌘/Ctrl+Z) and try again until you get the alignment correct. This trial and error is worth it because after you get one line to fall into place, others will follow.

Move across the light to the right and keep painting with short strokes. Notice that when you get to the line between the light brown area and the darker brown area, the vertical lines are still in alignment. You don't have to sample again until you get to the window, shown in the second frame of Figure 15-9.

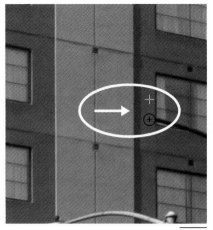

15-9

NOTE

Finding samples that line up with the area to be retouched is the name of the game when it comes to this kind of retouching. After you get the Clone Stamp's sample point and brush in alignment, you can retouch large areas without taking another sample.

22. Move to the right and down a bit and use the same technique to sample the horizontal line below the window and extend it through the arm that holds the light, as shown in the first frame of Figure 15-10.

Continue retouching without sampling until you're forced to take another sample. The second frame of Figure 15-10 shows how much I was able to remove without sampling again.

15-10

23. Zoom in closer and remove the leftovers from inside the window frame, shown in the upper left in the second image in Figure 15-10. Work with a small brush, and zoom in to 200 percent if you need to.

24. Start working your way down the pole with the Clone Stamp tool. Sample the top-center portion of the window frame one story above the window that needs retouching. Begin painting at exactly the same place right above the lower window so the sample and paint points stay in alignment.

Now when you paint on the lower window, a similar section of the window above is sampled. Use short strokes to remove the pole all the way down to the top of the next window, one story below, as shown in Figure 15-11.

RETOUCHING WITH COPY, TRANSFORM, AND MERGE

Here's another technique that's quite useful for this type of hard-edge retouching project because it enables you to work quickly with large areas.

Here's what you do: Instead of continuing to use the Clone Stamp tool to paint over specific details, you copy a similar area elsewhere on the building and then paste it over the entire area to be retouched.

A slight wrinkle on this project is that because you're retouching a subject with perspective, you also need to do some transformations to the copied information to get it to fit properly. Continue where you left off after Step 24, and follow these steps:

15-11

25. Choose the Lasso tool (L), and draw a selection around the window on the left, as shown in the first frame of Figure 15-12. After the selection is in place, choose Select⇨Modify⇨Feather. Enter a value of **1**, and click OK.

26. Copy the selection to a new layer by choosing Layer⇨New⇨Layer via Copy (⌘/Ctrl+J). Then use the Move tool to drag the new layer into position to the right, aligning it at the top of the window frame, as shown in the second frame of Figure 15-12.

27. Choose Edit⇨Transform⇨Scale. When the transformation handles appear, click the one at the center of the bottom and drag it upward until the bottom of the window is in alignment, as shown in the third frame of Figure 15-12.

15-12

Press Return/Enter to commit the transformation. Then merge the layer back into the Retouching layer by choosing Layer⇨Merge Down. Use the Clone Stamp tool to hide any telltale signs of the light post.

NOTE

The Transform command works only on the layer (or layers) that are currently active. If you want to transform two layers at the same time, you have to make both of them active by Shift+clicking them in the Layers panel to highlight them in blue.

28. Use the Clone Stamp tool to continue working your way down to the street, removing the pole as you go. When you find a sample point that's in perfect alignment, ride it as far as you can. Just be careful about leaving any cloning tracks behind. If you see any, clean them up.

Here's a chance to use the copy, transform, and merge technique again to remove the top of the remaining light post. This time, you'll modify the copied layer with a mask. Continue with these steps:

29. Use the Lasso tool to draw a selection similar to the selection in the first frame of Figure 15-13. Even though you need only a small area, it's often best to copy a large area and whittle it down to size as you fit it into place.

30. Copy the selected area to a new layer by choosing Layer⇨New⇨Layer via Copy (Ctrl/⌘+J).

31. Lower the opacity of the new layer to 50 percent so that you can partially see through it. This enables you to more easily align it with the layer below. Use the Move tool to drag the new layer into position over the light pole. Try to match the top-left corner of the top-left window.

Remember that you can use the arrow keys for fine-tuning the position.

PRO TIP

If you hold down the Shift key while you move the layer, movement is restricted to moving in a straight line; up and down or right and left. This helps to keep it in vertical alignment as you drag it downward.

15

Hands-on Architectural Retouching Project

15-13

32. Choose Edit➪Transform➪Distort. Work primarily with only the top right and bottom right handles adjusting them one at a time until you get all the lines to match up, as shown in the second frame of Figure 15-13.

Go back and forth between the handles until everything lines up, then commit the transformation by pressing Return/Enter.

33. Use the Masks panel to create a layer mask. Select the Brush tool, and use a large, soft brush with black paint at 100 percent to hide most of the new layer. Just leave enough of it to cover and blend the pole. Be sure to leave a bit of the pole showing above the wires, as shown in Figure 15-14. You'll place a cap on it in the next set of steps.

34. Return the layer's Opacity setting to 100 percent, and do a quick check to make sure the details line up. When you're happy with it, merge the new layer back into the Retouching layer.

15-14

NOTE

Normally, I'd leave this layer separate for a little longer, but in the interest of clarity, I decided to merge it now for this project.

Now all you need for this pole is a cap at the top. If you recall, the top of the pole you just removed had one. Fortunately, the Straight Lines layer still has the original pole and cap that you can copy.

15-15

35. Hide the visibility of the Retouching layer, and click the Straight Lines layer to make it active. Use the Lasso tool to draw a selection around the top of the original light post, as shown in the first frame of Figure 15-15. Copy the selection to a new layer using Layer⇨New⇨Layer via Copy (⌘/Ctrl+J).

36. In the Layers panel, drag the new layer upward in the layer stack until it's sitting just above the Retouching layer. Turn the visibility of the Retouching layer back on, but be sure to keep the new cap layer the active layer. You should now see the cap floating above the light post, as shown in the second frame of Figure 15-15.

Use the Move tool to position it. Use a mask or the Eraser tool (because this is a small thing) to quickly remove any of it that you don't want and then merge it into the Retouching layer. Take care of any cleanup with the Clone Stamp.

37. Use the Clone Stamp tool to trim the two pieces of pipe that are still sticking up on the right. Keep in mind that they don't have to be completely removed. They just need to blend in so they aren't noticeable.

NOTE

The technique you just used to retrieve a piece of information from a backup layer is one of the main reasons to keep these duplicate layers in the file.

38. Continue using the Clone Stamp tool to remove the white crosswalk sign and the large traffic light, as well as some of the wire it hangs from. Stop removing the wire when you get to the corner of the building. You'll use a different technique to work on the building's left face.

Retouching with Vanishing Point

Earlier you used the Transform command to adjust the perspective of copied layers to align them before merging. Sometimes, though, you can't use the copy, transform, and merge technique. What's needed in those cases is a set of retouching tools that work within any given perspective.

Fortunately, Photoshop has a feature that enables you to do just that. It's named Vanishing Point.

The Vanishing Point filter enables you to define a geometric retouching plane. Then any retouching, copying, or pasting is restricted to the angles in that plane. When the Vanishing Point dialog box opens, a set of tools is displayed on the left, as shown in Figure 15-16.

These tools have their own options bar at the top of the dialog box. Here are the more notable of these tools:

> **The Marquee tool (M):** Lets you create rectangular marquees that conform to the perspective of the retouching plane. The Marquee is used to easily copy and paste information while keeping it in perspective. This tool also has a healing feature that's activated by choosing On from the Heal menu.

> **The Stamp tool (S):** Similar to the Clone Stamp tool. It enables you to clone in perspective. This tool is great for working on large areas, but can be hard to control when working with details.

15-16

> **The Brush tool (B):** Enables you to paint in perspective.

> **The Transform tool (T):** Used to transform a scale or rotate a selection after it's in place.

Pick up where you left off after Step 38, and follow these steps:

39. Before opening the Vanishing Point dialog box, hide the visibility of your adjustment layers. Otherwise, their effects become magnified when you use the Stamp tool. Then click on the Retouching layer to make it the active layer.

40. Choose Filter⇨Vanishing Point to open the Vanishing Point dialog box. Then select the Create Plane tool — second from the top. This tool is used to define the retouching plane. Use it to click the four corners of the left face of the building.

    When you click on the fourth corner, a blue grid similar to the one in Figure 15-16 appears on the side of the building. If you see a red or yellow box, it means that you tried to define an axis that doesn't seem natural. You'll need to move one or more of the four points until the axis is accepted and changed to blue.

41. Change the Grid Size value to 200 in the tool options to open up the spacing on the grid. Notice that the grid has handles at its corners and sides. These handles are used to fine-tune the grid's shape by clicking and dragging them. Use them now if you need to do any adjustment to the alignment of the grid.

NOTE

After you create a plane, it stays with the image. That way, when you return to the Vanishing Point dialog box, the previous plane is still in place.

42. Zoom in so you can focus on the grid area and select the Vanishing Point's Marquee tool (M). In the tool options, change Feather to **0**. Draw a marquee around the three windows that are just above the wires holding the traffic light, as shown in the first frame of Figure 15-17.

    After you draw the selection, go back to the tool options and make sure that Move Mode is set to Destination.

15

Hands-on Architectural Retouching Project

15-17

43. Hold down the Alt key, and drag the selection downward until it covers the windows directly below it, as shown in the second frame of Figure 15-17. As you do, notice that the image content inside the original selection is dragged along with the selection.

By holding the Alt key you are copying the information inside the selection as you drag. You can use your arrow keys while holding the Alt key to nudge the copied information into place.

This selection is called a *floating selection*. As long as it's in place, the copied information acts like a separate layer. When you click outside the selection with the Marquee tool the selection is deactivated and its content is automatically merged back into the layer.

PRO TIP

You can press ⌘/Ctrl+H to hide the selection, enabling you to get a better look at the alignment before deselecting and merging.

44. If necessary, use the Transform tool to adjust the geometry of the selected content before deselecting. When you're happy with the alignment, click outside the selection using the Marquee tool to deselect and merge down.

45. Draw a new selection with the Marquee tool that encloses the two windows you just replaced, as well as the windows above it that were selected in Step 42, as shown in the first frame of Figure 15-18. This time, change the Heal setting in the tool options to On. This helps to blend the copied windows selection with the mottled reflections on the side of the building.

Hold down the Alt key while dragging the selection into place over the windows by the traffic light. Notice how the windows scale to the correct size as they're dragged, as shown in the second frame of Figure 15-18. When you're happy with the alignment, click outside the selection with the Marquee tool to deselect it.

15-18

46. Continue using the Vanishing Point's Marquee tool to copy and paste, covering as much of the wire and light as possible. Don't worry about removing all of it. Just focus on the easy areas. When you're finished retouching the left side of the building, click OK to apply all the changes.

As you can see, the Vanishing Point filter is perfectly designed for the type of retouching necessary with this project. You could have used it on the front face of the building as well.

47. Turn the visibility of the adjustment layers back on. You probably see something that needs to be fixed. The top of the light post at the corner is obscured. It needs to be painted back in.

48. Select the History Brush and use it to paint the top of the post back in from the history state previous to the Vanishing Point history state. Remember that to do this you need to first click in the box to the left of the previous history state in the History panel.

49. Use the Clone Stamp to finish removing any pieces of the wire that still show on the left side of the building.

This project has come a long way. To check your work, turn the visibility of the Retouching layer off and on a couple of times. It's almost as if someone peeled a layer of public utilities off of the scene.

If you see anything else you want to remove, like the cars or the fire hydrant, go for it. Leave the person crossing the street because she adds a human scale to the image. She also adds some action to an otherwise stagnant scene.

PHASE 3 WORKFLOW: FINISHING THE IMAGE

Give yourself a pat on the back for attempting this difficult retouching project. Now it's time to add some finishing touches and prepare the file for output printing. Begin with some burning and dodging.

LOCAL TONAL ADJUSTMENT

The biggest tonal problem with this image is the contrast on the left face of the building. The dark shadow on the lower half needs to be lightened, and the sunny area on the upper half needs to be darkened.

If you recall, this contrast was exaggerated when you created the Curves layer back in the Phase 1 section. Luckily, there's enough detail in the shadows and highlights that you can bring them closer together with a burn and dodge layer. However, before you do that, undo some of the Curves adjustment layer effect.

Pick up where you left off after Step 49, and follow these steps:

50. Click the Curves 1 adjustment layer to make it and its mask active. Use the Brush tool, with black paint at 100 percent opacity, to mask out the effect of the Curves layer on the upper half of the left face of the building. This returns that area to the darker tones it originally had.

51. Click the top layer in the Layers panel to make it active. Create a burn and dodge layer, and name it **Burn & Dodge**. (Create a new layer, and change its layer blending mode to Soft Light, as discussed in

Chapter 11.) This layer should be at the top of the layer stack, as shown in Figure 15-19.

52. Select the Brush tool. Work with a large, soft brush at an opacity of 15 percent. Paint the upper part of the left face of the building with black to darken it, and paint the lower section with white to lighten it.

Be careful around the edges and at the seam along the middle of the building where the light and dark meet. Lighten the dark windows along the bottom of the front face, too. When the building looks good, switch to a large brush and darken the outer edges of the sky with black paint.

This makes a huge improvement. Turn the Burn & Dodge layer's visibility off and on a couple of times to compare before and after the changes. If you see any of it bleeding from the building into the sky, use the Eraser tool to remove the paint from the Burn & Dodge layer.

The only things left to do with this image are final sizing and sharpening. Because that means you're going to make some permanent changes, you need to save this latest version of the master file before moving on. Do that now.

Using resampling to increase image size

This image currently measures 11.64 inches by 7.76 inches at 300 ppi. Because the objective is to make a 20×24 print, you need to increase its pixel dimensions by upsampling. As you may recall, image sizing and resampling were discussed in Chapter 9. Now's a good time to put that discussion to use. Begin with the image you saved in Step 52, and follow these steps:

53. Flatten all of the layers into a single layer by choosing Layer⇨Flatten Image. Then go ahead and clear the guides if you haven't already by choosing View⇨Clear Guides.

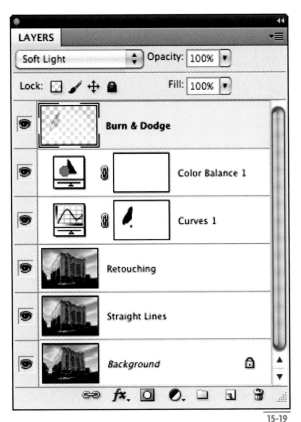

15-19

NOTE

You don't necessarily need to flatten here, but doing so makes the file size more manageable, especially after its size is increased to a 20×24. This flattened file will be about 155 megabytes at 20×24, while the layered file will be 612 megabytes. This size differential makes a big difference on a slower machine. Because you're only going to do a couple of things from here on out, it will be easy enough to back up and make adjustments to the layered master file if major changes are needed.

54. Open the Image Size dialog box by choosing Image⇨Image Size. Make sure the Constrain Proportions check box is selected and then change the Height dimension to **20 inches**.

When you do, the Width value changes proportionally to 30 inches, as shown in Figure 15-20. Click in the pop-up menu at the bottom of the dialog box, and change the resampling interpolation method to Bicubic Smoother. Click OK.

PRO TIP

One of the keys to effectively increasing image size with the Image Size dialog box is to use the correct interpolation method, as discussed in Chapter 9.

55. Now that the image is a 20×30, all you need to do is remove 6 inches from the width. Select the Crop tool and change its options to: Width = 24, Height = 20, and Resolution = 300. Draw a selection from the top of the image to the bottom so you include as much of the sky and foreground as possible, while using the full 20 inches of height.

This way the Crop tool won't resize the image during the cropping process. It only removes extra inches from the sides. Position the crop horizontally so the building is centered. Press Enter/Return to commit the crop. Your retouched and sized image should now look like Figure 15-21.

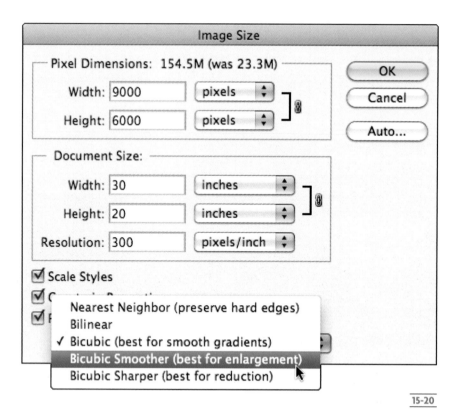

15-20

Applying output sharpening

The image is finally at its intended output size. Now you can complete the final step and apply output sharpening. Follow these steps to complete the process:

56. Zoom to the best zoom preset (33% or 50%) for sharpening, as discussed in Chapter 14. Use the Hand tool to pan the image so that you have a good view of the front face of the building. Choose Filter⇨Sharpen⇨Smart Sharpen.

57. Set the Amount value to 400 and the Radius value to 1.5. Be sure to select Lens Blur from the Remove menu. Click OK.

58. Choose File⇨Save As and save it as Building_ Remodel-20x24.jpg.

Phase 4 Workflow: Output and Archiving

This file is now sized, sharpened, and ready to print. Because inkjet printing was discussed in Chapter 14, it's a good idea to consider using a lab for printing in this section.

Having a lab handle printing

Inkjet printing isn't for everyone. It can be time consuming and expensive. Many of the photographers I know, especially the professionals, have their printing done by professional photolabs. Here are some of the main advantages to having a lab handle printing:

> **Real photo paper:** Although there's nothing wrong with using quality inkjet papers and inks, some people are not comfortable with them. Photolabs use the same types of printing paper that they've always used.

This gives you the opportunity to have your photos printed on papers like Kodak's Metallic or Fuji's Crystal Archive papers.

> **Finishing services:** Full-service labs offer a wide range of finishing services such as dry mounting and canvas mounting, as well as matting and framing.

> **Professional color management:** This is often the number one reason for using a lab, especially for photographers new to color management. That's

15-21

because the people who work in photolabs, especially prolabs, are experts at seeing and correcting color.

You can save time and improve your quality by letting them take care of your final color corrections until you're ready to take over the task.

When you work with a new lab it's important to ask lots of questions before placing your first order. That way you'll know exactly how to prepare your files. For example, what color space does the lab use — sRGB or Adobe RGB (1998)?

Knowing the answer to this question allows you to make sure that you use the same color space when editing, enabling you to better predict what the final color will look like when the prints are made.

X-REF

See Chapter 3 for a discussion of color spaces.

Another question to ask is: Does the lab prefer JPEG or TIFF files. Most prefer JPEG, but I know of some labs that work with both. If you're delivering TIFF files, be sure to flatten them.

Some labs prefer that you deliver files that are completely prepared for printing — that is, sized and sharpened — while others simply want a full-sized JPEG file. I always prefer to manage these variables myself, especially when I order large prints. I want to know that the image is cropped and sharpened exactly the way I like it.

However, if you don't have the time or the experience to make these decisions, you can let the lab do it for you. When you're more comfortable with your workflow, you'll be able to take on some of these duties yourself.

The most important thing to consider when working with a lab is communication. Discuss your needs and

expectations with the lab before placing an order. Make sure that it is willing to listen. When problems occur and your expectations aren't met, be sure to find out why. If the problem is related to your workflow, be willing to listen to suggestions from lab personnel.

These technicians work with lots of photographers so they see many of the same mistakes. If they point one out to you, thank them and consider modifying your workflow to fix it. If the lab is doing something wrong, be sure to let it know so it has the opportunity to fix the problem. If the lab isn't willing to do so, start looking for another lab.

PRO TIP

When working with a prolab it's always useful to develop a relationship with a specific contact person. After this person gets to know you and your work, he or she will be able to keep an eye on your orders and generally give you better service.

ARCHIVE IMPORTANT FILES

After all prints are made and everyone, including you, is happy, be sure that all files are archived. If you're retouching a job for someone else, it can be tempting to remove all files from your system to save space. If it's absolutely necessary, go ahead and do so.

But before you do, be sure to burn a disc for the client that has the finished file and the edited, layered file in case he needs to make changes down the road. Also be sure to tell him that he has the only copy of the project so he needs to treat it appropriately.

This brings us to the end of our journey together. Now you're ready to use everything you learned in this book and begin making better images. When a question arises, use this book as a reference guide.

If you become rusty on a particular technique, be sure to come back and explore relevant sections. And by all means, have fun!

Q & A

Throughout this book, you demonstrated different ways of accomplishing similar tasks. It's good to know there's more than one way to do things, but how do I know which is the best way?

The fact that there are a number of ways of accomplishing the same thing in Photoshop is both a blessing and a curse. It's great that you have lots of options as you approach a retouching problem. However, in the beginning it can be tough to know when one method is better than another.

Naturally, you'll always want to use the method that does the best job of solving the problem. If different techniques offer similar results, then the next thing to consider is speed. For example, in this chapter you learned two ways to retouch parts of the building. One was to use a traditional method with the Clone Stamp tool. The other was to use Vanishing Point. If you can get satisfactory results with Vanishing Point, you'll save time.

What I usually recommend is to master a basic set of tools and techniques. This toolset may vary for different people, depending on their needs. Throughout this book, I attempted to expose you to a range of tools and techniques, enabling you to try your hand at them. As you continue to work with them, you'll learn which are best for the way you work and the kinds of projects you tend to work on.

The difference between beginning and ending stages of this building project are huge. It looks much better, but is it a representation of reality? How do you know when you've gone too far?

Who's to say what "reality" is? The image the camera captured certainly doesn't look real to me when I look at this building. As a retoucher, my job is to make the subject look its best. At the same time, I don't want to draw attention to my work. In the case of the building project in this chapter, the goal was to remove a bunch of clutter from the scene. None of the things that were removed were part of the actual building.

If I had added additional floors to the building to make it 16 stories, or even cloned a door to add a new one, I would have changed the character of the building. Sometimes that's desirable, for example when preparing a composite for consultation with a construction contractor. But in most cases the goal is to improve the subject without doing anything that impinges on its integrity.

PRO GLOSSARY

additive color   Describes the way light waves combine to create color. This is the way humans see things, and it's how most color adjustment happens in Photoshop. This system is called additive because it begins with black (no light). A light source adds wavelengths that have a specific color. Equal amounts of pure red, green, and blue light added together create white. See also *subtractive color*.

Adobe Camera Raw   Photoshop's RAW file converter. See also *RAW*.

artifact   An unwanted visual distortion introduced by the digital process.

aspect ratio   The relationship of the height of an image to its width. For example, 4×5 is the same aspect ratio as 8×10.

banding   Occurs when intermediate tones are lost during the digital process. Because these tones are missing, color graduations show as bands rather than gentle tonal grades.

blending mode   Determines how pixels blend with previously existing pixels. Blending modes can be used with some tools, such as the Brush tool, to affect pixel blending for each stroke, or entire layers can be blended with underlying layers by changing the blending mode on the Layers panel.

Bridge   Adobe Bridge is the file browser that comes with Photoshop. It's named Bridge because it acts as a file browser for all of Adobe's design products.

burning   The process of locally darkening specific regions of an image without affecting the rest of the image. See also *dodging*.

cache   A Folder that contains hidden information about images that have been viewed in Bridge.

capture file format   A file format that's used in digital cameras to record captured images. Camera Raw and JPEG are the most common capture file formats. See also *editing file format* and *output file format*.

clipping   The loss of detail due to underexposure or overexposure, or image adjustments to the extreme shadows and highlights. Clipping occurs when a pixel's value is higher than the highest value or lower than the lowest value in the image.

cloning tracks   Artifacts caused by the retouching process, which often appear as repetitive details from sampled image content.

collection   A virtual group of files created in Bridge. When a photo is added to a collection, it isn't moved or copied. Instead, a visual reference to the photo is placed in the collection.

color editing space   Describes the total palette, or gamut, of colors available when editing a photo in Photoshop. Also called *working color space*. See also *color space*.

color mapping   The method used to translate tones from one color space to another.

color model   A mathematical model describing colors and their relationships to each other. RGB and CMYK are different color models.

color profile   A description of the gamut of a particular device, or a document that is attached to a file to describe the color space that was used to create or edit it.

color profile mismatch   A warning that appears when the working color space in Photoshop doesn't match the color space of the file that's being opened.

color space   A subset of a color model that contains a specific gamut of colors. Adobe RGB (1998) and sRGB are both color spaces that exist in the RGB color model.

combing   The effect on a histogram that occurs when image data is expanded by a tonal or color adjustment. It's called combing because the gaps in the histogram look like a comb. See also *spiking*.

complementary color   Pairs of colors that are opposite in hue. Red/cyan, green/magenta, and blue/yellow are all pairs of complementary colors.

Pro Glossary

compression   A system used to reduce the size of a file when saving it. See also *lossless compression* and *lossy compression*.

device-dependent color space   A color space describing the range of colors that a particular device can see and/or reproduce.

device-independent color space   Color spaces used to describe the range of colors in color editing spaces. These color spaces are not dependent on any particular device.

dodging   The process of locally lightening specific regions of an image without affecting the rest of the image.

dots per inch (dpi)   Refers to the number of dots per inch that an inkjet printer is capable of applying to a sheet of paper. Generally speaking, the higher the dpi, the better the output. See also *resolution*.

downsampling   The process of decreasing the number of pixels in an image through resampling. See also *upsampling*.

dynamic range   Refers to the range between the darkest and the lightest tones in an image or scene.

editing file format   A file format that's used for saving files during the editing process. TIFF and PSD are the most common, though JPEG can also be considered an editing file format. See also *capture file format* and *output file format*.

file browser   A program that allows the user to visually choose photo files by selecting thumbnails of the images.

file compression   A system used to decrease the size of a file when it's saved. See also *lossless compression* and *lossy compression*.

gamut   A description of the color that a device is capable of capturing or reproducing. The palette of colors it is able to work with.

gang scan   Scanning several images at the same time with the same settings into a single document. Each image must be cropped from the scan and saved as an individual document.

GPU (graphics processing unit)   Your system's graphics card. It controls all display functions in your computer.

grayscale   Another way of saying that the image has no color in it and only tones of gray are used to describe image content. Grayscale is also a color space where only tones of gray are available for editing.

hard-edge retouching   The use of retouching tools and techniques to maintain image detail and produce the most realistic rendition of the subject. See also *soft-edge retouching*.

Hide All layer mask   A layer mask that is all black and therefore hides all content on its associated layer. See also *Reveal All layer mask*.

image capture format   A file format that's used for capturing digital images. Most dSLR cameras are capable of capturing photos in the JPEG and/or RAW formats.

image interpolation   When an image is resampled, the color values of new pixels are based on the existing pixels surrounding it. The interpolation method used during resampling controls which type of calculations are used to assign the new colors. See also *resampling*.

intellectual property   Ownership of intangible assets, such as photographic images or artwork.

layer   Discrete segments of image information that are stacked on top of one another. The use of layers is the key to creating a nondestructive workflow.

layer mask   A system of using black and white paint to hide or reveal specific information on a layer.

layer transparency   A gray and white checkerboard that is Photoshop's way of indicating *transparency* — which means there's nothing there.

lossless compression When saving a file, all information is retained during file compression. This means that an image can be resaved and recompressed without compromising image quality. See also *compression*.

lossy compression When saving a file, data is permanently removed through compression. Higher levels of compression result in greater data loss. Every time a file is resaved with lossy compression, more data is lost. This cumulative data loss can greatly affect quality. See also *compression*.

marching ants Used to describe the moving dashed line that surrounds a selected area because it looks like ants marching in unison.

metadata A standardized set of information that describes characteristics of a photo file. Metadata, such as the date of creation and camera settings, is added to a file at the time of its creation. Additional metadata, such as keywords, are added after the file is created.

moiré A digital artifact created by digital capture devices such as scanners and cameras. It's usually found when one or more patterns are captured by the device.

monitor calibration A set of standards that refer to the color temperature, brightness, and contrast for monitor displays. A hardware calibration device measures these qualities in your monitor, and then you adjust your monitor (if possible) to bring it into alignment with the standards. If you cannot adjust your monitor, the calibration device modifies the settings on the computer's graphics card. See also *GPU*.

noise Digital artifacts (unwanted leftovers) that often show up as specs that have a grainy appearance. It's usually caused by shooting at high ISO speeds and by underexposure.

nondestructive workflow A working system that's designed to prevent permanent changes from occurring to the image. Using a nondestructive workflow insures the greatest amount of flexibility because you can alter or completely undo any previous changes at any time. See also *layer* and *workflow*.

OpenGL (Open Graphics Library) A standardized specification developed in 1992 by Silicon Graphics. It consists of a library of standard graphics routines for manipulating images on-screen. OpenGL is used by software manufacturers to speed up and customize the way images are shown on the monitor.

output file format A file format that's used for saving files intended for output. The most common output file formats are JPEG and TIFF. See also *capture file format* and *editing file format*.

Panel menu A menu you access by clicking the Panel menu button, just below the Close panel button that looks like an X.

Panel set Groups of similar panels that are stacked together to save space.

pixels per inch (ppi) A term used to describe the resolution of an image. The greater the number of pixels per inch, the higher the resolution. Generally speaking, higher resolution produces better quality when printing an image. See also *resolution*.

plug-in Third-party software that works within other software, such as Photoshop or scanner software.

RAW A generic term referring to a digital camera capture format that creates files containing unprocessed data from the camera's sensor. RAW files must be processed with conversion software before they can be opened in Photoshop. See also *Adobe Camera Raw*.

resampling Changing the amount of data in an image when resolution or pixel dimensions are changed. See *upsampling* and *downsampling*.

resolution A measurement of the detail in an image. Image resolution is measured in pixels per inch (ppi) and printer resolution is measured in dots per inch (dpi). See also *pixels per inch* and *dots per inch*.

Reveal all layer mask A layer mask that is all white and therefore shows all content on its associated layer. See also *Hide all layer mask*.

saturation The intensity of the color. A true gray has zero color saturation.

scanner driver   Software that enables your scanning equipment to interface with your computer.

Scrubby slider   The hand icon with double arrows that appears when you hover the cursor over a numerical input box. When this icon appears, you can click and drag to the left to decrease numerical values, or click and drag to the right in increase numerical values.

s-curve   The shape of the diagonal line in the Curves dialog box when midhighlights are lightened and midshadows are darkened.

sepia tone   A faded brown color that results from using specific darkroom chemicals to tone a black-and-white print. Historically, this was done to improve the longevity of the print, as well as add a visual element to it.

soft-edge retouching   The use of retouching tools and techniques to blend and soften details in order to enhance the subject. Mostly used in portrait retouching. See also *hard-edge retouching*.

spiking   The effect on a histogram that occurs when image data is compressed by a tonal or color adjustment, causing spikes to appear in portions of the histogram. See also *combing*.

spring-loaded keys   The ability to momentarily switch to a different tool by pressing and holding its shortcut key. When the key is released, the selected tool springs back to the original tool.

subtractive color   Describes the way pigments, such as paints, dyes, inks, and natural colorants reflect light. When white light strikes a pigment, the pigment absorbs some wavelengths of light and reflects the unabsorbed wavelengths. The wavelengths that are reflected are the colors we see and what give the pigment its color. See also *additive color*.

thumbnail   A small graphical representation of a full-sized image used in Bridge to render images more quickly because the original image does not need to be accessed.

twirly   A triangular icon that is used to reveal hidden information. When it points to the side, the information is hidden. When it points downward, the information is revealed.

upsampling   The process of increasing the number of pixels in an image through resampling. See also *resampling* and *downsampling*.

virtual memory   The use of empty hard drive space for overflow memory when the system's RAM (Random Access Memory) is full.

workflow   1) The order in which editing steps are taken to insure that each is executed in the correct sequence. 2) A systematic methodology that insures each step is performed in the correct order. 3) A repeatable system designed to enhance efficiency.

index

continued

continued

continued

347